# Best of the Best

the best recipes from the 25 best cookbooks of the year

from the editors of
**FOOD & WINE**

FOOD & WINE BEST OF THE BEST VOL. 7

**EDITOR** Kate Heddings
**ART DIRECTOR** Liz Quan
**SENIOR EDITOR** Pamela Mitchell
**COPY EDITOR** Lisa Leventer
**ASSISTANT EDITOR** Melissa Rubel
**PRODUCTION MANAGER** Matt Carson
**REPORTERS** Nicole A. Cloutier, Ruby Cutolo, Charlotte Druckman,
Carla Ranicki, Jane Sigal, Ratha Tep

FOOD & WINE MAGAZINE

**EDITOR IN CHIEF** Dana Cowin
**CREATIVE DIRECTOR** Stephen Scoble
**MANAGING EDITOR** Mary Ellen Ward
**EXECUTIVE EDITOR** Pamela Kaufman
**EXECUTIVE FOOD EDITOR** Tina Ujlaki
**ART DIRECTOR** Patricia Sanchez

**SENIOR VICE PRESIDENT, CHIEF MARKETING OFFICER** Mark V. Stanich
**VICE PRESIDENT, BOOKS AND PRODUCTS** Marshall Corey
**DIRECTOR, BRANDED SERVICES AND RETAIL** Tom Mastrocola
**CORPORATE PRODUCTION MANAGER** Stuart Handelman
**MARKETING MANAGER** Bruce Spanier
**SENIOR OPERATIONS MANAGER** Phil Black
**BUSINESS MANAGER** Doreen Camardi

**COVER**
**PHOTOGRAPH BY** Tina Rupp
**FOOD STYLING BY** Joe Maer

**FLAP PHOTOGRAPHS**
**DANA COWIN PORTRAIT BY** Andrew French
**KATE HEDDINGS PORTRAIT BY** Emily Wilson

AMERICAN EXPRESS PUBLISHING CORPORATION

ISBN 1-932624-00-7
ISSN 1524-2862

Published by American Express Publishing Corporation
1120 Avenue of the Americas, New York, New York 10036

Manufactured in the United States of America

# Best of the Best

the best recipes from the 25 best cookbooks of the year

**FOOD&WINE**
BOOKS

American Express Publishing Corporation, New York

AMERICAN BOULANGERIE

FRENCH PASTRIES AND BREADS FOR THE HOME KITCHEN

PASCAL RIGO

Steven Raichlen's
BBQ USA

425 FIERY RECIPES from all across AMERICA

Bernard Clayton's New Complete Book of Breads

bitter sweet

RECIPES AND TALES FROM A LIFE IN CHOCOLATE

ALICE MEDRICH

Rose Levy Beranbaum

the bread bible

The Cakebread Cellars
NAPA VALLEY COOKBOOK

WINE AND RECIPES TO CELEBRATE EVERY SEASON'S HARVEST

DOLORES AND JACK CAKEBREAD
with resident chef BRIAN STREETER

césar

RECIPES FROM A TAPAS BAR

1950 PORT

Come for Dinner

Memorable Meals to Share with Friends

LESLIE REVSIN

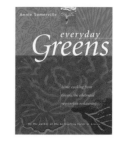

EAST OF PARIS

THE NEW CUISINES OF AUSTRIA AND THE DANUBE

DAVID BOULEY

MARIO LOHNINGER AND MELISSA CLARK

Annie Somerville

everyday Greens

home cooking from Greens, the celebrated vegetarian restaurant

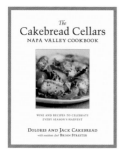

food network kitchens cookbook

AS SEEN ON STYLE NETWORK
FOREVER SUMMER

NIGELLA LAWSON

Author of Nigella Bites

LAURA CALDER

French Food at Home

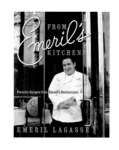

FROM Emeril's KITCHEN

Favorite Recipes from Emeril's Restaurants

EMERIL LAGASSE

ANNE WILLAN

Good Food NO FUSS

150 RECIPES AND IDEAS FOR EASY-TO-COOK DISHES

I am almost always hungry

Lora Zarubin

DAVID ROSENGARTEN

IT'S ALL AMERICAN FOOD

THE BEST RECIPES FOR MORE THAN 400 NEW AMERICAN CLASSICS

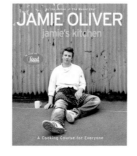

JAMIE OLIVER
jamie's kitchen

A Cooking Course for Everyone

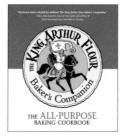

THE KING ARTHUR FLOUR
BAKER'S COMPANION

THE ALL-PURPOSE BAKING COOKBOOK

FUCHSIA DUNLOP

land of plenty

The Maccioni Family Cookbook

Egi Maccioni with Peter Kaminsky

The SLOW MEDITERRANEAN KITCHEN

Recipes for the Passionate Cook

PAULA WOLFERT

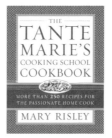

THE TANTE MARIE'S COOKING SCHOOL COOKBOOK

MORE THAN 250 RECIPES FOR THE PASSIONATE HOME COOK

MARY RISLEY

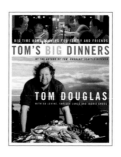

BIG TIME HOME COOKING FOR FAMILY AND FRIENDS

TOM'S BIG DINNERS

TOM DOUGLAS

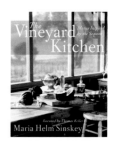

The Vineyard Kitchen

Maria Helm Sinskey

# Contents

# Contents continued

# Recipes

## Poultry

## Meat

## Vegetables & Sides

## Desserts

# Foreword

In our search for the 25 best cookbooks of the year, we read and tested recipes from at least 150 candidates. Sometimes the winners came as no surprise to us because they were from authors we already revere, such as Paula Wolfert (*The Slow Mediterranean Kitchen*) and Rose Levy Beranbaum (*The Bread Bible*). Among the most gratifying discoveries were terrific books from first-time authors, including Laura Calder (*French Food at Home*) and Olivier Said, James Mellgren and Maggie Pond (*César*). And we were delighted to find great books from such unusual sources as Food Network's test kitchen and the King Arthur Flour Company. The diversity of global recipes kept us intrigued as well: Tuscan, Austrian and Sichuan, to name just a few.

Selecting the 25 best books took us several months, but singling out the 95 most delicious recipes in those books was even harder. This year some of our favorites were Maria Helm Sinskey's Salt and Herb–Crusted Prime Rib with Horseradish Cream, David Bouley's Roast Chicken with Paprika Sauce and Alice Medrich's unbelievable Melting Chocolate Cookie Tartlets.

As in previous years, you'll find each recipe reproduced here exactly as it appears in the original cookbook, but we've added helpful cooking tips to troubleshoot any potential problems along the way. We've also included insightful interviews with the authors, revealing how they got their start, highlighting their most prized ingredients and equipment and listing cookbooks *they* turn to for advice or inspiration.

We've done 100 percent of the work to ensure that you derive 100 percent of the pleasure from the very best recipes in the very best cookbooks of the year.

Dana Cowin
Editor in Chief
FOOD & WINE MAGAZINE

Kate Heddings
Editor
FOOD & WINE COOKBOOKS

# The American Boulangerie

## PASCAL RIGO AND THE BAKERS OF BAY BREAD

INTERVIEW BELOW WITH PASCAL RIGO

**BACKGROUND** Born in Paillet, outside Bordeaux, France; lives in San Francisco.

**EDUCATION** "When I was young, my mother would send me to our village *boulangerie* to get baguettes. I felt at home there and began an informal apprenticeship when I was seven. In my teens I worked in nearby Lestiac for a man named Bernard Contraire who was a member of a select artisanal baker's guild. He taught me everything from the Parisian style of baking to the different regional specialties. It's unusual for someone like me to become a baker—my father was a diplomat! My parents encouraged me, though. They told me, 'Fine, you can do your baking, but don't neglect your studies.' My grandfather was a *courtier en vins,* a wine broker, and I spent many days with him in the winery, breathing in the aromas and learning about *levure,* the airborne yeast that makes both grape juice and bread dough ferment."

**EXPERIENCE** "When I moved to Los Angeles, I developed the bread recipes for Michel Richard's Broadway Deli. That led to my starting a wholesale bakery that served 70 of the top restaurants and hotels in the city. When I moved to San Francisco, I opened Boulangerie with the intention of selling mainly wholesale breads; the bakery attracted a lot of customers, though, and soon I was making and selling croissants, cookies and more than 50 other items. The current bakery, Boulangerie Bay Bread, is a descendant of those two wholesale ventures."

**RECIPE INSPIRATIONS** "Each of the recipes in this book is based on a personal experience, either a very special or simple moment. The Chaussons aux Pommes (apple turnovers) are the same as those I had every day at school in Paillet for four years. The croissant is similar to my favorite at Dalloyau in Paris. The Tarte Tropezienne, a brioche filled with pastry cream, reminds me of vacations at Saint-Tropez. I grew up with the Cannelés de

**BREAD BAKER'S MOTTO** "Making bread is like making wine: You have to pay attention. You have to be patient."

Bordeaux, crunchy pastries with a custardy center. The pound cake is my mom's."

**MOST IMPORTANT BREAD BAKING LESSON** "Taste the bread once it's baked and take notes: What does it taste like? Is there too much salt? Is it too acidic? Not acidic enough? Is the color what you're looking for? The next time, you'll make changes in the recipe and take notes again; eventually you'll arrive at a loaf of bread that is exactly what you want. People go too fast when making bread. Read about the subject. Imagine the process and the final product. Always think along the way about the result you want. Use your good judgment."

**TIP FOR THE BEGINNING BAKER** "Be patient and bake only what you would most like to eat."

**RIGO'S GOAL** "The recipes in my book are only a starting point. At the end of the process, you want to come away with your own signature *pain de campagne* or lemon tart. My recipes become yours."

**RECIPES THAT DIDN'T MAKE IT INTO THE BOOK** "A few recipes are too hard to make at home. For example, a very dense, sticky chestnut-flour bread is a real challenge."

**ESSENTIAL EQUIPMENT** "A good oven, convection or not. Preferably lined with a baking stone to help distribute the heat evenly."

**ESSENTIAL BAKING INGREDIENTS** "Great organic flour. *Sel de mer* (sea salt), because the the iodine in it gives foods a lot of flavor; you don't taste it in breads so much, but you do in *sablés* and *petits gâteaux*. *Levain* (starter) is like a pet that needs to be taken care of every day. Plugra, a European-style butter, has less water than American butters; it's a 'fat' butter, and an expensive one. And chocolate: I like Valrhona, but it's a very personal choice."

**HIS OPINION OF PARCOOKED BREAD** This increasingly popular bread is partially baked, flash-frozen and sent to stores, mainly supermarkets, to finish baking. "I think it's a good thing. We make parcooked bread for Whole Foods stores. Parcooking guarantees freshly baked bread every hour or two. The fact is, all warm bread is good whether it's industrial or artisanal. But it's also a question of education: If you know what good bread tastes like, you'll demand good bread from your baker whether he works at your supermarket or at a local artisanal bakery. And just because a baker calls his bread artisanal doesn't mean that it's good!"

# Gâteau Fondant au Chocolat

*bittersweet chocolate cake*

**MAKES ONE 10-INCH CAKE**

This is the only chocolate cake we make, and once you try it, it might become the only one you make, too. Its stroke of genius is marbling ganache into the already ultra-chocolatey cake batter. It may not be the most spectacular-looking cake when it comes out of the oven, but once you slice it and present it on a nice plate with a big dollop of whipped cream, it's something truly beautiful. I highly recommend warming each slice for a few seconds in the microwave just before garnishing and serving: The ganache will soften and the flavors will become even more intense.

12 ounces bittersweet chocolate, finely chopped (approximately 2 cups)

4 ounces (½ cup) unsalted butter

2 tablespoons unsweetened cocoa powder

4 extra-large eggs, separated

2 extra-large egg whites

Pinch of salt

½ cup sugar

½ cup Chocolate Ganache (recipe follows), melted

1. Preheat the oven to 325°. Spray a 10-inch springform pan with vegetable oil spray and line the bottom with a circle of parchment paper. Set aside.

2. In a large, heat-resistant bowl set over a pot of simmering water, melt the chocolate and butter, stirring occasionally. Remove the bowl from the heat and whisk in the cocoa powder. In a small bowl, whisk the egg yolks to break them up, and then whisk into the chocolate mixture. Set aside.

3. In the bowl of an electric mixer fitted with the whisk attachment, whip the egg whites and salt on medium speed until foamy. Increase the speed to high and gradually add the sugar. Continue to whip to medium-firm peaks—the

peaks will droop slightly when you lift up the whisk. Stir the egg whites, rather vigorously, into the warm chocolate mixture, until there are no white streaks visible. You need not be gentle, as this cake is best without a lot of air incorporated into it. Transfer the batter to the prepared pan, smooth it out, and pour the ganache on top. Using a spoon, or your fingers, marble the ganache into the batter.

**4.** Bake in the center of the oven for 35 to 40 minutes or until the center of the cake no longer looks shiny. The cake will be puffed up and wobbly in the center but set on the edges. It's a soft cake that will firm up as it cools. Cool the cake completely, on a wire rack, before removing the side from the pan.

**5.** To slice the cake (easiest when it is chilled), run a long knife under hot water, then wipe it off with a towel, and cut the cake into 12 slices. The cake can be kept 3 days at room temperature or up to 5 days if refrigerated.

## on rigo's nightstand

I'm a fan of *The Italian Baker* by **Carol Field.** I love the old French book by **Professor R. Calvel,** *La Boulangerie Moderne,* and **Lionel Poilâne's** French cookbooks. And I am a faithful reader of *Saveurs* magazine, published in France.

## Chocolate Ganache

1    cup plus 2 tablespoons
     heavy cream

4    ounces semisweet chocolate,
     coarsely chopped
     (approximately ¾ cup)

4    ounces bittersweet chocolate,
     coarsely chopped
     (approximately ¾ cup)

1    tablespoon light corn syrup

In a small saucepan, bring the
cream to the scalding point over
medium-high heat. In a medium
heat-resistant bowl, combine
the semisweet chocolate, bittersweet
chocolate, and corn syrup.
Pour the scalded cream over the
chocolate mixture and gently
whisk until the chocolate is
completely melted and smooth.

# Financiers

*brown butter hazelnut cakes*

**MAKES 18 CAKES**

In France, these rich, buttery nut cakes run a close second to madeleines in terms of popularity. Traditionally, they're made with ground almonds, but we give ours a special twist and a deeper, toastier flavor by using ground hazelnuts instead. The whole key to *financiers* is getting the brown butter right. It should be a true *beurre noisette*—a deep brown butter that smells like toasted hazelnuts, and the trick is to remove it from the heat a split-second before it burns. *Friand* or *financier* molds are small, rectangular molds with angled sides, available at specialty cookware shops. They measure 4-inches long by 2-inches wide. You may substitute mini-muffin pans or madeleine pans.

*food & wine tip*

To prepare the hazelnuts for this recipe, place them in a food processor and pulse them until they are very finely ground. Be careful not to overprocess or you'll end up with hazelnut butter.

8   ounces (1 cup) unsalted butter

2¼ cups powdered sugar

½   cup plus 3 tablespoons all-purpose flour

3½ ounces (1 cup) finely ground hazelnuts

⅛   teaspoon salt

8   extra-large egg whites

½   teaspoon vanilla extract

1   cup fresh blackberries or raspberries

1. To make the browned butter: In a 2-quart saucepan, melt the butter over low heat. Once the butter is melted, turn the heat up to medium and continue cooking, swirling the pan occasionally. At first the butter will bubble wildly, and then the solids will start to sink to the bottom of the pan and turn brown. When the butter is deep brown and smells nutty and delicious, it's ready. Be careful not to let it burn; the difference is a matter of seconds. Remove the pan from the heat and set aside in a warm place.

2. In the bowl of an electric mixer fitted with the whisk attachment, combine the powdered sugar, flour, hazelnuts, and salt on low speed. With the mixer

off, pour in the hot browned butter, making sure to scrape the tasty brown bits off the bottom of the saucepan. Mix on low speed until combined. Still on low speed, slowly add the egg whites and vanilla extract and mix thoroughly, scraping down the sides and bottom of the bowl as necessary. Transfer the batter to an airtight container and refrigerate for about 1 hour or until firm. The batter can be kept in the refrigerator for up to 3 days.

3. To bake, preheat the oven to 375°. Arrange the nonstick 4 x 2-inch *friand* or *financier* molds on a cookie sheet and fill three-quarters full with batter. If using muffin pans, spray them with vegetable oil spray and fill them one-third full with batter. Top each with 2 to 3 berries of your choice.

4. Bake for 25 minutes, or until golden brown and springy to the touch. Cool for 5 minutes in the pans, then unmold (if needed, run a knife around the edges) onto a wire rack. Dust with powdered sugar and serve warm or at room temperature. They are best the day they are baked.

# Macarons de Paris

*parisian macaroons*

**MAKES ABOUT 16 FILLED MACAROONS**

They're called *"macarons"* in Paris, but these small almond cookies sandwiched around a variety of flavored fillings are more like almond meringues—crunchy on the outside and soft inside. They're often made with almond paste, but we prefer the texture and flavor of finely ground almonds. Use sliced, blanched almonds finely ground in small batches in a coffee grinder. You can have a lot of fun playing with different cookie and filling flavors. Tinted in pastel shades with food coloring, these make nice Easter cookies, and because they're made without flour, they're suitable for Passover, too. Eat them as is or choose a filling or two to fill them with (see the Variations and Buttercream recipe that follow).

1¼ cups plus 1 teaspoon powdered sugar

4    ounces (1 cup) finely ground, sliced, blanched almonds

¼    cup plus 2 tablespoons fresh egg whites (about 3 extra-large egg whites)

Pinch of salt

¼    cup granulated sugar

1. Preheat the oven to 350°. Sift together the powdered sugar and ground almonds into a bowl. In the bowl of an electric mixer fitted with the whisk attachment, whip the egg whites with the salt on medium speed until foamy. Increase the speed to high and gradually add the granulated sugar. Continue to whip to stiff peaks—the whites should be firm and shiny. With a flexible spatula, gently fold in the powdered sugar mixture until completely incorporated.

2. Line baking sheets with parchment paper. Fit a piping bag with a ⅜-inch, number 4, stainless steel round tip and fill the bag with the macaroon batter. Pipe batter into 1-inch disks onto the parchment-lined baking sheet, 2 inches apart. The batter will spread a little; this is normal. Let them dry at room temperature for 15 minutes, or until a soft skin forms on the top of the macaroons and the shiny surface turns dull.

**3.** Bake, with the door of the oven slightly ajar, for 15 minutes or until the surface of the macaroons is completely dry. Remove the baking sheet to a wire rack and let the macaroons cool completely on the baking sheet before gently peeling them off the parchment. The tops are easily crushed, so take care when removing them from the parchment. In an airtight container, the macaroons can be refrigerated up to 2 days or frozen up to 1 month.

**4.** When filling the macaroons, fill a pastry bag with the desired prepared filling (see Variations that follow). Turn over all the macaroons so their flat bottoms face up. On half of them, pipe out about 1 teaspoon filling and sandwich them with the remaining macaroons, flat-sides down, pressing on them slightly to spread the filling to the edges.

VARIATIONS

chocolate Make the Chocolate Ganache (page 16) using ½ cup heavy cream, 3 ounces bittersweet chocolate, and 1 teaspoon light corn syrup. Set aside. In step 1, sift 2 tablespoons unsweetened cocoa powder with the ground almonds and powdered sugar. In step 4, use the ganache for filling.

**raspberry** In step 1, add 2 drops red food coloring to the egg whites after they are whipped. In step 4, use ⅓ cup good-quality raspberry jam for filling.

**hazelnut** In step 1, substitute ½ cup (2 ounces) finely ground, toasted hazelnuts for the ground almonds. In step 4, blend ⅓ cup Buttercream (recipe below) with ⅓ cup finely ground hazelnuts for the filling. If desired, add ½ teaspoon hazelnut extract to the filling.

**coffee** In step 1, sift 1 teaspoon freshly ground coffee beans with the ground almonds and powdered sugar. In step 4, blend ⅓ cup Buttercream (recipe below) with 2 teaspoons espresso powder for the filling.

## Buttercream for Variations

**MAKES 3 CUPS**

3   egg whites
1   cup sugar
8   ounces (1 cup) unsalted butter, at room temperature, cut into slices

1. In the bowl of an electric mixer, whisk together the egg whites and the sugar. Set the mixer bowl over a pot of simmering water and heat the mixture, whisking often, until it feels warm to the touch and the sugar is dissolved, 3 to 5 minutes.

2. Transfer the bowl to the electric mixer and fit with the whisk attachment. Whip the warm egg mixture on high speed until stiff and shiny, 3 to 5 minutes. Add the butter, one slice at a time, and continue mixing until all the butter is thoroughly incorporated. The Buttercream can be kept, covered and refrigerated, up to 1 week. Bring to room temperature before stirring and proceeding.

*food & wine tip*

The Buttercream recipe makes twice as much filling as you'll need for these cookies. Either cut the recipe in half or use the extra to frost a layer cake or to fill cupcakes.

# BBQ USA

## STEVEN RAICHLEN

**BACKGROUND** Born in Japan and raised in Baltimore; lives in Miami.

**EDUCATION** "I majored in French literature, and for me food was a way to understand the society of the Middle Ages. After college I spent two years in Europe, mainly France, studying medieval cooking. While I was there I also trained at both La Varenne and Le Cordon Bleu cooking schools in Paris."

**MENTOR** Anne Willan of La Varenne. "She's set the bar for writing cookbooks that work."

**HOW HE STARTED WRITING ABOUT FOOD** "When I came back from Europe I wrote a magazine article on restaurants in Boston, which led to my becoming the restaurant critic for *Boston* magazine. I wrote my first cookbook in 1979, and last fall I finished my twenty-fifth."

**THE APPEAL OF BARBECUE** "People get so passionate about barbecue. *BBQ USA* shows how much it's part of our culture. George Washington wrote about barbecue. Abraham Lincoln's parents celebrated their marriage with a barbecue."

**WHAT MAKES AMERICAN BARBECUE DIFFERENT FROM GRILLING IN THE REST OF THE WORLD** "We not only grill, we also smoke foods a lot. Plus, in America grilling cuts across all socio-economic levels. People grill in asphalt parking lots and chic California restaurants. They use oil drums or $10,000 stainless-steel supergrills."

**HOW HE RESEARCHED THE BOOK** "I did lots of traveling. I flew to Santa Maria, California, the home of beef tri-tips—a $5 meal that, with flights and a rental car, ultimately cost $400. I drove around the Olympic Peninsula to observe a traditional Pacific Northwest Indian salmon roast."

**WHY HE WROTE THE BOOK** To provide a recipe from or inspired by every part of America. "There might be three good barbecue recipes in Wyoming and 300 in Texas, but there's interesting live-fire cooking in every state."

**GRILLING MOTTO** "Keep it hot (preheat the grill), keep it clean (scrape the grate with a wire brush) and keep it lubricated (oil the grate)."

MOST CHALLENGING RECIPE ADAPTATIONS "Pit masters can use some gross stuff to make a delicious sauce, like cheap salad dressing in a marinade or powdered bouillon cubes in a dry rub. I don't do that, so sometimes I had to do things like create a homemade Italian dressing to replicate the taste of a bottled one."

INVENTIONS "In New Orleans there's not much grilling, so I created some dishes that are Cajun in spirit and flavor, like the Cajun "Hunger Killer," a version of South American *matambre* (rolled flank steak) stuffed with andouille sausage and tasso ham."

WEIRDEST FOODS HE EVER SAW BEING GRILLED Sweetbreads in the United States, nori seaweed in Japan and whole eggs in Vietnam.

ESSENTIAL EQUIPMENT Good spring-loaded tongs. "They work as a mover, spatula, oiler (use them to rub a folded, oiled paper towel on the grate), even a grill brush when they hold crumpled aluminum foil. And here's a tip: The more expensive the tongs, the less well they perform—their arms tend to bend when you try to pick up a whole chicken. Go with cheap and basic."

GRILLING PANTRY Extra-virgin olive oil, coarse salt, freshly ground black pepper, lemon juice, garlic. "Of course, there is an American tradition of using drinks like root beer and Coke in barbecue sauces, so I always have them on hand. And I use a lot of coffee in sauces, too."

GRILLING TRENDS "We're pushing the envelope in what we're grilling. We once grilled just the main course, but now we're grilling the whole meal, from salads to dessert. We're grilling cheese, fruits like pineapple—everything. And ten years ago tandoori and yakitori were exotic; now they're a basic part of American barbecue."

GRILLING PREDICTIONS "More international barbecue—from the current focus on Brazilian and Argentinean barbecue to the newer Korean and Peruvian varieties— as well as authentic Indonesian saté bars."

FUTURE PROJECTS "A book on indoor grilling, using everything from a fireplace to a George Foreman. Also I'd like to bring some of my restaurant ideas to life."

## BIGGEST GRILLING MISTAKES

"Putting a sweet sugar- or tomato-based sauce on too early, so the sauce burns and the meat stays raw: This is particularly common with chicken. Also, running out of gas or charcoal halfway through."

# The Ultimate Hamburger

For historic continuity, ferociously loyal community support, and an atmosphere that you could spread with a knife, you can't beat the hamburger joint Louis' Lunch, in New Haven, Connecticut. Since 1898, the Lassen family has been grinding its own beef daily, hand shaping patties to order, and grilling burgers on antique cast-iron broilers in front of live flames. (This answers the question once and for all—the proper way to cook a hamburger is by grilling, not by frying it on a griddle.) And as any regional American culinary landmark should be, Louis' Lunch is sufficiently quirky to allow melted processed cheese but militantly prohibit ketchup and mustard as accompaniments to its signature burgers. Here, then, is the granddaddy of all burgers; it's the next best thing to elbowing your way up to the counter at Louis'.

1¼ pounds ground chuck

1¼ pounds ground sirloin

Coarse salt (kosher or sea) and freshly ground black pepper

½ medium-size onion, cut into 8 thin wedges

16 slices sandwich bread

3 tablespoons butter, melted (optional)

1 large or 2 medium-size gorgeous, luscious, ripe red tomatoes, thinly sliced

8 Boston lettuce leaves or iceberg lettuce slices

Cheese Sauce (optional; recipe follows)

1. Set up the grill for direct grilling (see page 26 for charcoal or gas) and preheat to high.

2. Place the chuck and sirloin in a large mixing bowl and mix with a wooden spoon, or mix the meat in a stand mixer fitted with a dough hook. If possible, avoid mixing the meat with your hands so your fingers don't warm it.

**3.** Wet your hands with cold water and divide the meat into 8 equal portions. Working quickly and with a light touch, pat each portion into a ½-inch-thick squarish patty. Generously season each patty on both sides with salt and pepper. Press an onion wedge into one side of each patty so that it's flush with the meat.

**4.** Lightly brush the bread slices with the butter, if using. Arrange the tomatoes and lettuce leaves on an attractive serving platter.

**5.** When ready to cook, brush and oil the grill grate. Place the burgers on the hot grate, onion side down. Grill the burgers until cooked to taste, 3 to 4 minutes per side for medium-rare. To test for doneness, insert an instant-read meat thermometer through the side of a burger into the center. The internal temperature should be about 145°F for medium-rare or, if using commercial ground beef, cook it to at least medium, 160°F.

**6.** Meanwhile, place the bread slices on the hot grate and grill until lightly toasted, 1 to 2 minutes per side.

**7.** To serve, place a lettuce leaf on top of a slice of toast. Top with a burger, tomato slice, and Cheese Sauce, if using. Slap a piece of toast on top and serve at once.

DIRECT GRILLING

As the name suggests, direct grilling involves cooking food directly over a fire, usually three to six inches above the flame. This method is used to cook relatively small, thin, tender pieces of food—steaks, chops, chicken breasts, fish fillets, vegetables, tofu, sliced pineapple—foods that cook quickly, benefiting from the searing heat of the fire. To grill using the direct method, all you do is place the food on the grate over your heat source. The challenge

## on raichlen's nightstand

If I could take one cookbook to a desert island, it would be the original 1931 edition of *Joy of Cooking.* One of the most intellectually stimulating books I've read recently is *Raw* by **Charlie Trotter** and **Roxanne Klein.** Even though raw food and grilling are antithetical, I was inspired by the way Trotter and Klein deconstructed dishes and put them back together in a new way. **Rick Bayless's** books are very good, as are **Anne Willan's.** And I love the way **Rose Levy Beranbaum** gets into the subject of baking and really digs deep. **Thomas Keller's** *The French Laundry Cookbook* is a great chef's book that's also very human.

of direct grilling—especially when using charcoal—is to control the heat. One way to do this is to build a three-zone fire.

**A three-zone charcoal fire** To build a three-zone fire in a charcoal grill, rake half of the lit coals into a double layer on one side of the grill, so that they cover about a third of the bottom grate (you can use a garden hoe to rake out the coals). The rest of the coals go in a single layer in the center of the bottom grate. Leave the remaining third bare. This gives you three heat zones—a hot zone for searing, a medium zone for cooking, and a cool or safety zone where you can move what you are grilling if it starts to burn or keep cooked food warm.

**A three-zone gas fire** To control the heat on a gas grill, you could adjust the burner controls, but I prefer to set up a three-zone fire here, too. Turn one burner on to high heat, then turn one or two burners on to medium. Leave the remaining burner turned off. If your grill has only two burners, use the warming rack as your safety zone.

**A two-zone fire (charcoal and gas)** When you are grilling only a couple of steaks or chicken breasts, you can use a two-zone fire. Depending upon what you are cooking, if you are using a charcoal grill, spread the coals out in an even layer, leaving a quarter of the grill bare, or make a double layer of coals in half of the grill and a single layer in the other half. If you are using a gas grill, preheat half or two out of three of the burners to the desired temperature; leave the rest turned off. This gives you a hot zone for grilling and a cooler zone for dodging the flames or resting the meat.

## Cheese Sauce

**MAKES ABOUT 1¼ CUPS**

The Grilling Guru has a moral dilemma. To be strictly faithful to Louis' Lunch, he should tell you to top your hamburger with a liquid processed cheese, like Cheez Whiz. The Grilling Guru doesn't use Cheez Whiz himself, however, so he feels awkward about calling for it. So he's created a made-from-scratch cheese sauce that will satisfy the purist, while remaining faithful to the lurid orange cheese topping used by Louis'.

½   clove garlic

1   cup beer

2   cups (about 8 ounces) coarsely grated Colby cheese or orange cheddar cheese

2   teaspoons cornstarch

2   teaspoons prepared mustard

Coarse salt (kosher or sea) and freshly ground black pepper

1. Rub the bottom and side of a heavy saucepan with the cut garlic. Place the garlic clove in the pan, add the beer, and bring to a boil over high heat.

2. Meanwhile, place the cheese and cornstarch in a bowl and toss to mix. Sprinkle the cheese into the boiling beer, stirring it with a wooden spoon. Let the sauce come back to a boil; it will thicken.

3. Reduce the heat slightly, stir in the mustard, and season the sauce with salt and pepper to taste. Let the sauce simmer gently until smooth and rich-tasting, 3 to 5 minutes, stirring steadily with the wooden spoon. The purist can fish out and discard the garlic clove; otherwise, one lucky person will get to eat it.

# Maple Mustard Pork Chops

**SERVES 4**

food & wine tip

Even if you don't have
time to make the
barbecue sauce, these
chops are fabulous
on their own—simple,
juicy and flavorful.

Advance Preparation: 30 minutes for marinating the chops

4    pork chops (½ to ¾ inch thick and 6 to 7 ounces each for
     boneless chops or 8 to 10 ounces each for bone-in chops)

Coarse salt (kosher or sea) and freshly ground black pepper

About 3 tablespoons dry mustard

About 3 tablespoons soy sauce

½    cup maple syrup

3    tablespoons vegetable oil

Maple Mustard Barbecue Sauce (optional; recipe follows)

1. Place the pork chops in a baking dish and season generously on both sides
with salt and pepper. Sprinkle the pork chops on both sides with the mustard
powder, using about 1 teaspoon per side and rubbing it onto the meat with
a fork or your fingertips. Drizzle the soy sauce over the chops, patting it onto
the mustard with a fork to make a flavorful paste. Place the maple syrup
and oil in a small bowl and stir with a fork to mix. Pour this mixture over the
chops, turning to coat both sides, and let marinate in the refrigerator,
covered, for 30 minutes.

2. Set up the grill for direct grilling (see page 26 for charcoal or gas) and
preheat to high.

3. When ready to cook, brush and oil the grill grate. Drain the marinade from
the chops and discard the marinade. Arrange the chops on the hot grate,
placing them on a diagonal to the bars. Grill the chops until cooked through,
4 to 6 minutes per side, depending on the thickness of the chops. Rotate
the chops a quarter turn after 2 minutes to create an attractive crosshatch of
grill marks. When ready to turn, the chops will be nicely browned on the
bottom. To test for doneness, use the poke method; the meat should be firm

but gently yielding. Or insert an instant-read meat thermometer sideways into a chop: The internal temperature should be about 160°F.

4. Transfer the grilled chops to a platter or plates and let rest for 2 minutes. Serve the chops with the Maple Mustard Barbecue Sauce, if desired.

## Maple Mustard Barbecue Sauce

**MAKES ABOUT 1¼ CUPS**

1    tablespoon butter

2    slices bacon, cut into ¼-inch slivers

1    small onion, finely chopped (about ¾ cup)

1    clove garlic, minced

1    tablespoon tomato paste

¾    cup maple syrup

6    tablespoons Dijon mustard

2    tablespoons cider vinegar, or more to taste

Coarse salt (kosher or sea) and freshly ground black pepper

1. Melt the butter in a nonreactive saucepan over medium heat. Add the bacon, onion, and garlic and cook until golden brown, 4 to 5 minutes. Stir in the tomato paste and cook for 1 minute.

2. Stir in the maple syrup, mustard, and vinegar and let the sauce simmer until thick and flavorful, about 10 minutes. Taste for seasoning, adding salt and pepper to taste and more vinegar as necessary. You can serve the sauce hot or at room temperature. It can be made up to 2 days ahead and refrigerated, covered. Bring the sauce to room temperature before serving.

# Bourbon-Brined Chicken

**SERVES 4**

Desperate times call for desperate measures. In the past thirty years, all meat in the United States has gotten leaner, and the boneless, skinless chicken breast is no exception. This popular cut is about as low in fat as meat can be. So what's the problem? Well, fat is what carries flavor and it's what keeps meat from drying out during grilling. That's where brining comes in—this traditional American technique puts moisture back in meat. And the bourbon? Well, this distinctly American whiskey adds a smoky sweetness that's perfect for grilled chicken.

Advance Preparation: 2 to 3 hours for brining the chicken

For the brine

¼   cup bourbon

¼   cup coarse salt (kosher or sea)

¼   cup firmly packed brown sugar

4   slices (each ¼ inch thick) lemon

2   cloves garlic, peeled and gently crushed with the side of a cleaver

1   tablespoon black peppercorns

1   tablespoon mustard seeds

1   tablespoon coriander seeds

For the chicken

2   whole skinless, boneless chicken breasts (each 12 to 16 ounces), or 4 half breasts (each half 6 to 8 ounces)

2   tablespoons melted butter or olive oil

Your favorite barbecue sauce, for serving

You'll also need

2   cups wood chips or chunks (optional; preferably hickory or oak), soaked for 1 hour in water to cover, then drained

1. Make the brine: Combine the bourbon, salt, brown sugar, lemon slices, garlic, peppercorns, and mustard and coriander seeds in a large nonreactive bowl with 4 cups of water and whisk until the salt and brown sugar dissolve.

2. If using whole chicken breasts, cut each breast in half. Trim any sinews or excess fat off the breasts and discard. Rinse the breasts under cold running water, then drain. Place the chicken breasts in a large resealable plastic bag and add the brine. Let the breasts brine in the refrigerator for 2 to 3 hours, turning the breasts twice so that they brine evenly.

3. Set up the grill for direct grilling (see page 26 for gas or charcoal) and preheat to high. If using a gas grill, place all of the wood chips or chunks, if desired, in the smoker box or in a smoker pouch and run the grill on high until you see smoke. If using a charcoal grill, preheat it to high, then toss all of the wood chips or chunks, if desired, on the coals.

4. When ready to cook, drain the brine off the chicken and blot the breasts dry with paper towels. Discard the brine. Lightly brush both sides of the breasts with the melted butter. Brush and oil the grill grate, then arrange the chicken breasts on the hot grate, placing them on a diagonal to the bars. Grill the breasts for 2 minutes, then rotate them a quarter turn to create an attractive crosshatch of grill marks. Continue grilling the breasts on that side for 2 minutes longer. Turn the breasts over and grill until cooked through, 4 to 6 minutes longer, again rotating them after 2 minutes to create a crosshatch of grill marks. The total cooking time will be 8 to 10 minutes, depending on the thickness of the chicken breasts. To test for doneness, poke a breast in the thickest part with your finger; it should feel firm to the touch. Transfer the grilled chicken breasts to a platter or plates and serve at once with your favorite barbecue sauce.

# Bernard Clayton's New Complete Book of Breads

**BERNARD CLAYTON, JR.**

## the book

*Bernard Clayton's New Complete Book of Breads* by Bernard Clayton, Jr. (Simon & Schuster), $35, 685 pages, black-and-white illustrations.

## the gist

A revision of the 1973 classic that extols the joys of homemade bread through well-researched and refined recipes.

## the ideal reader

The serious bread baker interested in experimenting with a broad range of flavors and international styles.

## the extras

Terrific sections in the back of the book on proper bread storage, troubleshooting, even building your own adobe oven.

**BACKGROUND** Born in Rochester, Indiana; lives in Bloomington, Indiana.

**EDUCATION** "My father was the owner of a small-town newspaper, so early on I was a reporter-writer. I went to college for two or three years. Then off to work, because of the Depression."

**EXPERIENCE** "I was picture editor at *Life* magazine, and opened bureaus for them in Chicago and San Francisco. Then I was in Hawaii for three years during World War II, in charge of photographers and reporters covering Pearl Harbor. For the last six months, I went with MacArthur's staff to the Philippines. Then I traveled to Europe, and when I came back I looked for some of the breads I had tasted in England, Ireland and France. I couldn't find them in bakeries in the United States, so I decided to try making them myself."

**COOKING SCHOOL EXPERIENCE** "I did go to a number of cooking schools—never as the student, always as the instructor! I also taught many classes in my home."

**MENTOR** "I didn't really have one, although I'd say my dear friend Julia Child got me started in the kitchen. It was a cold and miserable winter in Indiana. I made one of the recipes from *Mastering the Art of French Cooking*, and from then on I was a fan. However, I started totally on my own, learning from my own experience. I tried a number of bread books—remember, this was 35 years ago, and there were only a few bread books out at the time—and there was something not right about all of them. Invariably, some recipes worked, some didn't. So I sort of rewrote favorite recipes my way, so that the person who used them would have a pretty good idea of how to make that loaf of bread."

**FIRST BAKING FAILURE** "The first loaf of bread I made was a disaster. I gave it to my neighbor and she said that it dropped to the floor and sounded like a bomb."

**TIP FOR PERFECT DOUGH** "Slap your hand down on the dough and count to ten. If you lift your hand and no dough is sticking to it, then you're set to go."

CAREER BREAKTHROUGH "I was making some pretty good handmade breads, and I sent a loaf of my California sourdough to an editor at Simon & Schuster publishers along with a letter. Then she called—I'll never forget, it was just two days before Christmas—and said that she loved the bread I had just sent, and that if my recipes were as good as the bread, she would like to see me write a cookbook."

CAREER THRILL "I ended up showing Barbara Walters how to bake bread on *The Today Show* when my first book, *The Complete Book of Breads,* was published in 1973. I was delighted and she enjoyed making the dough, even though she was a little upset when we scattered flour around and got it all over her dress."

**FAVORITE STORE-BOUGHT BREAD** "My good friends at Mrs. London's bakery in Saratoga Springs, New York, ship me some of their outstanding bread to put in the freezer for the days when I don't bake my own."

ORIGINAL TITLE FOR HIS BOOK "It was 'Breads to a Man's Taste.' But the publisher said I was cutting out the female sector with that title, so they wouldn't use it."

ESSENTIAL EQUIPMENT "You better have a good oven, an oven that keeps the heat even. And an oven thermometer. You simply cannot bake bread in an oven that's too cold or too hot—you need the right temperature."

SURPRISING EQUIPMENT ENDORSEMENT The bread machine. "In the very beginning I didn't think much of it. I figured people would use it once a year and then put it away and forget it. But it's a very good dough maker—as well as a loaf baker. As a matter of fact, you can make many of my recipes in a bread machine. I don't own one, though; I've had to borrow one."

FAVORITE BREAD PANS "Many years ago I made my own bread pans out of stovepipe—it is an excellent baking tin because it absorbs rather than reflects the heat. I knew an old man who owned a country store, so I baked bread for him with soft crusts (he didn't have any teeth) in exchange for the stovepipes. I still use those pans—they make great baguettes."

INGREDIENT PET PEEVE "I just don't need all the variations of flour being made today. Flax flour, almond flour, low-carb flour…I don't do those. If you want to cut the amount of carbs you're eating in half, then just eat half a slice of bread!"

# Cinnamon Oatmeal Bread

**2 LOAVES**

*food & wine tip*

Place a baking sheet under the loaf pans while the bread is baking to prevent the sugary filling from overflowing onto the oven floor.

Miss Lucetta J. Teagarden, of Austin, Texas, has been my friend for years, though we have never met. She was one of my first readers and we have corresponded ever since. She is always on the hunt for recipes she likes, and which I, too, might like.

This Cinnamon Oatmeal Bread is one of them. She and a friend bake 15 loaves each year for Christmas giving, but I think it is too good to hold just for a special occasion. It is a special bread for anytime.

The large amount of oatmeal creates the effect of finely chopped nuts, and gives a slightly nutty flavor.

1½ cups rolled oats

1½ cups boiling water

3 tablespoons butter or margarine

3 tablespoons honey

1 tablespoon brown sugar

2 teaspoons salt

½ cup raisins

1 package dry yeast

2 eggs, room temperature

4 to 5 cups bread or all-purpose flour, approximately

3 tablespoons butter, melted

1 cup granulated sugar

2 tablespoons ground cinnamon

Equipment 2 medium (8"-x-4") loaf pans, greased or Teflon (this dough makes excellent rolls, so half could be shaped into a loaf, while the balance could be made into small rolls)

Preparation: 10 mins. In a large bowl mix together the rolled oats and boiling water. Stir to blend, and add the butter or margarine, honey, brown sugar, salt, and raisins.

If using a processor, attach the plastic dough blade; pulse the rolled oats and boiling water together in the work bowl. Let stand for a few moments to be certain the oats have absorbed the water. Remove the cover and add the butter or margarine, honey, brown sugar, salt, and yeast. Pulse.

Let the mixture cool to no more than 130°.

By hand or mixer: 12 mins. Add the yeast. Add the eggs and 2 cups flour. With a wooden spoon or with the mixer flat beater, stir vigorously for 2 to 3 minutes.

Work in additional flour, ½ cup at a time, with the spoon first and then with your hands—or dough hook, if you are using a mixer. The dough will become a soft mass that can be picked up and placed on the work surface, or left under the hook.

Kneading: 8 mins. Knead with a strong push-turn-fold rhythm, adding flour if the dough is slack or wet and sticky. Knead for 8 minutes, or until the dough is soft and elastic. If under the dough hook in the mixer, add sprinkles of flour if the dough should cling to the sides of the bowl.

By processor: 5 mins. With the machine running, add the eggs and 2 cups flour. Add additional flour, ¼ cup at a time, until the dough becomes a soft mass that whirls with the blade and, at the same time, cleans the sides of the bowl. Work in the raisins by hand.

Kneading: 50 secs. Process to knead for 50 seconds.

**First rising:** 1 hour Place the dough in a buttered bowl, cover the bowl with plastic wrap, and put the dough aside to rise at room temperature until double in bulk, about 1 hour.

**Shaping:** 10 mins. Turn the dough out of the bowl and divide into 2 pieces. With your hands and a rolling pin, shape each piece into a rectangle about 8" wide and 12" long. Butter the dough and sprinkle on the sugar and cinnamon.

Roll up the dough as for a jelly roll, and press the seams securely together. Drop each into a pan, seam down, and push into the corners and ends with your fingers.

**Second rising:** 45 mins. Cover the pans with wax paper and put aside to rise until the center of the dough is slightly above the edge, about 45 minutes.

**Preheat** Preheat the oven to 375° 20 minutes before baking.

**Baking:** 375° 40 mins. (If using a convection oven, reduce heat 50°.) Bake on the middle rack of the oven until the crusts are nicely browned, about 40 minutes. The bottom crust may be sticky with the melted sugar (which will harden as the loaf cools), but tap the crust to make certain it sounds hard and hollow.

**Final step** When the loaves come from the oven, brush with more melted butter and turn out onto a metal rack to cool before serving.

# Blue Ribbon French Bread

**2 LOAVES**

The blue ribbon won by this loaf at the Indiana State Fair almost 20 years ago has hung over my desk since I started to write cookbooks—to buoy me when it seemed there were more good recipes to be baked than there were words to describe them. Somehow I have always managed to find both.

A personal note: my mother and my sister were consistent award winners for their baked goods at the fair. It was a time of year when it seemed both were baking night and day. And then came the euphoric moment when the morning newspaper carried the names of the winners. There they were—the names of my mother, Lenora, and Martha as blue ribbon winners. Both the challenge of entering my breads in the state fair, and the happy moment of winning many years later, were heightened by my memories of those moments a long time ago.

| | |
|---|---|
| 1 | package dry yeast |
| 2 | tablespoons nonfat dry milk |
| 1 | tablespoon sugar |
| 1 | tablespoon salt |
| 4 to 5 cups all-purpose flour, approximately |
| 2 | cups hot water (120° to 130°) |
| 1 | tablespoon butter, room temperature |
| 1 | tablespoon *each* cold water and coarse salt |

Equipment 1 baking sheet, greased or Teflon

**By hand or mixer: 15 mins.** In a large mixing or mixer bowl stir together the yeast, dry milk, sugar, salt, and 2 cups flour. Pour in the hot water and add the butter. Blend with 100 strong strokes with a wooden spoon, or for 2 minutes with the flat beater of the mixer. Stir in the balance of the flour, ½ cup at a time, first with the spoon and then by hand, or in the mixer. The dough will be

**on clayton's nightstand**

**Marion Cunningham** is a favorite of mine, as is **Carol Field**; I love *The Italian Baker*. I go back to *Joy of Cooking* once a month, perhaps. I also have technical books— *Bakery Technology, Practical Baking*. I use *Larousse Gastronomique* an awful lot—it's tremendous. I also refer to **Beth Hensperger's** *Bread Lover's Bread Machine Cookbook*.

a shaggy mass, elastic but not sticky; it will clean the sides of the bowl. If, however, it continues to be moist, sprinkle on additional flour.

Rest: 10 mins. Turn the dough onto a lightly floured work surface and let it rest for 10 minutes.

Kneading: 10 mins. Knead with the rhythmic 1-2-3 motion of push-turn-fold. The dough will become smooth and elastic, and bubbles may rise under the surface of the dough. Break the kneading rhythm by throwing the dough down hard against the work surface. Knead by hand or with the mixer for 10 minutes.

By processor: 5 mins. Use the steel blade. Measure the dry ingredients and 2 cups flour into the work bowl. Pulse to blend. Pour in the hot water and add the butter. Pulse 4 or 5 times to mix thoroughly.

With the processor on, add additional flour through the feed tube, ¼ cup at a time, until the dough forms a mass and rides atop the steel blade as it whirls around the bowl. When this happens turn off the machine and allow the dough to rest for 10 minutes.

Kneading: 50 secs. Turn on processor and knead for 50 seconds.

First rising: 1¼ hours Place the dough in a greased bowl, cover tightly with plastic wrap to retain moisture, and leave at room temperature until the dough doubles in volume, about 1¼ hours.

Shaping: 15 mins. Punch down the dough and turn it onto the lightly floured work surface again. Knead for 30 seconds to press out the bubbles, cut into 2 pieces, and form each into a ball.

For a round loaf, place the dough on a corner of a baking sheet or in a small basket, lined loosely with a cloth and sprinkled with flour.

For a long loaf, roll the ball into a rectangle, about 10"x16". Roll the dough under your palms into a long loaf which can be placed directly on the baking sheet or in a long cloth-lined basket. Later, after it has risen, it will be turned from the basket directly onto the baking sheet.

Second rising: 45–50 mins. Place the baking sheet and/or the baskets in a warm place and cover the loaves carefully with a length of wax paper. Leave until the loaves have doubled in volume, about 45 to 50 minutes.

Preheat Prepare the oven by placing a large, shallow roasting pan under the bottom shelf of the oven. Preheat the oven to 400° 20 minutes before baking. Three minutes before placing the loaves in the oven, pour 1 pint hot water in the pan. Be careful of the steam that will suddenly erupt.

Baking: 400° 45 mins. (If using a convection oven, reduce heat 25°.) If the loaves have raised in baskets, simply tip the raised loaf into your hand and quickly turn the loaf right side up and onto the baking sheet. Brush with cold water and sprinkle with the coarse salt.

With a razor blade or a sharp knife, slash the round loaves with a tic-tac-toe design, the long loaves with diagonal cuts.

Bake the loaves until they are golden brown, 45 minutes. Turn over one loaf and tap the bottom crust; a hard hollow sound means the bread is baked. If not, return to the oven for an additional 10 minutes. Midway during baking and again near the end of it, shift the loaves on the baking sheets so they are exposed equally to the temperature variations of the oven.

Final step Remove the loaves from the oven and place them on wire racks to cool. This bread is delicious reheated. Place uncovered in a 350° oven for 20 minutes. It also keeps well frozen at 0°.

# Roquefort Cheese Bread

**2 MEDIUM LOAVES**

### food & wine tip

This cheese-flavored bread would be excellent for sandwiches, especially roast beef or turkey.

The cheesemakers of the small French town of Roquefort-sur-Soulzon have for centuries stood militant over the good name and incomparable flavor of their much-prized cheese. If it is not made with sheep's milk or aged in the region's extraordinary limestone caverns, it is *not* Roquefort. And these cheesemakers will pursue to the ends of the world anyone who dares call his blue-veined cheese, no matter the quality, a Roquefort!

A slice of deep brown Roquefort bread is as delicious as Roquefort crumbled in a salad or spread on toast. Because the veins running through the cheese are a deep blue, the bread, understandably, is colored a rich off-white.

This recipe is from those vigilant Roquefort cheesemakers, and while I have made respectable loaves with a domestic blue-veined cheese, it is just not the same as the genuine article.

There is a glorious smell in the house when this bread is baking.

1½ cups milk

4    ounces (1 cup) Roquefort cheese, room temperature, crumbled

2    tablespoons butter, room temperature

1    egg, beaten

¼    cup sugar

1    teaspoon salt

4½ to 5 cups bread or all-purpose flour, approximately

2    packages dry yeast

Equipment 2 medium (8"-x-4") loaf pans, greased or Teflon

**By hand or mixer: 15 mins.** In a medium saucepan heat the milk and add the crumbled cheese, butter, egg, sugar, and salt. Stir until the cheese has melted into the liquid. Set aside.

In a mixing or mixer bowl measure in 3½ cups flour and the yeast. Stir to blend. By hand or with the mixer flat beater, stir the milk-cheese mixture into the flour to become a thick batter. Beat with 50 strong strokes, or for 2 minutes in the mixer. Add flour, ¼ cup at a time, until the dough forms a shaggy ball and can be lifted from the bowl to a floured work surface. In the mixer, the dough will clean the sides of the bowl and at the same time form a ball around the dough hook.

Kneading: 10 mins. Knead by hand with the strong motion of push-turn-fold, adding sprinkles of flour if the dough is sticky. The dough is rich in butterfat and will be soft and elastic under the hands. Knead by hand or with the dough hook for 10 minutes.

By processor: 8 mins. Heat the milk and other ingredients, as above, and set aside.

Attach the short dough blade. Measure 3½ cups flour into the work bowl and sprinkle on the yeast. Pulse to blend. With the motor on, slowly pour the milk-cheese mixture through the feed tube. Stop the machine. The dough will be a thick batter and quite sticky. With the processor running, add flour, ¼ cup at a time, through the feed tube. The dough will form a ball that cleans the sides and bottom of the work bowl.

Kneading: 1 min. Process for 1 minute to knead.

Stop the machine, uncover, and pinch off a small piece of dough the size of a golf ball. If it can be pulled and stretched with your fingers, it is sufficiently kneaded. If necessary, to achieve an elastic ball, return the dough to the work bowl with a small bit of flour to process for a few more seconds.

First rising: 1 hour Place the dough in a greased bowl, cover with plastic wrap, and put aside to double in volume, about 1 hour.

**Shaping:** 4 mins. Place the dough on a floured work surface, then divide the dough in half. Work and roll each half into a tubular shape the length of the loaf pan. Press the dough down into the corners of the pan with your fingers.

**Second rising:** 40 mins. Cover the loaves and allow to rise to ½" above the edge of the pan, about 40 minutes.

**Preheat** Preheat the oven to 375° 15 minutes before baking.

**Baking:** 375° 30–40 mins. (If using a convection oven, reduce heat 50°.) With a razor blade or sharp knife, cut a ½"-deep slit down the length of each loaf.

Place the loaves on the middle shelf of the moderately hot oven. The cheese-rich dough will brown quickly, so after 20 minutes cover the loaves with a length of foil. Turn the loaf pan around midway during baking so the loaves are exposed to an equal range of temperatures.

**Final step** Remove the bread from the oven. Allow to cool completely on a wire rack before slicing.

The Roquefort cheesemakers suggest storing the loaf in a covered container that has a few tiny openings for ventilation. I don't want to cross them, but I find it more convenient to keep my cheese bread in an ordinary paper sack (to retain a crisp crust) or a plastic bag. This bread freezes beautifully. In reheating or toasting, the loaf casts a wonderful fragrance throughout the house—an ideal loaf to bake before a prospective buyer comes to visit.

# Fresh Strawberry Bread

I MEDIUM LOAF

| | |
|---|---|
| 1 | pint fresh strawberries, washed and hulled |
| 1¾ | cups bread or all-purpose flour |
| 1 | teaspoon baking soda |
| 1 | teaspoon salt |
| ¼ | teaspoon baking powder |
| ¾ | cup sugar |
| ⅓ | cup butter or other shortening |
| 2 | eggs |
| ⅓ | cup water |
| ½ | cup chopped walnuts |
| | Cream cheese, softened (optional) |

**Equipment** 1 medium (8½"-x-4½") loaf pan, greased or Teflon, long sides and bottom lined with buttered wax paper

**Preheat** Preheat the oven to 350°.

**Preparation: 5 mins.** Crush enough of the strawberries to fill 1 cup. Pour into a small saucepan and heat over a medium flame. Cook for 1 minute, stirring constantly. Cool. Slice the remaining strawberries and chill.

**By hand: 8 mins.** In a medium bowl combine the dry ingredients, except the sugar. In a large mixing bowl cream the sugar and butter or other shortening; then add the eggs and water, mixing until light and fluffy. Add the flour mixture to the creamed mixture, mixing well to blend. Stir in the crushed strawberries and walnuts. Pour or spoon the mixture into the prepared pan.

**Baking: 350° 1 hour** (If using a convection oven, reduce heat 50°.) Bake for 1 hour, or until a pick inserted in the center comes out clean.

**Final step** Remove the bread from the oven. When the loaf has cooled in the pan for 10 minutes, turn onto a rack to cool. Present to your guests thin slices spread with softened cream cheese and topped with the reserved chilled strawberries. Families will like it, too.

*food & wine* **tip**

This scrumptious breakfast bread is also delicious with strawberry preserves.

# BitterSweet

## ALICE MEDRICH

**BACKGROUND** Born in Temple City, California, outside Los Angeles; lives in Berkeley, California.

**EDUCATION** Studied history as an undergraduate at the University of California at Berkeley in the early 1970s; also pursued an MBA there.

**EXPERIENCE** "For years and years I owned a chocolate and pastry shop in Berkeley called Cocolat and amassed a collection of recipes. I compiled these in my first book, *Cocolat: Extraordinary Chocolate Desserts*. It came out when all kinds of new culinary things were happening, and I tried to describe my own experience of that era."

**PREVIOUS BOOKS** Following *Cocolat* came *Chocolate and the Art of Low-Fat Desserts, Alice Medrich's Cookies and Brownies* and *A Year in Chocolate: Four Seasons of Unforgettable Desserts*.

**WHAT MAKES THIS BOOK DIFFERENT** "In some ways *BitterSweet* is breaking a lot of new ground because I was baking with chocolates that are more flavorful and less sweet and trying to figure out how to incorporate them in the recipes we are accustomed to. People usually add a ton of sugar and fat to chocolate in order to enjoy it in desserts. I wanted to address the notion that chocolate is not just a generic flavor, it's many flavors, and you don't want to mask the nuances. I wanted to talk about chocolate a little bit more as a specialty not so different from wine, coffee or cheese. My intention was to give people some tools—ideas and recipes— to use these new chocolates and to start to experiment on their own."

**HOW SHE CAME TO LOVE CHOCOLATE** "I grew up on chocolate, like a lot of Americans. I started out with Hershey bars and M&Ms. Then as a really young woman I tasted some chocolate things in Paris that heightened my understanding of what chocolate could be. My landlady's chocolate truffle was a real turning point."

**PET PEEVE** Multiflavored chocolate desserts. "Some of the ways that exotic flavors are combined with chocolate are so heavy-handed."

FAVORITE CHOCOLATE INDULGENCE "I love all the Scharffen Berger chocolates, and all their many tastes: tart, fruity, assertive, subtle. On my book tour I traveled around with tiny wrapped squares of all of Scharffen Berger's different chocolates. If I was tired, annoyed or lonely, I'd unwrap one and pop it in my mouth. My hotel rooms would be littered with little paper squares."

HOW BAKING CAN BE RELAXING "It's important to pay attention to details—they make all the difference—but the process can also be meditative. Just go from beginning to end, methodically. It's a little dance."

BEST ADVICE FOR NOVICE BAKERS "Pick a simple recipe, be accurate in your measurements—and spend your money on a chocolate you love."

NEWEST CHOCOLATE DISCOVERY Cocoa nibs, which are roasted, hulled and broken cocoa beans. "When I tasted them, I suddenly realized that chocolate doesn't have to be used only in sweet desserts. The flavor and texture of those nibs reminded me of a wonderfully complex, earthy, tart-fruity nut. What a fabulous crunch! So I tried sprinkling them on some greens in a simple salad just the way you would toasted nuts—and they were terrific. Once I tried *that,* I was inspired to try the nibs with all kinds of savory foods. It was fun to discover that those flavor combinations really work well."

**LESS IS MORE** "I'm in a minimalist period. Ninety percent of the time I'd just as soon eat a small piece of plain chocolate as I would a chocolate dessert."

MOST UNUSUAL USE OF CHOCOLATE IN THE BOOK Chopped Eggplant with Cocoa Nibs and Chopped Chicken Livers with Sherry-Cocoa Pan Sauce.

ON LOWER-FAT CHOCOLATE RECIPES "More and more I'm replacing cream with milk. That interests me—the whole business of decreasing the sweetness and fat in order to get more flavor out of a dish, including dessert."

ESSENTIAL EQUIPMENT Microplane zesters. "I just adore them. I went through a period when I made every food you can imagine with citrus zest."

CHOCOLATE TRENDS "I see a lot more interest in the origins of chocolate and in the complexity of its flavors. Americans love to become connoisseurs. When they get their hands on a product they like, they grab it and go. Fine chocolate is next."

# Marble Cheesecake

**SERVES 10 TO 12**

Updated and improved, this is one of the best cheesecakes I make, even though a slice has only about two hundred calories and less than eight grams of fat. What it does have is plenty of cheese flavor and a satisfying swirl of rich dark chocolate without the excessive sweetness of commercial cheesecake. I often teach this recipe alongside luxuriously rich and decadent desserts. It is only from the ingredients list, never from the taste or texture, that students realize that this cake has a fraction of the fat of a traditional cheesecake.

Avoid nonfat cream cheeses and spreads because they taste artificial. I like the flavor of Neufchâtel cream cheese and low-fat cottage cheese or quark, which is an excellent creamy type of yogurt cheese available at cheese shops and also at the best supermarkets. I have also added simple steps to make the texture richer and less *wet* (the bane of some low-fat homemade cheesecakes). Thus the cottage cheese or quark is drained and the cake pan is lined with absorbent coffee filters. And I use real ground vanilla beans, if possible, rather than vanilla extract. It's still a simple recipe, but, as always, the details make a difference!

Instead of one 8-inch cake, you can make two 6-inch cheesecakes from this recipe. Bake 5 to 10 minutes less. For best flavor and texture, make this one day before serving.

One 16-ounce container low-fat (2%) quark or small-curd cottage cheese

3     tablespoons premium cocoa powder (natural or Dutch-process)

¼     teaspoon instant espresso powder (such as Medaglia d'Oro) or coffee powder

1     cup plus 1 tablespoon sugar

3     tablespoons water

1½ teaspoons strained fresh lemon juice (if using cottage cheese)

One 8-ounce package Neufchâtel cream cheese (Kraft in the box is good—don't buy the kind in the tub)

3     cold large eggs

## on medrich's nightstand

It's hard to name only a few favorite authors. In the dessert world, I love **Flo Braker, Carole Walter, Lindsey Shere** and **Marion Cunningham.** Among my favorites beyond desserts are **Barbara Tropp, Joyce Goldstein, Carol Field, Rick Bayless, Shirley Corriher** and **Harold McGee.**

¾   teaspoon ground vanilla beans, or 1 tablespoon pure vanilla extract

¼   teaspoon salt

¼   cup graham cracker crumbs or chocolate wafer crumbs,
     homemade or store-bought

Special equipment An 8-inch round cake pan (not a springform) at least
2 inches deep

4 round coffee filters at least 8 inches in diameter (iron or weight them if
necessary to flatten them), or several cone-shaped filters

An 8-inch cardboard cake circle (optional)

Line a sieve with several layers of folded paper towels topped with 1 of the
coffee filters. Scrape the quark or cottage cheese on top and set the sieve
over a bowl. Cover and refrigerate for at least 30 minutes to drain. (Don't worry
if the cheese does not exude much liquid; some brands do, some don't.)

Position a rack in the lower third of the oven and preheat the oven to 350°F.
Line the bottom of the cake pan with coffee filters: Lay round ones on top of
one another, or arrange cone-shaped filters in an overlapping pattern to cover
the bottom of the pan. Lightly grease the sides of the pan. Put a kettle of
water on to boil.

In a small bowl, whisk the cocoa, coffee powder, 1 tablespoon of the sugar,
and the 3 tablespoons water until smooth. Set aside.

Place the drained cheese (if using cottage cheese, add the lemon juice now) in
a food processor for 2½ to 3 minutes, until silky-smooth, scraping the sides and
bottom of the bowl once or twice as necessary. Leave the cheese in the processor.

Soften the Neufchâtel cheese in the microwave on high (100%) power for about
30 seconds. Or warm it gently in the top of a double boiler. Stir until smooth
and soft, like thick mayonnaise. Scrape into the processor. Add the eggs, the

remaining 1 cup sugar, the vanilla, and salt. Pulse only until all the ingredients are incorporated and the mixture is perfectly smooth. Do not overprocess or the batter will become too thin.

Stir 1 cup of the batter into the cocoa mixture. Pour all of the plain batter into the prepared pan (on top of the coffee filters). To prevent the chocolate batter from sinking into the vanilla batter, pour or spoon it gently—in several puddles—over the top, making sure it doesn't cover all of the vanilla batter. Draw a knife or teaspoon through the puddles to marble the batters without really mixing them together. (The cake tastes best and most chocolatey with separate pockets of vanilla and chocolate rather than a blend.)

Place the cheesecake pan in a baking pan at least 1 inch larger all around than the cake pan, pull out the oven rack, and set the pans on the rack. Carefully pour boiling water around the cheesecake pan to a depth of about 1 inch. Slide the oven rack in gently and bake until the cheesecake has puffed and risen slightly around the edges and is just beginning to shrink from the edges of the pan, 40 to 45 minutes. Remove the cheesecake from the water bath and cool on a rack. When completely cool, cover and chill for at least 12 hours, or for up to 2 days, before serving.

To serve, run a thin knife blade around the side of the pan to release the cake. Cover the pan with tightly stretched plastic wrap. Place a flat dish upside down over the plastic. Invert the pan and dish and rap the pan gently until the cheesecake is released from the pan. Remove the pan and peel the coffee filters from the bottom of the cake. Place a cake circle or serving plate on the cake and carefully invert again so that the cake is right side up. Remove the plastic wrap. Press the crumbs around the sides of the cake. Cut with a sharp thin knife dipped in hot water and wiped dry between cuts.

CHOCOLATE NOTE I get good results with either natural or Dutch-process cocoa. However, I don't like the Dutch-process cocoas called "black" cocoa.

# Melting Chocolate Cookie Tartlets

**MAKES 8 TO 10 TARTLETS**

*food & wine tip*

The tartlet dough here is extremely soft and a little difficult to work with. Don't worry—it's supposed to be that way, and it will yield a fabulous buttery, tender crust.

These rustic-looking craggy-topped tartlets with a crunchy crust and chewy-yet-soft-centered chocolate filling were the inspiration of one of my students. Alicia Hitchcock makes thousands of tartlets by filling my melted butter shortbread crust with my melting chocolate meringue cookie batter. Here's "our" recipe.

For the crust

| | |
|---|---|
| 8 | tablespoons (1 stick) unsalted butter, melted |
| 3 | tablespoons sugar |
| ¾ | teaspoon pure vanilla extract |
| ⅛ | teaspoon salt |
| 1 | cup all-purpose flour |

For the filling

| | |
|---|---|
| 6 | ounces bittersweet or semisweet chocolate, coarsely chopped |
| 2 | large egg whites, at room temperature |
| ⅛ | teaspoon cream of tartar |
| ½ | teaspoon pure vanilla extract |
| ¼ | cup sugar |
| ¾ | cup chopped pecans or walnuts |

Special equipment Eight 4-inch (measured across the top) or ten 3½-inch fluted tartlet pans (about ¾ inch deep)

Position a rack in the lower third of the oven and preheat the oven to 350°F.

To make the crust Mix the butter, sugar, vanilla, and salt in a medium bowl. Add the flour and mix just until well blended. Don't worry if the dough seems too soft. Divide the dough into 8 or 10 equal pieces. Press one piece of dough very thinly and evenly across the bottom and up the sides of each tartlet pan. This takes some patience—there is just enough dough. Place the pans on a cookie sheet. Bake for 15 to 20 minutes, until a deep golden brown.

While the crusts are baking, make the filling: Melt the chocolate in a medium heatproof bowl set in a wide skillet of barely simmering water, or in the microwave on medium (50%) power for 3½ to 4 minutes, stirring frequently until the chocolate is almost completely melted. Remove from the heat and stir until completely melted. Set aside.

In a large bowl, beat the egg whites with the cream of tartar and vanilla until soft peaks form when you lift the beaters. Gradually add the sugar and continue to beat until the egg whites are stiff but not dry. Pour the nuts and all of the warm chocolate over the egg whites and fold with a rubber spatula until the color of the batter is uniform.

As soon as the tartlet crusts are ready, divide the filling equally among them. Make sure that batter touches the crust all around the edges. Return to the oven and bake until the filling is dry or slightly cracked on top, about 10 minutes. Cool on a rack.

To unmold, use the point of a paring knife to loosen one edge of the crust from the pan, then tip the tarts into your hand. Serve warm or at room temperature.

Ideas Fold into the filling 2 ounces crystallized ginger, finely chopped; 4 ounces moist prunes, chopped into ¼-inch pieces; or 4 ounces candied chestnuts, chopped. Substitute toasted pine nuts for the pecans.

CHOCOLATE NOTES You can use standard bittersweet or semisweet chocolate (without a percentage on the label), or any marked 50% to 62%.

To use chocolate marked 64% to 66% instead of standard bittersweet: Use 5 ounces chocolate.

To use chocolate marked 70% to 72% instead of standard bittersweet: Use 4½ ounces chocolate, and increase the sugar to ⅓ cup.

# Tiger Cake

**SERVES 12**

A chocolate marble cake made with extra virgin olive oil and a pinch of white pepper? Stay with me. The flavors are subtle and delicious, the cake is moist with a close-to-pound-cake texture, it's not too sweet, and the stripes are beautiful. The pepper does its work sotto voce, accentuating the olive oil flavor and somehow adding an elusive almond flavor with just a little heat. Too esoteric? The five-year-old boy who named the cake (for the stripes, of course) says it's his favorite, but grown-ups like it too. It's a little sneaky in that it seems plain at first, then you notice you've eaten the whole piece and have started slicing seconds.

This cake is even better on the second day. Toasting brings out more flavor too; try a slice for breakfast. Finally, the cake is easy to make and seems to be self-marbling: The liquid layers of batter sink and mingle in the oven of their own accord, with gorgeous results.

½    cup natural cocoa powder (not Dutch-process)

½    cup sugar

⅓    cup water

3    cups all-purpose flour

2    teaspoons baking powder

¼    teaspoon salt

2    cups sugar

1    cup flavorful extra virgin olive oil

1    teaspoon pure vanilla extract

½    teaspoon finely ground white pepper

5    cold large eggs

1    cup cold milk

Special equipment A 10- to 12-cup tube or Bundt pan or two 6-cup loaf pans

*food & wine* **tip**

Using a good-quality olive oil is key to the success of this recipe. Look for one that is super fruity and tastes delicious all by itself.

Position a rack in the lower third of the oven and preheat the oven to 350°F. Grease and flour the cake pan or line the loaf pans with parchment.

In a small bowl, whisk the cocoa, sugar, and water together until well blended. Set aside. Mix the flour, baking powder, and salt thoroughly and sift together onto a piece of wax paper. Set aside.

In a large mixer bowl (with the whisk attachment if you have it), beat the sugar, oil, vanilla, and pepper until well blended. Add the eggs one at a time, beating well after each addition. Continue to beat until the mixture is thick and pale, 3 to 5 minutes. Stop the mixer and add one-third of the flour mixture. Beat on low speed just until blended. Stop the mixer and add half of the milk. Beat just until it is blended. Repeat with another third of the flour, the remaining milk, and then the remaining flour.

Pour 3 cups of the batter into another bowl and stir in the cocoa mixture. Pour one-third of the plain batter into the prepared tube pan (or divide it between the loaves) and top with one-third of the chocolate batter. Repeat with the remaining batters. Don't worry about marbling the batters—that happens beautifully during the baking.

Bake until a cake tester comes out clean, about 1 hour and 10 minutes for either the tube pan or loaf pans. Cool the cake in the pan(s) on a rack for about 15 minutes. Slide a skewer around the tube pan or slide a thin knife around the sides of the loaf pans to release the cake(s). Invert the pan(s) and invert again, setting the cake right side up on a rack to cool completely.

CHOCOLATE NOTE Natural cocoa powder is a *must* here. Dutch-process adds an unpleasant taste because it reacts with the leavening and the olive oil in the cake.

# Cocoa Nib Panna Cotta

**SERVES 6**

This dreamy, delicately set dessert is flavored with an infusion of roasted cocoa beans. Measure the gelatin like a miser . . . or risk turning an exquisite confection into a dish of Jell-O.

½   cup cocoa nibs, coarsely chopped into smaller bits

3¼ cups heavy cream

2¾ teaspoons unflavored gelatin

1    cup whole milk

¼   cup plus 2 tablespoons sugar

Pinch of salt

Fresh blackberries or blackberry puree, well sugared

Special equipment Instant-read thermometer

6 wide margarita glasses (or six 6-ounce ramekins)

Bring the nibs and cream to a boil in a medium saucepan over medium-high heat. Remove from the heat, cover, and let steep for 20 minutes. Meanwhile, sprinkle the gelatin over the cold milk in a small bowl and set aside to let the gelatin soften.

Strain the cream, pressing lightly on the nibs to extract all the liquid. Discard the nibs. Return the cream to the saucepan, add the sugar, and bring to a simmer. Pour into a heatproof bowl. Gradually stir in the milk, then the salt. Set the bowl in a larger bowl of ice cubes and water and stir frequently until the mixture thickens and registers 50°F on an instant-read thermometer. Divide evenly among the margarita glasses (or ramekins). Cover with plastic wrap and chill overnight.

Serve the panna cotta in their glasses or ramekins. Or, wrap each ramekin in a hot wrung-out wet towel and unmold onto dessert plates. Accompany with well-sugared berries or berry puree.

# The Bread Bible

## ROSE LEVY BERANBAUM

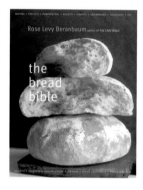

**BACKGROUND** Born in Far Rockaway, New York; lives in Manhattan.

**EDUCATION** Attended the University of Vermont and then New York University, where she studied food science and culinary arts. She went on to earn her master's in food science from NYU.

**EXPERIENCE** "I began my food career in the test kitchen at *Ladies' Home Journal*—a great experience. I always envied the head of the test kitchen because that person got to make all the special cakes. I went on to study cake decorating at the Wilton School in Chicago. Then I started food styling and writing about food for magazines and cookbooks."

**HOW SHE CAME TO LOVE FOOD** "I didn't grow up around good food. My mother was a dentist, and she was too busy working to have the time to cook. When I went away to college I realized just how good food could be. Then I met a woman who worked in the test kitchen at American Can Company, and I found her job and the environment she worked in simply amazing. I saw for the first time that if you knew how to cook, you could have wonderful food all the time, every day."

**PREVIOUS BOOKS** Beranbaum has written seven other cookbooks, six of them about baking (she considers herself a "missionary of baking"). Her baking books include *The Cake Bible, Rose's Christmas Cookies* and *The Pie and Pastry Bible*.

**IDEAL COAUTHOR** "I would love to write a book with Pat Conroy. I sent him a letter once asking for a duck recipe that he describes beautifully in his novel *The Prince of Tides*. His wife wrote back and said it was all fiction, and that Pat's mother actually made fish sticks. But he did send me a recipe that he said inspired the dish in the story. We became friends and he even put a character similar to me in his book *Beach Music*. He has a very special food sensibility."

## ESSENTIAL EQUIPMENT
A pizza stone. "It helps the oven heat more evenly, and it retains heat so you don't lose as much every time you open the oven door."

**MENTOR** Dieter Schorner, associate professor of baking and pastry arts at The Culinary Institute of America. "He is truly a culinary treasure. All you need to do is look at his hands, and watch how he handles the dough with such love."

**WHAT SHE LOVES MOST ABOUT BAKING BREAD** "I often feel like an alchemist. Bread is like magic: You have four basic ingredients and you can make variations simply by changing the rising time or the amount of water. Bread also connects people—every culture has it. It's fundamental to human existence."

**WHY SHE WROTE THE BOOK** "I find instructions in many cookbooks are very vague, especially in baking books. A lot of recipes, for instance, don't explain how you can tell when bread is fully risen, and if you get that wrong, you can ruin the flavor and texture. I always give the specifics. People are already frightened when it comes to baking; my goal is to make the process transparent, to have it make sense so people can jump right in."

**FAVORITE NEW YORK CITY BAKERIES** "I love the rosemary focaccia at Sullivan Street Bakery, the raisin pecan bread made by Eli's Bread and the amazing sticky buns at Balthazar Bakery."

**RECIPES THAT DIDN'T MAKE THE BOOK** "There are a hundred that didn't make the book. I'm an explorer, a researcher; I'm always trying new things. One recipe that was cut was Heartbeat Bread. I added beet juice to the dough to make it red and shaped it into a heart. My editor said it looked too realistic. Another one was Swiss Black Pear Bread: The pear is not America's favorite fruit."

**MOST COMMON BAKING MISTAKE** "Recipes often call for 'all-purpose flour,' which is very misleading. You need to use different kinds of flour for different kinds of bread; in my recipes I always specify which kind. For quick-bread recipes that call for solid butter, always use bleached flour. For yeast breads, always use unbleached flour. Even professionals get this wrong."

**COOKBOOK TRENDS** "There are so many cookbooks for people who want things faster, easier and better. But what I love about the craft of baking is that people are willing to treat it more as a hobby, and so they are also more willing to dedicate time to it; they don't necessarily expect immediate results. Although, when you really get into it, you learn that baking bread is quite simple."

# Southwestern Corn Spoon Bread

**SERVES 4**

My friend and longtime collaborator David Shamah is a font of ingenious ideas. This recipe was inspired by one of his suggestions, and it is the best spoon bread I've ever had. It forms a crisp and golden cheesy crust on top, and inside it is light yet moist and full flavored. It's terrific as an accompaniment to barbecued chicken, pork chops, sausages, or ham—I actually love this spoon bread so much I think of these other dishes more as an accompaniment to it!

Oven Temperature: 375°F    Baking Time: 30 to 35 minutes

| Filling ingredients | MEASURE | WEIGHT | |
| --- | --- | --- | --- |
| room temperature | volume | ounces | grams |
| unsalted butter | 4 tablespoons | 2 ounces | 57 grams |
| 1 small onion, chopped | ⅔ cup | 3 ounces | 86 grams |
| chipotle chile in adobo (see step 2), or ½ jalapeño pepper, seeded and finely chopped | about 1 tablespoon | – | 12.5 grams 11 grams |
| 1 large garlic clove, minced | 2 teaspoons | 0.25 ounce | 7 grams |
| ½ roasted red bell pepper, peeled, seeded, and chopped | ½ cup | 3 ounces | 85 grams |
| 2 small ears corn—husked and cooked, kernels | 1 cup (or 11-ounce can niblets, drained) | 5 ounces | 142 grams |
| cilantro, chopped | ¼ cup | – | 20 grams |

Equipment A 4- to 6-cup ceramic casserole or soufflé dish, buttered or greased with cooking spray or oil

1. Preheat the oven Preheat the oven to 375°F 20 minutes before baking.

2. Sauté the filling Place a medium (10-inch) skillet over medium-low heat and add the butter. When it is melted, add the onion and jalapeño (if not using the chipotle). Sauté, stirring occasionally, until the onion is softened and golden.

Add the garlic and sauté, stirring constantly, for 30 seconds. Remove the pan from the heat and stir in the red pepper, corn, and cilantro. If using the chipotle, remove most of the seeds and chop it fine. Combine it with enough of the adobo sauce to make 1 tablespoon and stir into the filling. Cool completely.

| Batter ingredients | MEASURE | WEIGHT | |
|---|---|---|---|
| room temperature | volume | ounces | grams |
| *bleached* all-purpose flour (such as Gold Medal or Pillsbury) | ½ cup plus ½ tablespoon | 2.5 ounces | 75 grams |
| yellow cornmeal, preferably stone-ground (such as Kenyon's) | ½ cup | 2.25 ounces | 64 grams |
| sugar | 3 tablespoons | 1.3 ounces | 38 grams |
| baking powder | 1 ¼ teaspoons | — | 6 grams |
| salt | ¾ plus ⅛ teaspoon | — | 5.8 grams |
| black pepper | ⅛ teaspoon | — | — |
| heavy cream | ⅓ liquid cup | 2.75 ounces | 80 grams |
| milk | ⅓ liquid cup | 2.75 ounces | 80 grams |
| 1 large egg, divided: yolk | 1 tablespoon plus ½ teaspoon | 0.65 ounce | 18.6 grams |
| white | 2 tablespoons | 1 ounce | 30 grams |
| cream of tartar | ⅛ teaspoon | — | — |
| sharp cheddar cheese, shredded | 1 heaping cup, divided | 2.5 ounces | 70 grams |
| *Optional:* red pepper flakes, if not using the chipotle | ⅛ teaspoon | — | — |

3. **Mix the batter** In a medium bowl, stir together the flour, cornmeal, sugar, baking powder, salt, and black pepper. In a glass measuring cup or small bowl, lightly whisk together the cream, milk, and egg yolk.

## on beranbaum's nightstand

For bread, one of my favorite books is **Peter Reinhart's** *The Bread Baker's Apprentice.* Also **Artisan Baking Across America** by **Maggie Glezer.** For food, I love **Judy Rodgers's** *The Zuni Café Cookbook.* I always go to *Joy of Cooking* and **Doubleday Cookbook** when I have questions.

In a medium bowl, whisk the egg white until foamy. Add the cream of tartar and whisk until stiff peaks form when the beater is lifted slowly.

Stir the egg/milk mixture and corn mixture into the flour mixture just until it is evenly moistened. Fold in all but ½ cup (1 ounce/28 grams) of the cheese, then fold in the egg white just until incorporated.

4. Bake the spoon bread Pour the batter into the prepared casserole. Sprinkle with the remaining cheese and the optional red pepper flakes. Bake for 30 to 35 minutes or until the top is puffed and golden brown and springs back when lightly pressed in the center with your finger (an instant-read thermometer inserted in the center will read about 160°F). Serve at once.

STORE Any leftovers can be refrigerated for up to 5 days.

POINTERS FOR SUCCESS To roast a red pepper, line a gas burner with foil to catch any dripping juices. Hold the pepper over the heat with tongs, turning it occasionally so that the skin blisters and chars all over. (Or, if you have an electric range, roast it under the broiler.) Place it in a plastic bag for a few minutes to steam, to help separate the skin from the pepper. Then remove and discard as much of the skin as possible.

To cook the fresh corn, boil the ears in unsalted water for 5 to 7 minutes or until just tender when pierced with a cake tester or skewer. Canned niblets are the best alternative to fresh corn. An 11-ounce can of niblets, drained, equals 9.6 ounces/272 grams; half is 4.8 ounces/113 grams. If niblets are unavailable, use frozen corn, thawed.

The spoon bread reheats well, particularly in a microwave.

The recipe can be doubled easily.

# Big Banana Muffins

**MAKES 5 MUFFINS**

This recipe is adapted from my banana cake, one of the most popular recipes in my book *The Cake Bible*. The texture and flavor of the toasted walnuts, or poppy seeds or chocolate, are a great new addition. I bake them in a Texas muffin pan, which has cups that have an 8-ounce capacity, compared to the usual 6 ounces. Texas, the largest state in America, is big on big, which is how this muffin pan got its name! It seemed particularly appropriate for these muffins because they are big on flavor as well as size. This batter can also be baked in a loaf pan, and can feature chocolate chips. (See the variation on page 62 and the pointers at the end of the recipe on page 63.)

**beranbaum's tip**

For calculation purposes if making these muffins in larger quantities, it is useful to know that the banana peel represents about 25 percent of the weight of the banana.

**Oven Temperature: 350°F     Baking Time: 25 to 30 minutes**

| Ingredients | MEASURE | WEIGHT | |
|---|---|---|---|
| room temperaure | volume | ounces | grams |
| 1 very ripe banana, peeled and lightly mashed | ½ cup | 4 ounces | 113.5 grams |
| sour cream | ¼ cup | about 2 ounces | 60 grams |
| 1 large egg | 3 tablespoons | 1.75 ounces (weighed without shell) | 50 grams |
| grated lemon zest | 1 teaspoon | — | 2 grams |
| pure vanilla extract | ¾ teaspoon | — | — |
| *bleached* cake flour or *bleached* all-purpose flour | 1 cup scant ¾ cup | 3.5 ounces | 100 grams |
| sugar, preferably turbinado | 6 tablespoons | 2.6 ounces | 75 grams |
| baking powder | ½ teaspoon | — | 2.4 grams |
| baking soda | ½ teaspoon | — | 2.5 grams |
| salt | ¼ teaspoon | — | 1.7 grams |
| unsalted butter, softened | 5 tablespoons | 2.5 ounces | 71 grams |
| walnuts, toasted and chopped medium-fine | ½ cup | 1.75 ounces | 50 grams |

## beranbaum's banana loaf variation

This recipe can also be baked in an 8-by-4-inch bread pan for 40 to 50 minutes or until a wooden skewer inserted in the center comes out clean.

Equipment A heavy-duty stand mixer with paddle attachment or a hand-held mixer; a Texas muffin pan lined with foil or paper liners, preferably lightly sprayed with Baker's Joy or cooking spray

1. Preheat the oven Preheat the oven to 350°F 20 minutes before baking. Have an oven shelf at the middle level.

2. Mix the batter In a food processor fitted with the metal blade, process the banana and sour cream until smooth. Add the egg, lemon zest, and vanilla and process until blended.

In a mixer bowl or other large bowl, combine the flour, sugar, baking powder, baking soda, and salt and beat on low speed (#2 if using a KitchenAid, with the paddle attachment) for about 1 minute, until well mixed. Add the butter and half the banana mixture and beat until the dry ingredients are moistened. Raise the speed to medium (#4 KitchenAid) or high if using a hand-held electric mixer and beat for 1½ minutes. Scrape down the sides of the bowl. Add the remaining banana mixture in two parts, beating for about 20 seconds after each addition or until well mixed. On low speed, beat in the walnuts.

3. Fill the muffin containers Spoon or pipe the batter into the muffin containers, filling them three-quarters full. Pour a little water into the unfilled muffin cup to prevent uneven baking.

4. Bake the muffins Bake for 25 to 30 minutes or until the muffins spring back when pressed lightly in the center.

5. Cool the muffins Remove the muffins from the oven and unmold them at once onto a wire rack. Turn top side up and cool until just warm or room temperature.

STORE Stored airtight at room temperature, these have just as lovely a texture and flavor the next day. The muffins can be reheated for about 4 minutes in a 400°F oven.

POINTERS FOR SUCCESS Use *bleached* all-purpose flour for a firmer, more bread-like texture. Use cake flour for a softer, lighter crumb.

For finely grated zest, use a citrus zester (a small implement with tiny scraping holes), a vegetable peeler, or fine grater to remove the yellow portion only of the peel. The white pith beneath is bitter. If using a zester or peeler, finish by chopping the zest with a sharp knife.

For the best flavor and sweetness, use a banana that is very ripe, with black spots all over the skin.

It is not necessary to sift the flour if you are weighing it. However, if you measure it, be sure to sift it into the cup and then level it off, without shaking or tapping the cup at all.

A #30 ice cream scoop (2-tablespoon capacity) works well for transferring the batter to the muffin containers. But I find it easiest to use a heavy-duty gallon zip-seal bag as a disposable piping bag. Scrape the batter into the bag, zip it closed, and cut off the tip.

The muffins can be frozen for up to 3 months. Frozen muffins can be reheated in a preheated 400°F oven for 15 to 20 minutes or until a metal cake tester inserted briefly into the center feels warm.

These are also delicious made with 2 tablespoons poppy seeds instead of the walnuts.

For a chocolate chip version, fold ¼ cup/1.5 ounces/42 grams of mini chocolate chips (or chocolate chopped medium fine) into the finished batter.

For a chocolate swirl version, stir 1 ounce/28 grams melted cooled bittersweet chocolate into ½ cup of the batter. Add it to the top of the batter in the loaf pan or muffin cups and swirl it in.

# Dutch Baby

SERVES 4 TO 6

A Dutch baby is actually a giant crater-shaped popover, perfect for accommodating a filling of sautéed caramelized apples, peaches, or fresh berries and a billow of crème fraîche or whipped cream.

As is so often the case, it is the simplest things that require the most work to perfect. My goal was for a Dutch baby that had crisp, puffy sides but a tender, almost custardy bottom (as opposed to an eggy/rubbery one). The final result of many tests is this crunchiest, puffiest, and most tender version. The secrets are coating the flour with the butter before adding the milk, and adding 2 extra egg whites and enough sugar to tenderize and flavor the batter.

Advance Preparation: minimum 1 hour, maximum 24 hours

Oven Temperature: 425°F    Baking Time: 1 hour

| Batter ingredients | MEASURE | WEIGHT | |
| --- | --- | --- | --- |
| room temperature | volume | ounces | GRAMS |
| *bleached* all-purpose flour (use only Gold Medal or Pillsbury) | 1 cup | 5 ounces | 142 grams |
| sugar | 3 tablespoons | 1.3 ounces | 37 grams |
| salt | ¼ teaspoon | — | 1.7 grams |
| unsalted butter, melted | 4 tablespoons, divided | 2 ounces | 56 grams |
| milk | 1 liquid cup | 8.5 ounces | 242 grams |
| 2 large eggs plus 2 large egg whites | 5 fluid ounces | 5.6 ounces | 160 grams (weighed without shells) |
| pure vanilla extract | 1 teaspoon | — | — |

Equipment An 11-inch steel Dutch baby pan or cast-iron skillet (if using the skillet, lower the initial 425°F to 400°F)

1. Mix the batter

**FOOD PROCESSOR METHOD** In a food processor with a metal blade, process the flour, sugar, and salt for a few seconds to mix. Add 2 tablespoons of the melted butter and process until it is the size of tiny peas, about 20 seconds. Scrape the sides of the container. With the motor on, add the milk, eggs and egg whites, and vanilla and process for about 20 seconds or until the batter is smooth.

**HAND METHOD** In a medium bowl, stir together the flour, sugar, and salt. Add 2 tablespoons of the melted butter and use a fork to mash and mix it in until it is the size of tiny peas. With a rotary beater or whisk, slowly beat in the eggs and then egg whites one at a time, beating for about 1 minute after each addition. Then beat until the batter is fairly smooth (small lumps of butter will remain visible). Beat in the vanilla extract.

2. Let the batter rest Allow the batter to sit at room temperature for 1 hour before baking, or cover and refrigerate it for up to 24 hours. Allow it to come to room temperature and beat it lightly before baking.

3. Preheat the oven Preheat the oven to 425°F 30 minutes before baking. Have a rack in the bottom third of the oven.

4. Prepare the pan Remelt the remaining 2 tablespoons butter in the pan. Use a small pastry feather or brush to coat the entire interior with the butter.

Three minutes before baking, place the pan in the oven and heat it until the butter is hot and bubbling.

5. Fill the pan and bake the Dutch baby Remove the pan from the oven and pour the batter on top of the hot butter. Bake for 15 minutes. Lower the heat to 350°F and continue baking for 30 minutes or until puffed around the edges above the sides of the pan and golden brown. About 15 minutes before the end of the baking time, open the oven door and quickly make 3 small slits in the center of the Dutch baby to release the steam and allow the center to dry more.

*food & wine tip*

This puffy popover would make a delicious dessert simply topped with ice cream or whipped cream.

| Apple filling ingredients | MEASURE | WEIGHT | |
|---|---|---|---|
| room temperature | volume | ounces | grams |
| unsalted butter, softened | 4½ tablespoons | 2.2 ounces | 63 grams |
| 2 pounds Granny Smith or other tart apples (about 6 medium), peeled, cored, and sliced ¼ inch thick | 6 cups sliced | 25 ounces | 717 grams |
| freshly squeezed lemon juice | 2 teaspoons | — | 10 grams |
| light brown sugar | 3 tablespoons | 1.5 ounces | 40 grams |
| granulated sugar | 3 tablespoons | 1.3 ounces | 38 grams |
| ground cinnamon | ¾ teaspoon | — | — |
| nutmeg, preferably freshly grated | ¼ teaspoon | — | — |
| salt | ¼ plus ⅟₁₆ teaspoon | — | — |
| *Optional garnish:* crème fraîche or whipped cream | 1 cup | about 8 ounces | 232 grams |

6. While the Dutch baby is baking, prepare the apples In a large nonreactive frying pan, melt the butter over medium heat until bubbling. Add the apple slices and sprinkle them with the lemon juice, brown sugar, granulated sugar, cinnamon, nutmeg, and salt. Sauté the apples, stirring occasionally, for 12 to 15 minutes. After about the first 5 minutes of cooking, the apples will begin to exude liquid. Raise the heat slightly until it evaporates, then lower the heat to medium and continue cooking until the slices are glazed and tender when pierced with a cake tester or sharp knife. Turn off the heat and cover to keep warm.

7. Fill the Dutch baby and serve Slide the Dutch baby onto a serving plate (slip a spatula between the sides of the pan and the pastry if necessary to dislodge it) and fill it with the apples. If desired, spoon some crème fraîche or whipped cream on top, and pass the rest.

REHEAT Place the Dutch baby on a baking sheet and heat it in a preheated 350°F oven for about 10 minutes. The texture of the dough will not be as moist and tender as when freshly baked.

POINTERS FOR SUCCESS To core and slice the apples, cut them in half and use a melon baller to scoop out the cores. Slice each half into quarters, and then each piece into 3 slices, or 4 if the apples are very large.

If you prefer a more chewy, slightly less puffy version, simply leave out the extra egg whites.

UNDERSTANDING Letting the batter rest allows the flour to absorb the liquid evenly. Coating some of the flour with the melted butter keeps the proteins in the flour from absorbing as much of the milk and forming gluten. A certain amount of gluten development is necessary in order to support the puff. I tried using one-quarter cake flour instead of coating the flour with butter, and the batter would not puff at all! Replacing the milk with buttermilk decreased the puffing by three-quarters due to the effect of the buttermilk's acidity on the gluten. Adding powdered buttermilk to the milk for flavor, however, has no effect on the puffing.

Adding extra whole eggs to the basic recipe would toughen the dough, making it rubbery, but the extra egg whites make it airier, crisper, and more tender.

This batter is actually quite similar to cream puff pastry dough, with half the butter, 1 less egg, and 1 less egg white. Cream puff dough is cooked slightly before baking, making it stiff enough to pipe. The extra butter in cream puff dough keeps it from becoming rubbery because of the extra egg, and the resulting puff is crisper on the outside than the Dutch baby, but the insides of the two are actually quite similar.

The leavening in this batter is provided entirely by the egg.

## beranbaum's variation

For a Baby Dutch Baby, to serve 2, simply divide the recipe in half and use an 8-inch ovenproof skillet (preferably cast-iron). Decrease the baking time at 350°F to 15 minutes and make the slits 10 minutes before the end of the baking time.

# The Cakebread Cellars Napa Valley Cookbook

### DOLORES AND JACK CAKEBREAD WITH BRIAN STREETER

## the book

*The Cakebread Cellars Napa Valley Cookbook: Wine and Recipes to Celebrate Every Season's Harvest* by Dolores and Jack Cakebread with Brian Streeter (Ten Speed), $35, 228 pages, color photos.

## the gist

A look at daily life at a Napa Valley winery, with appealing recipes and lots of useful wine information.

## the ideal reader

The cook who enjoys serving wine with meals.

## the extras

Behind-the-scenes photographs of the winery.

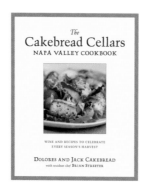

**BACKGROUND** Jack was born in Oakland, California; Dolores was born in Sheboygan, Wisconsin and moved to California when she was nine. They live at their winery in Rutherford, in the Napa Valley. "Jack and I started dating when we were 14 and got married at 19," Dolores says. "We've been married 53 years."

**WINERY EXPERIENCE** "I'm basically a car mechanic and photographer by trade," Jack says. Dolores adds, "We got into the Napa wine business 32 years ago. For the first 19 years we worked at our garage in Oakland during the day and would come up to the winery on nights and weekends. We started with just 22 acres of vineyards and we made 157 cases of wine a year. Now we have 300 acres of vineyards and we make 95,000 cases of wine a year."

**COOKING EXPERIENCE** Dolores says, "I have three sons and Jack, and when you have four men in your house with a name like Cakebread, there's a whole lot of eating going on! I didn't know how to cook when I first got married, so I studied *Joy of Cooking*. My favorite dish was pork chops with tomato and bell pepper sauce, which Jack says I made for dinner all the time. I started taking some cooking classes locally. Then I prepared all the family holiday dinners and cooked for our church and even for the Oakland Camera Club."

**ON COOKING FOR A CROWD** "When we started out in Napa, we didn't have a kitchen at the winery, so I'd make meals in Oakland and bring them up. I'd cook dinner for 20 people every Friday night at home and serve it the next day to everyone who helped out at the winery. People who had tasted our wines and wanted to pitch in would come to the winery and help bottle the wine or weed the grounds or do construction on the buildings. I never knew beforehand how many people would come, so if there were 10, we'd have a feast, and if there were 30, we'd have to skimp."

**TASTE SENSATION** "We served Sauvignon Blanc the other morning at 7 o'clock with scrambled eggs. They're delicious together."

# featured recipes

**WHAT DOLORES COOKS MOST OFTEN FOR JACK** "Jack travels a lot, and his favorite comfort meal when he comes home is mashed potatoes, meat loaf and fresh carrot salad. He doesn't eat potatoes anymore, so I use pureed celery root or cauliflower instead—the recipe's in the book. On our 50th wedding anniversary, Jack got bottles of 1976 Krug Champagne, 1980 Cakebread Chardonnay and 1974 Cakebread Cabernet from our cellar, and we drank them with that very meal."

**HOW "THE CAKEBREAD CELLARS NAPA VALLEY COOKBOOK" CAME TO BE** "Some of the recipes are from our annual American Harvest Workshop. Each year we invite chefs from across the country to come here to learn about wine and, along with our resident chef, Brian Streeter, develop new dishes using ingredients from local farmers and food artisans. The bulk of the recipes in the book, however, are ones that I've prepared at the winery for the past 30 years for meals with wine distributors, restaurateurs and other visitors."

**HOW THE COOKBOOK RECIPES WERE TESTED** "We gave out the recipes to our staff at the winery—home cooks with ordinary kitchens—and got their feedback. Then we incorporated any changes we felt were needed."

**HOW TO PAIR FOOD WITH WINE** "The main thing to remember is to match like flavors. And always keep in mind that pairing wine with food is all very subjective. People in the wine business can sometimes make choosing wines too complicated. Wine is meant to be enjoyed—and you don't have to be a connoisseur to enjoy it."

**FAVORITE FOOD AND WINE PAIRINGS** "We love lamb or salmon with Pinot Noir and, with Zinfandel, osso buco—or peanut butter."

**TIPS FOR COOKING WITH WINE** "Always have a glass of wine while you're cooking and toss some into the pan. For instance, if you are serving an off-dry wine with dinner, be sure to add some to your sauce—this will help bridge the flavors. Never cook with wine you won't drink. Food and wine go together like husband and wife; they're natural complements."

## TOP FOOD-FRIENDLY WINES
Dry wines with medium acidity. "Wines with a very low acidity are flat. Wines with medium acidity add that tang, zippiness or zing to your food."

# Liberty Duck Breast with Dried Cranberry–Apple Bread Salad

**SERVES 4 TO 6**

This recipe was adapted from a dish that Debbie Gold created when she participated in our 2000 American Harvest Workshop. It is made with duck breasts from Sonoma County Poultry, which is owned by Jim Reichardt, a purveyor with whom we have enjoyed a wonderful relationship for a long time. A third-generation duck farmer, Jim left the family business to grow his own ducks in Penngrove, a small town on the eastern side of Sonoma County. There, he raises his Liberty ducks exclusively for chefs and gourmet food markets.

4  (6- to 8-ounce) boneless Liberty or Pekin duck breasts

2  cups dry red wine

½  cup dried cranberries

½  cup plus 1 tablespoon extra virgin olive oil

4  cups crustless sweet French bread cubes

½  cup pecans, toasted and chopped

1  tablespoon chopped flat-leaf parsley

1  teaspoon fresh thyme

Kosher salt

Freshly ground black pepper

1½ pippin or Braeburn apples, peeled, cored, and diced (2 cups)

½  cup Brown Chicken Stock (recipe follows)

Trim the duck breasts, score the skin, and set aside.

Combine the wine and cranberries in a medium saucepan and bring to a boil over medium-high heat. Remove from the heat and let sit for 20 minutes, until the berries are plump and moist.

While the berries are sitting, heat the ½ cup olive oil in a large nonstick saucepan over high heat. Add the bread and toss to coat evenly with the oil. Cook for 5 minutes, until lightly browned on all sides, tossing occasionally to prevent burning. Transfer to a large bowl.

Drain the cranberries over a small saucepan to catch the wine. Set the cranberries aside. Return the wine to a boil over high heat. Cook for 10 to 15 minutes, until reduced to about ¼ cup.

Add the cranberries, pecans, parsley, and thyme to the bowl with the bread.

Season the duck with salt and pepper. Heat the 1 tablespoon olive oil in a large sauté pan over high heat. Add the duck, skin side down, reduce the heat to medium, and cook for 6 to 7 minutes, until golden brown. Turn and cook the other side for 3 to 4 minutes, until firm. Transfer the duck to a plate, drain all but 2 tablespoons of the fat from the pan, and return to high heat. Add the apples and cook for 3 to 5 minutes, until soft and golden brown. Add to the bread mixture.

Return the skillet to high heat and add the stock. Pour any duck juices that collect on the plate into the skillet. Bring to a boil and scrape the sides and bottom with a wooden spoon to loosen any stuck bits of duck or apple. Cook on a rapid simmer for 2 to 3 minutes, until thick. Add to the bread salad and toss to mix well. Season to taste with salt and pepper.

Cut the duck breasts into thin slices. Place a spoonful of the bread salad on the center of the plate. Arrange the sliced duck over the bread salad, spoon a small amount of the reduced wine around the plate, and serve.

WINE Enjoy with Cakebread Cellars Benchland Select or Pinot Noir, or a full-bodied red wine with lots of ripe red fruit flavors.

## Brown Chicken Stock

**YIELDS APPROXIMATELY 8 CUPS**

| | |
|---|---|
| 6 | pounds chicken backs or wings |
| 2 | yellow onions, coarsely chopped |
| 2 | carrots, peeled and chopped |
| 1 | stalk celery, chopped |
| 1 | cup dry white wine |
| 12 | cups cold water |
| 3 | ripe plum tomatoes, chopped |
| 4 | cloves garlic, smashed |
| 3 | sprigs parsley |
| 2 | prigs thyme |
| 1 | bay leaf |
| 4 | black peppercorns |

Preheat the oven to 450°.

Heat a large roasting pan in the oven until hot. Add the chicken and bake for 30 minutes, until dark brown. Tilt the pan and discard all but 2 tablespoons of the oil that collects in the corner. Add the onions, carrots, and celery to the pan and stir to coat with the oil. Bake for 10 minutes.

Transfer the chicken and vegetables to a large stockpot. Add the wine to the roasting pan and cook for 2 to 3 minutes, scraping the bottom and sides of the pan. Add to the stockpot. Cover with the water and bring to a boil over high heat. Remove any impurities that rise to the surface. Add the tomatoes, garlic, parsley, thyme, bay leaf, and peppercorns. Return to a boil. Decrease the heat to low and cook uncovered on a low simmer for 4 to 6 hours, until the flavor is completely extracted from the chicken and vegetables. Pour through a fine-mesh strainer into a large bowl set in an ice water bath. Transfer to small airtight containers and refrigerate for up to 3 days or freeze for up to 2 months.

# Pork Chops with Mushroom-Caper Pan Sauce

**SERVES 4 TO 6**

When Brian cooks a meat dish that requires transferring the meat to a plate while the pan is used for a sauce, he sets a bowl upside down on a plate and leans the meat against it. The juices collect in the plate but the meat isn't lying in them and they are easier to add back to the pan to make the sauce. We use thick pork chops for this recipe because they stay juicier.

4    (1½-inch-thick) boneless pork loin chops

Kosher salt

Freshly ground black pepper

1    tablespoon unsalted butter

2    tablespoons extra virgin olive oil

¾    pound cremini mushrooms, wiped clean

1    cup dry sherry

1½ cups Brown Chicken Stock (see page 73)

3    sprigs thyme

2    tablespoons capers, drained

Preheat the oven to 450°.

Season the pork chops with salt and pepper on both sides. Combine the butter and olive oil in an ovenproof skillet large enough to hold the pork in a single layer. Heat over high heat. Add the pork chops and cook for 2 to 3 minutes per side, until browned. Transfer the pork chops to the oven, reserving the butter and olive oil mixture. Bake the pork chops for 10 minutes, until cooked nearly all the way through. Transfer the chops to a plate.

Return the pan with the butter and olive oil to the stove and heat over high heat. Slice the mushrooms ¼ inch thick, add to the pan, and cook for 1 to 2 minutes, until soft. Add the sherry and cook for 4 to 5 minutes at a rapid boil,

*food & wine* tip

While the pork chops are resting, cover them with aluminum foil to keep them warm while you make the sauce.

until the liquid evaporates. Add the stock and thyme and cook for 8 to 10 minutes, until the liquid is reduced by half. Add the capers and any juices from the pork chops that have collected on the plate and cook for 1 to 2 minutes. Remove the thyme sprig from the sauce before serving. Arrange the pork chops on 4 warm plates. Spoon the sauce over the pork chops and serve.

WINE Enjoy with Cakebread Cellars Chardonnay Reserve or a luscious chardonnay with tropical fruit flavors and vanilla and oak characteristics.

# Mushroom Caps Stuffed with Leeks and Fromage Blanc

**SERVES 4 TO 6**

You can use ricotta as a substitute for fromage blanc in this recipe. Just wrap the ricotta in cheesecloth and hang it over a bowl in the refrigerator overnight to eliminate any excess moisture.

1   large leek, white part only, julienned (2 cups)

2   tablespoons extra virgin olive oil

½   teaspoon kosher salt plus additional for seasoning

4   ounces fromage blanc

2   tablespoons finely grated Parmigiano-Reggiano

Freshly ground black pepper

18   large cremini mushrooms, wiped clean and stemmed

White truffle oil (optional)

Preheat the oven to 400°. Brush a baking sheet with olive oil.

Heat the leeks and olive oil in a small sauté pan over medium heat. Add the ½ teaspoon salt. Cook, stirring often to prevent browning, for 8 to 10 minutes, until wilted and tender, but not browned. Transfer to a small bowl and let cool.

Add the fromage blanc and Parmigiano to the leeks and stir to mix well. Season with salt and pepper. Scoop up about 1 heaping teaspoon of the mixture and spoon into the bottom of the mushrooms. Set on the prepared baking sheet. Bake in the top third of the oven for 10 to 12 minutes, until the cheese mixture begins to brown and the mushrooms become tender to the bite. Transfer to a serving plate and drizzle with a few drops of truffle oil.

**WINE** Enjoy with Cakebread Cellars Napa Valley Chardonnay or a chardonnay with great structure and rich fruit flavors.

*food & wine tip*

In addition to ricotta, a good substitute for fromage blanc is a soft and creamy goat cheese, feta cheese or even cream cheese. Be sure the cheese is at room temperature so that it's easy to work with.

# Wild Mushrooms, Butternut Squash, and Baby Spinach Salad

**SERVES 4 TO 6**

In autumn, when the days become shorter and the weather cools down, the garden crops change dramatically and, as a result, so do our menus. When Brian begins to serve this salad, we know that autumn has officially arrived. Farmers' markets are often the best resource for buying a selection of mushrooms. Fresh mushrooms should feel heavy, plump, and supple, and should not be wrinkled or frayed on the edges.

1½ pounds assorted wild mushrooms (such as chanterelle, shiitake, or oyster)

2 cups water

2 tablespoons soy sauce

3 cloves garlic

1 sprig thyme

2 pounds butternut squash, peeled and cut into ½-inch cubes

⅓ cup plus ¼ cup extra virgin olive oil

Kosher salt

Freshly ground black pepper

1 tablespoon fresh thyme

1 tablespoon fresh lemon juice

½ cup walnut oil

5 ounces baby spinach leaves

½ head radicchio, torn into bite-sized pieces

1 head Belgian endive, cut into bite-sized pieces

1 ounce dry jack cheese

Preheat the oven to 400°.

Wipe clean and stem the mushrooms, reserving the stems. Cut the caps into 1-inch pieces.

Combine the water, mushroom stems, 1 tablespoon of the soy sauce, 1 of the garlic cloves, and the sprig of thyme in a small saucepan. Bring to a boil over medium heat. Reduce the heat to low and simmer for 30 minutes. Strain the mushroom broth into a clean saucepan.

Spread the squash on a baking dish. Pour the ¼ cup olive oil over the squash and toss to coat evenly. Sprinkle with salt and pepper. Bake for about 20 minutes, until the center is tender and the outside is browned.

Spread the mushrooms out in a baking dish and drizzle with the ⅓ cup olive oil and the remaining 1 tablespoon soy sauce. Add the thyme leaves. Chop the remaining 2 garlic cloves and add to the mushrooms. Sprinkle with salt and pepper and cover with aluminum foil. Bake for 20 minutes, until the mushrooms are soft. Remove from the oven and remove the foil. If there are any juices in the bottom of the dish, strain them into the mushroom broth.

Increase the oven temperature to 500°. Return the mushrooms to the oven, uncovered, and cook for 10 to 15 minutes, until browned and crisp.

Bring the mushroom broth to a boil over high heat and cook for 10 to 15 minutes, until reduced to one-quarter of the amount. Add the lemon juice. Whisk in the walnut oil.

Combine the spinach, radicchio, and endive in a large bowl. Add the squash, mushrooms, and vinaigrette. Toss to coat. Divide among serving plates and shave the dry jack cheese over the top.

WINE Enjoy with Cakebread Cellars Napa Valley Chardonnay or Rubaiyat as a nice complement to the rich, earthy flavors of the salad. Or select a chardonnay with concentrated fruit flavors or a light-bodied red wine that can be served slightly chilled.

*food & wine tip*

To remove the skin from butternut squash, use a heavy-duty vegetable peeler or a small, sharp paring knife.

# Fennel-Crusted Ahi with Garden Herb Salad

**SERVES 4 TO 6**

*food & wine tip*

The easiest way to crush fennel seeds for this recipe is to place them in a resealable plastic bag and smash them lightly with a rolling pin or the side of a meat cleaver.

The salad part of this recipe really pays tribute to the herbs in our garden. Almost every type of herb we grow is included, as well as the leaves from the delicate celery stalks in the heart of the bunch. Brian often adds these leaves to salads because they provide a subtle celery taste. The tuna, which is seared and then chilled before being served, should be the best quality you can find. If you can, buy sushi-grade pieces and slice the fish into steaks at home.

½ cup Aioli (recipe follows)

1 small fennel bulb, outer leaves removed, halved, cored, and cut into paper-thin slices, fronds reserved

½ cup fennel fronds

4 radishes, cut into paper-thin slices

1 cup loosely packed assorted torn basil

1 cup flat-leaf parsley

½ cup yellow celery leaves (from the heart)

½ cup tarragon leaves

2 tablespoons chopped fresh chives

¼ cup crushed fennel seed

Kosher salt

Freshly ground black pepper

2 (8-ounce, 2-inch-thick) ahi tuna fillets

4 tablespoons extra virgin olive oil

1 tablespoon fresh lemon juice

Prepare the Aioli as directed.

Combine the fennel, fennel fronds, radishes, basil, parsley, celery leaves, tarragon, and chives in a large bowl. Set aside.

Sprinkle the fennel seeds, salt, and pepper over both sides of the tuna. Heat a large skillet over high heat. Add 2 tablespoons of the olive oil. Add the tuna and cook for 1½ minutes on each side, until slightly browned. Transfer to a plate and refrigerate.

Pour the remaining 2 tablespoons olive oil and the lemon juice over the salad and toss to coat well. Season to taste with salt and pepper.

Cut the tuna into ½-inch-thick slices and arrange a few slices on each of 4 plates. Drizzle with the Aioli and top with equal amounts of the salad.

WINE Enjoy with Cakebread Cellars Chardonnay Reserve or Rubaiyat, or a dry chardonnay with pineapple, lemon, and melon flavors. A light, dry, fruity red wine that can be served chilled makes a good choice as well.

## Aioli

**YIELDS ABOUT 1 CUP**

1    clove garlic, peeled and coarsely chopped

¼    teaspoon kosher salt

1    egg yolk

1    tablespoon fresh lemon juice

½    cup extra virgin olive oil

½    cup grapeseed or vegetable oil

Place the garlic and salt in a mortar and mash it to a paste. (Alternatively, put the garlic and salt on a cutting board and mash it using the tip and side of a wide chef's knife. Press the garlic against the board, pushing down with the knife to smash the garlic into a paste.)

Put the mashed garlic, egg yolk, and lemon juice in a bowl and whisk to combine. Whisk in the olive oil and grapeseed oil in a slow, thin stream. Whisk continuously until the oil is completely blended in. Cover with plastic wrap and refrigerate for up to 1 week.

# César

**OLIVIER SAID AND JAMES MELLGREN WITH MAGGIE POND**

INTERVIEW BELOW WITH OLIVIER SAID

## the book
*César: Recipes from a Tapas Bar* by Olivier Said and James Mellgren with Maggie Pond (Ten Speed), $29.95, 212 pages, color and black-and-white photos.

## the gist
A lively compilation of classic and innovative Spanish recipes and cocktails from the acclaimed tapas bar César in Berkeley, California.

## the ideal reader
Anyone who entertains.

## the extras
An excellent guide to creating a tapas pantry as well as useful information on Spanish sherries and bartending at home.

**BACKGROUND** Born in Paris; lives in Berkeley, California.

**EXPERIENCE** "My family has owned restaurants in France since 1840. My great-great-grandfather ran a bistro in Auvergne. My mother owned a very busy restaurant in Paris called Le Troudes Halles, where as a kid I assisted a giant chef who looked like Rasputin but seemed twice the size in the tiny kitchen. I worked my way up from washing dishes to preparing desserts. I tried a lot of things outside the restaurant business—I was a sound and video engineer, I went to school to become a pilot, I did photography—but I came back to food. After working several jobs at restaurants in Los Angeles and Paris, I became a managing partner at César."

**WHY HE LOVES TAPAS** "At César you can try so many different things on small plates. People can come taste a huge array of flavors and not be confined to only one little area, which is so much more interesting. I just love to see people have fun with the food here. César is loud and energetic, and we don't take ourselves too seriously—that's not what people are coming for."

**HOW THE COOKBOOK REFLECTS THE RESTAURANT** "The book is exactly like the restaurant. At César we do 50 percent drink and 50 percent food, so the book had to reflect that. César is a bar with food. To convey the casual atmosphere here, I took the black-and-white photographs in the book with a digital camera."

**HOW THE RESTAURANT REFLECTS THE CLIENTELE** "People come to César with bags of mushrooms or quince for us to create new recipes with, and we just say okay. Neighbors or people who hear about us bring two cases of something, and we'll play with that."

**ON PAIRING WINE AND FOOD** "We don't do pairings—we don't really believe in

## WHY TAPAS ARE TRENDY
"When you go to a tapas bar you can decide to eat or not to eat. There's no pressure to order a full meal. It's noncommittal and very entertaining."

them. There are so many different types of food that we serve every day, and so many different types of alcohols, wines and sherries, it would be crazy to limit ourselves. Dennis Lapuyade, who creates the beverage list, tries to get things nobody else has. We have about 500 different kinds of liquor on our list and 500 different kinds of wine. And I've tried every one of them."

PARALLELS BETWEEN CÉSAR AND ITS NEXT-DOOR NEIGHBOR, CHEZ PANISSE "We decided to take the same approach to the food as Chez Panisse does—everything is organic, except for some hard-to-get products from Spain. We use a lot of the same purveyors as Chez Panisse. We try to use the freshest ingredients. In fact, we have no freezer. We have no room for one anyway because the kitchen is tiny; the cooks have to prepare things *à la minute*."

RECIPE ADAPTATIONS "At the restaurant Maggie Pond [César's chef] makes batches of tapas for 50 or 100 people. So to create recipes that would serve between six and eight people, we'd estimate amounts, give instructions to home cooks we knew and then have them bring the finished dishes to a little potluck party. We were very surprised to see how closely those recipes matched what we served at César."

ESSENTIALS FOR THE TAPAS PANTRY Piquillo peppers, *pimentón* (smoked paprika from Spain), caperberries and *pimientos de Padrón*—"little peppers originally from Spain. We get them from the Happy Quail Farm in East Palo Alto. Eating them is like playing Russian roulette because some are hot and some are sweet, so we tell people to watch out. It's becoming sort of a game at the restaurant. We fry the peppers and send them out, then we look at the customer—and then we wait."

FAVORITE LOCAL RESTAURANTS "In Berkeley I like Chez Panisse. There's also a great seafood restaurant here called Downtown. In San Francisco I like Rose Pistola in North Beach and Bix right at the edge of the Financial District—it's beautiful."

FUTURE PROJECTS "We're contemplating opening a little Spanish delicatessen—a César Mercado. I'm also writing a bar book about liquor from around the world."

## RECENT DRINK DISCOVERIES

"I tried a gin made with saffron, called Old Raj. It was beautiful and it smelled so good. And I also tasted a rum flavored with orange rind, called Pyrat XO Reserve."

MAGGIE POND

# Portuguese-Style Fish Stew

**SERVES** 8

This thick, tomatoey fish stew recalls similar fisherman's stews found on both sides of the Atlantic. Hearty and satisfying, these dishes commonly sustain the fearless men and women who survive by extracting food from the cold, treacherous ocean waters. You can stretch this recipe to feed a few more people simply by adding more seafood; it's a good dish to serve for a dinner party because the sauce and croutons can be made a day in advance. When you sit down to eat, hoist a glass to intrepid fisherfolk everywhere.

**on said's nightstand**

I like **Fiona Dunlop's** book ***New Tapas: Today's Best Bar Food from Spain**—it's really lively. I prefer books with graphics and pictures. I don't always read them.

Sauce

½    cup extra virgin olive oil

3    yellow onions, diced

4    teaspoons finely chopped garlic

6    tablespoons finely diced celery

2    large carrots, peeled and grated

⅓    cup finely chopped piquillo peppers (see Said on Piquillo Peppers, page 86)

4    cups canned diced tomatoes, with liquid

1⅓ cups water

Grated zest of 1 orange

1    tablespoon salt

1    teaspoon freshly ground black pepper


16 to 20 black mussels (about 1 pound), scrubbed

16 to 20 clams (about 1 pound), scrubbed

1    pound grouper or sea bass fillet, cut into bite-sized pieces

¼    cup finely chopped fresh mint

¼    cup finely chopped fresh basil

Salt and freshly ground black pepper

8    sliced Fried Croutons (recipe follows)

These small peppers, sold
in jars, are grown in
Navarre in the north of
Spain and are so
distinctive that they
have been given the
prestigious DO
(*denominación de origen,*
the Spanish government's
seal of authenticity).
They are about an inch
across the top, no more
than two or three inches
long, and intensely red.
They are always
hand-picked, roasted
over an open beechwood
fire, and hand-peeled to
preserve the flavor
(no water is ever used).
Slightly spicy and wildly
delicious, *piquillos* can be
eaten out of the jar or
incorporated into an array
of beguiling tapas. They
are perfect for stuffing
with cheese, seafood, or
vegetables and are one
of the true glories of the
Spanish pantry.

To make the sauce, heat the oil in a large nonreactive pot over medium heat. Add the onions and cook, stirring occasionally, until translucent, about 10 minutes. Increase the heat to medium-high, add the garlic, and cook until lightly browned, another 10 minutes. Add the celery and cook for 5 minutes. Add the carrots and cook until they begin to soften, about 10 minutes. Add the peppers, tomatoes, and water and simmer, stirring frequently, until the mixture concentrates, about 45 minutes. Stir in the zest, salt, and pepper.

To assemble the stew, increase the heat to high and add the mussels, clams, and fish pieces. Cover and cook until the shellfish have opened, 2 or 3 minutes. Add the mint and basil and adjust the seasoning. Remove from the heat and discard any shellfish that have not opened.

To serve, place a crouton slice in the bottom of each bowl and ladle the stew over the top.

## Fried Croutons

The croutons can be made several days ahead of time and stored in an airtight container.

1   day-old baguette
2   cups olive oil
Salt and freshly ground black pepper

Cut away the crust on the baguette, and tear the bread into ½-inch, irregularly shaped pieces; or cut into ¼-inch slices, leaving the crust on. In a deep, heavy-bottomed pan, heat the oil to 375°F. Fry the bread in small batches until a light golden brown. Remove the croutons with a slotted spoon and drain on paper towels, then toss them in a large bowl with salt and pepper to taste. If not using immediately, cool and store in an airtight container.

# Chorizo and Apples in Hard Cider

**SERVES** 8

*Sidra*, or hard apple cider, is the regional drink of Asturias in northwestern Spain, home to hearty stews and boldly flavored cheese. *Sidra* is consumed in a curious ritual that dates back centuries. You stand with the bottle raised in your hand, over the top of your head, while the pint glass is held low at arm's length alongside the thigh. It is important that the cider falls in a steady stream down to the glass, resulting in a burst of foam that is the very essence of the drink. Apples and pork seem to go together naturally, and this regional dish grew from the love of both in a land famous for its apples. This is a great tapa for the fall months when a chill begins to fill the air and the apples are at their best.

16   small (1-inch) links chorizo

2    Gala apples, cored and each cut into about 16 cubes

2    cups hard cider

In a large Dutch oven or traditional *cazuela* (a flameproof terra-cotta casserole), combine the chorizo, apples, and cider. Bring to a boil and then turn the heat down to a simmer and cook until the apples are tender and the sausages are cooked through, about 30 minutes. Remove the apples and chorizo from the pan. Continue to cook the cider down to a thick syrup, reducing it to ½ cup, about 5 minutes. Return the chorizo and apples to the pan, reheating and glazing them with the reduced cider syrup. Serve immediately.

# Spicy Tuna Salad

**MAKES 6 TO 8 SANDWICHES**

This is probably not the tuna salad your mother used to make. But then again, you're all grown up now, and perhaps you have discovered that tuna is not really a chicken of the sea but, in the right hands, a delicious and versatile fish. Be sure to use the best-quality tuna you can find (at César we use an imported Spanish tuna that is packed in olive oil). Our tuna salad has just enough heat from the chiles and plenty of zest from the capers. The method we use to make hard-boiled eggs results in slightly soft yolks that won't have a gray ring. We serve this salad in a *bocadillo*, but it is also a great choice for stuffing tomatoes or *piquillo* peppers (see page 86), spreading on *crostini*, or serving on a bed of fresh greens.

Hard-boiled eggs

8   cups water

1   teaspoon distilled white vinegar

Pinch of salt

6   eggs

Tuna salad

12   ounces (two 6-ounce cans) tuna in oil

20   green olives, pitted and finely chopped

2   scallions, white and green parts, chopped

⅔   cup salt-packed capers, rinsed and coarsely chopped

⅓   cup finely chopped fresh flat-leaf parsley

1   jalapeño chile, minced

1½ cups extra virgin olive oil

2   teaspoons dried red chile flakes

Juice of 3 lemons

3 or 4 baguettes

Salt

2   cups loosely packed arugula leaves

To cook the eggs, combine the water, vinegar, and salt in a nonreactive saucepan and bring to a rapid boil. Gently place the eggs into the water and set a timer for 9 minutes. Meanwhile, prepare a bowl of ice water. When the timer goes off, remove the eggs immediately and drop them into the ice water to stop the cooking. Let them chill in the ice water for at least 20 minutes before you peel them. If cooked and peeled ahead of time, store the eggs in cold water until needed.

To make the salad, open the tuna and discard the top layer of oil. Do not rinse the tuna. Place in a large bowl and add the olives, scallions, capers, parsley, jalapeño, oil, chile flakes, and lemon juice. Fold together gently. Do not break apart the tuna too much; there should be a nice mix of small and large pieces.

To assemble, cut the baguettes into 10-inch lengths, and then slice them in half lengthwise, leaving a hinge. Spread the tuna mixture over the bread. Slice the hard-cooked eggs crosswise ⅛ inch thick and layer them on top. Sprinkle with salt and top with arugula leaves.

# Spinach Tortilla

**SERVES 8**

How the Mexican tortilla got its name is something of a mystery, since the only thing it has in common with the Spanish original is its shape. Unlike the Mexican flatbread made of either corn or wheat, a tortilla (literally "little cake") in Spain is a round, relatively flat omelet, or what the Italians call a frittata. They are ubiquitous in tapas bars throughout the country. There are two ways to cook a tortilla, both requiring a little practice. The first is to cook the eggs halfway and then invert the omelet and slide it back into the pan to finish cooking. In Spain, they actually use a ceramic disk with a handle designed specifically for flipping tortillas, but you can use a relatively flat plate or pot lid as long as it's bigger in diameter than the pan. Another method is to use a cast-iron pan and, after the initial cooking stage, slip the whole pan under the broiler to finish. It's easier than trying to flip the tortilla, and it produces a wonderfully golden brown top. Whichever method you choose, this is a terrific dish in which to use up leftovers since almost anything can go into it, such as cooked vegetables and potatoes, roasted peppers, mushrooms, bits of ham, and even pasta. Our version can make a meal unto itself, accompanied by a salad and a glass of wine.

1½ pounds spinach, tough stems removed and rinsed

¼ cup dried currants

½ cup pine nuts

½ cup extra virgin olive oil

2 yellow onions, thinly sliced

1 tablespoon finely chopped garlic

⅛ teaspoon ground nutmeg

⅛ teaspoon cayenne pepper

½ teaspoon salt

7 eggs

Freshly ground black pepper

Pickled red onions, for garnish

Blanch the spinach by plunging it into boiling salted water for about
30 seconds. Remove and drain. When the spinach is cool enough to handle,
squeeze out the excess water and chop coarsely.

Put the currants in a small bowl of warm water, let soak for 15 minutes, and
then drain. Meanwhile, toast the pine nuts in a dry skillet (preferably cast-iron)
over medium heat, stirring frequently, until golden brown, about 7 minutes.

Heat ¼ cup of the oil in a skillet over medium heat, and slowly caramelize the
onions, cooking them until they take on a deep amber color, about 30 minutes.
Add the garlic and cook for another 5 minutes. Remove from the heat and
drain off the oil.

In a large bowl, mix the onions and garlic with the spinach, currants,
pine nuts, nutmeg, cayenne, and salt. In another large bowl, whisk the eggs
and season with salt and black pepper. Fold in the spinach mixture.

Heat the remaining ¼ cup oil in a 10-inch nonstick skillet over medium heat.
Pour in the spinach-egg mixture and scramble lightly. Turn down the heat to
medium-low and cook until the tortilla has begun to form a bottom crust,
about 5 minutes. Using a plate or a pot lid, invert the tortilla, slide it back into
the pan, tucking in the edge to form the shape, and continue to cook until
it feels firm to the touch, 3 to 4 minutes. Cut into wedges and garnish with
pickled red onions.

# Come for Dinner

**LESLIE REVSIN**

**BACKGROUND** Born in Chicago; lives in Seattle.

**EDUCATION** Graduated with a degree in painting from McCallister College in Saint Paul, Minnesota. Studied cooking at the New York City College of Technology in Brooklyn, New York.

**EXPERIENCE** "In the mid-1960s I was a young, married mother, and I needed to be doing more. A friend had become a very good cook, and when she came back from a trip to France, she had us over for a dinner that was so wonderful, the desire to cook professionally took hold of me. I became a lunatic, driven to find a way to go to cooking school. After City Tech I got a job at the Waldorf-Astoria in Manhattan as a 'kitchen man' (that was the title they gave me so I could join the union), ostensibly hauling food around from one of the hotel's kitchens to another. Getting the job was a big deal because it was before women really worked in professional kitchens. I was the first female in the kitchen there, starting in the cold-food section, *garde manger*. Then I moved to the fish station. Later I opened my own bistro in Greenwich Village, Restaurant Leslie; then I became the chef at One Fifth, also in New York City, and The Inn at Pound Ridge in northern Westchester County in New York."

**PREVIOUS BOOKS** *Great Fish, Quick* and *Simply Elegant: Delicious Dinners in an Hour.*

**HOW SHE CAME TO LOVE FOOD** "I grew up around food; my father was quality-control manager of a large bakery and caterer in Chicago, which is where I got my first taste of desserts. He left our home when I was young, and the immediacy of that work experience faded. When I was little, I wanted to be a popcorn lady in the park, then an archaeologist. It wasn't until I got older that the whole food thing kicked in."

**WHAT SHE LEARNED ABOUT HOME COOKING FROM BEING A CHEF** "One thing you do in a professional kitchen is deconstruct dishes. Essentially I took that concept of preparing

**WHY GIVING PARTIES IS STRESSFUL** "It's a huge push-pull dynamic: being in the kitchen versus in the living room."

hearts of romaine with sherry-basil dressing **94** chicken breasts roasted with honey, pine nuts, and thyme **96** orzo "risotto" with roasted tomatoes and hot sausage **98** lamb chops with provençal tomatoes **100**

parts of the meal ahead of time, so there's less pressure at the last minute, and applied it to entertaining at home. A lot of anxiety about cooking for a party comes from feeling so conflicted when you have friends over: You want to spend time with them but still produce a beautiful meal. The book is about a better balance. I wanted to reduce anxiety but not compromise the food."

**TIP FOR THE BEGINNER COOK** "Just start. Think of something that you like to eat, get a recipe for it and make it. Don't overthink, don't agonize."

**MOST INSPIRING MEAL** "When I was in Spain, I had a salad dressed in a vinaigrette that had such life—it was the essence of a good dish because it was so pure. The garlic was cooked until it was lightly golden and nutty, then mixed with vinegar and good olive oil. I came home and applied the vinaigrette to a recipe for golden garlic shrimp. I remember that vinaigrette in Spain so well."

**CHEF SHE MOST ADMIRES** André Soltner, the former chef and longtime owner of Lutèce in New York City. "I always wanted to work and study with him, but he never hired me. He didn't have women in his kitchen; none of the French chefs did, until later. His whole approach was very simple, not fussy. I've always disliked fussiness in anything, but especially in food; I don't like tons of flavors mixed together and muddied. His food was always pure taste, without all kinds of unnecessary elements, so that a dish's sauce highlighted the basic quality and character of the ingredients themselves. That's what I really responded to in him. He's also a down-to-earth person, a very kind man, very humble."

**FAVORITE RESTAURANTS** Jean-Georges Vongerichten's. "There's a delightfulness to his inventions. They can be clever, but they aren't ponderous or overly contrived."

**COOKBOOK TRENDS** "I think there will always be great chefs' cookbooks because they are great entertainment. You're not really going to do all the recipes at home, but they're certainly fun to read about, and they offer you a look into a different world. These cookbooks document what's currently popular in restaurants. More power to the chefs who write them."

> **REVSIN'S MENU STRATEGY**
> "Choose at least a few dishes that can be prepared far ahead of time and kept in various pieces. Then assemble them right before serving."

# Hearts of Romaine with Sherry-Basil Dressing

**6 SERVINGS**

The satisfying crunch of crisp inner leaves of romaine lettuce makes the perfect conterpoint for this light and creamy basil-infused dressing.

½   cup less ½ tablespoon extra-virgin olive oil

6½ tablespoons mayonnaise

3   tablespoons aged Spanish sherry vinegar (available in some supermarkets, specialty stores, and by mail order) or other wine vinegar

Salt and freshly ground pepper

3   tablespoons finely diced shallots (see How to Dice Shallots and Onions on next page)

1   small garlic clove, minced

¼   cup fresh basil, torn into bite-size pieces

3   hearts of romaine lettuce or whole heads

1. Place the olive oil, mayonnaise, and vinegar in a blender or food processor and combine them on low speed until smooth and creamy, about 1 minute. Pour the dressing into a bowl, season it with salt and pepper, and stir in the shallots, garlic, and basil. Cover and refrigerate until ready to use or for at least 10 minutes to allow the basil flavor to permeate the dressing.

2. Meanwhile, if you have only whole heads of romaine, remove the dark green, coarse outer leaves, saving them for another use, to reach the lighter colored, crisp ones at the core. Trim and discard the root ends. Figuring six to seven medium leaves per person, separate enough of the leaves. Wash and dry them well.

3. Arrange the leaves slightly overlapping on plates, stir the dressing to recombine if it has separated, and drizzle it over the lettuce. Grind a little pepper over the top of each salad and serve right away.

Do-ahead option Refrigerate the dressing for up to a week. If it has separated, whisk it well to recombine, but either way, it will still taste fine.

HOW TO DICE SHALLOTS AND ONIONS

Chopping shallots and onions with a dull knife is more like hammering them into submission than cutting them. This bludgeoning, though well meant, makes them taste somewhat like gasoline. To avoid this sad start, use a sharp knife and follow these steps for dicing shallots and onions:

1. Cut a thin slice off the top and bottom of the shallot or onion.

2. Score through the skin and first layer, then peel and discard them (or save for a broth).

3. Cut the shallot or onion lengthwise in half and lay the halves cut side down, parallel to you.

4. Hold the top of one (so it doesn't slide) and, starting from the bottom, make horizontal cuts at equal intervals (⅛ to ¼ inch or wider, depending on the size dice you want), cutting up to but not through the end.

5. From the top, cut down but not through the end at ⅛- to ¼-inch (or wider) intervals.

6. Finally, cut crosswise at ⅛- to ¼-inch (or wider) intervals and watch it fall into dice. Cut the end into small pieces and repeat the process with the other half.

As you can see, the size of the dice is determined by the width of the cuts. Once you get the hang of it, it's easier to do than to read about.

## on revsin's nightstand

I would have to say my favorite authors are **Diana Kennedy,** who writes about Mexican food, and **Julie Sahni,** who covers Indian cooking. My favorite cuisines are Mexican and Indian, which may be surprising because they have almost nothing to do with most of the food that I have cooked professionally. I love them because they're totally unpretentious and have deep cultural roots. Their flavors are earthy, yet they can be delicate, too.

# Chicken Breasts Roasted with Honey, Pine Nuts, and Thyme

**6 SERVINGS**

Chicken breasts cooked in a mixture of honey, olive oil, and herbs emerge from the oven studded with pieces of golden nuts looking almost radiant as they await their last-minute gloss of light, syrupy pan juices.

3    tablespoons honey

4½ tablespoons olive oil

2    tablespoons freshly squeezed lemon juice

¾    teaspoon Worcestershire sauce

¾    teaspoon dried thyme

¾    teaspoon dried oregano

¼    teaspoon ground mace

4½ tablespoons pine nuts, somewhat finely chopped

Salt and freshly ground pepper

6    split chicken breasts on the bone, each about ¾ pound (4½ pounds total), excess skin trimmed

½    cup dry vermouth (see Revsin on Dry Vermouth on next page) or dry white wine

1. Preheat the oven to 400°F with the rack in the center and a heavy roasting pan large enough to hold all the chicken with plenty of room around each piece.

2. Mix the honey, 3½ tablespoons of the olive oil, the lemon juice, Worcestershire sauce, thyme, oregano, and mace in a medium bowl until smoothly combined. Stir in the pine nuts, season with salt and pepper to taste.

3. Dry the chicken breasts with paper towels and season them generously with salt and pepper. Set a large heavy skillet over medium-high heat with the

remaining 1 tablespoon olive oil. When it's hot, brown the breasts in batches, skin side down, adding more oil if needed, until they're golden and the fat from the skin is rendered, 3 to 5 minutes per batch.

4. When all the breasts are browned, transfer them to the roasting pan, skin side up, and coat each with the honey mixture, spreading it with the back of a spoon (some will drip into the pan). Pour the vermouth around the breasts and place the pan in the oven.  Roast until the chicken is just cooked through, 15 to 18 minutes (to check, make a cut in the thickest part of one breast to see if it's white in the center). If at any time the juices threaten to evaporate and burn, add a little more wine or water.

5. Transfer the chicken to a warm platter or plates and reserve the pan. Set the pan directly over low heat (or transfer the juices to a small saucepan) and cook them down with any accumulated platter juices, stirring, until they become a flavorful, light syrup. Season with more salt and pepper if you like, spoon them over the breasts, and serve hot.

Do-ahead options Mix the honey, olive oil, Worcestershire sauce, thyme, oregano, and mace up to 2 days ahead and store it at room temperature. Stir in the lemon juice and nuts and season with salt and pepper right before cooking.

Brown the breasts up to an hour ahead. Right before cooking, coat them with the honey mixture and finish them in the oven in the preheated pan.

## revsin on dry vermouth

You may not always have an open bottle of white wine available or want to open one for the small amount of wine used in cooking. Dry white vermouth is the answer. I always have it in my pantry, and much of the time I prefer its rich, herbal, white wine flavor because of the way it combines with food. A bottle lasts almost forever unrefrigerated, and its screw-on cap is not a sign of lesser quality; it's just how vermouth is capped.

# Orzo "Risotto" with Roasted Tomatoes and Hot Sausage

**8 SERVINGS**

*food & wine tip*

This is a perfect recipe for entertaining. Not only do you end up with a dish similar to risotto without having to stand over the stove and stir for half an hour, but it also tastes great at room temperature, so you can make it ahead of time.

Orzo is the diminutive Italian pasta that looks like rice (or the tiniest footballs imaginable). Cooked until just al dente, its comforting grains roll on your tongue like silken beads. Here, plenty of Parmesan cheese stirred in at the end of cooking makes it creamy like risotto.

1½ pounds ripe plum tomatoes, rinsed and dried

⅓ cup olive oil

1 medium onion, thinly sliced (1 cup)

3 garlic cloves, minced

4 links hot or sweet Italian sausage (about ¾ pound)

1½ cups dried orzo, preferably Italian

1 cup chicken broth

Salt and freshly ground pepper

1 cup freshly grated imported Parmesan cheese, plus more for garnish

Torn fresh basil leaves, coarsely chopped flat-leaf parsley, or coarsely chopped fresh oregano, for garnish

1. Preheat the oven to 500°F with the rack at the top. Roast the tomatoes in one layer on a large baking pan until blistered and very soft, 20 to 25 minutes, depending on their size. Transfer them, with any skins that have popped off, to a plate. Let cool, then coarsely chop the tomatoes, skin and all (to measure about 1½ cups).

2. Meanwhile, set a large heavy skillet over low heat with the olive oil. When it's hot, add the onion and cook, stirring frequently, until tender and slightly golden, about 8 minutes. Stir in the garlic, cook for 1 minute more, and remove the pan from the heat.

3. Peel off and discard the sausage casing. Break enough of the meat into small pieces to measure 2 generous cups.

**4.** Bring a large pot of water to a boil, salt it generously, and cook the orzo until al dente, 8 to 10 minutes.

**5.** Reheat the onion mixture over low heat, add the sausage, and cook, stirring occasionally, until the meat is half done, about 3 minutes. Stir in the tomatoes and cook 2 to 3 minutes more, stirring occasionally. Stir in the broth, season with salt and pepper, and remove the skillet from the heat. When the orzo is ready, drain it in a colander and give it several good shakes to eliminate as much water as possible.

**6.** Return the orzo to its cooking pot set over low heat and dry it for about 30 seconds, stirring. Stir in the tomato-sausage mixture and heat for about 1 minute, stirring frequently. Stir in 1 cup of the cheese. Spoon the orzo onto warm plates, sprinkle with herbs, if using them, and serve right away with more grated cheese on the side.

**Do-ahead options** Chop the garlic a day ahead.

Roast and chop the tomatoes up to 3 days ahead.

# Lamb Chops with Provençal Tomatoes

**4 SERVINGS**

It seems like a hundred years ago that I cooked order after order of noisettes of lamb Provençal at a Manhattan bistro called P.S. 77, but its earthy flavors will still be appealing for a hundred years to come because they are so satisfying. I like to sear the chops in a hot pan so they get a good crust and then slide them into a moderate oven to finish so their middles stay pink and juicy. But if high-heat sautéing seems like too much, you can grill or broil them instead. And in cold weather or for more of a crowd, you could roast a leg or a couple of racks in place of the chops and serve them with double the tomatoes.

3½ tablespoons extra-virgin olive oil

4 large garlic cloves, finely chopped

1 teaspoon dried *herbes de Provence*

1 can (35 ounces) plum tomatoes, drained, then crushed or coarsely sliced

2½ tablespoons pitted and coarsely chopped Mediterranean olives, both black and green (see Revsin on How to Pit Olives on next page)

¼ to ½ teaspoon hot crushed red pepper flakes

Salt and freshly ground pepper

8 loin or rib lamb chops, cut 1 to 1¼ inches thick

¼ cup dry vermouth, or dry white or red wine

Basil or sprigs of another fresh herb, for garnish

1. Preheat the oven to 350°F with the rack in the center. Heat 2 tablespoons of the olive oil in a large skillet set over high heat. Stir in the garlic and dried herbs, immediately followed by the tomatoes. Cook over high heat, stirring occasionally, until the watery liquid has evaporated but the mixture is still very moist, 4 to 6 minutes. Remove from the heat and stir in the olives. Season with the red pepper flakes and salt and black pepper to taste; cover to keep warm.

**2.** Season both sides of the chops with salt and pepper. Heat a very large heavy, ovenproof skillet over high heat with the remaining 1½ tablespoons olive oil. Add the lamb chops and sauté until brown on one side, about 2 minutes. Turn them over and lightly brown the second side, about 1 minute (that side will finish browning in the oven). Stand the chops on their fatty edge to crisp before turning them back to their less browned side. Discard the fat in the skillet and transfer the skillet to the oven.

**3.** Cook the chops 5 to 8 minutes for medium-rare to medium, or 2 to 3 minutes longer for more well done. Transfer the chops to a platter. Set the skillet back over medium-low heat, pour in the vermouth or wine, and scrape up any brown bits from the bottom of the pan. Add any accumulated juices from the platter. Boil slightly to intensify the flavor and season with salt and pepper to taste.

**4.** Quickly reheat the tomatoes, if necessary. Make a bed of the tomatoes on a warm platter or plates. Arrange the chops on top, spoon the pan juices over them, garnish with the basil, and serve right away.

Do-ahead option Prepare the tomatoes up to 4 days ahead and add the olives when you reheat them.

**revsin on
how to pit olives**

Press the flat side of a large knife on top of a few olives at a time and exert a little pressure until they split open enough to pull out the pits. The softer flesh of the purple and black ones makes them a little more accommodating than the green ones, but either way it's simple to do.

# East of Paris

## DAVID BOULEY, MARIO LOHNINGER AND MELISSA CLARK

INTERVIEW BELOW WITH DAVID BOULEY

### the book
*East of Paris: The New Cuisines of Austria and the Danube* by David Bouley, Mario Lohninger and Melissa Clark (Ecco), $34.95, 346 pages, color photos.

### the gist
A singular interpretation of Austrian cuisine, the basis for chef and restaurateur David Bouley's Danube in New York City.

### the ideal reader
The confident, accomplished cook who's looking for new culinary territory.

### the extras
Behind-the-scenes restaurant anecdotes.

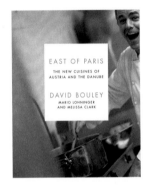

**BACKGROUND** Born in Storrs, Connecticut; lives in New York City.

**EDUCATION** "After high school I went to the University of Connecticut to study business administration, and at the same time I worked in a nearby restaurant with two very creative and knowledgeable Canadian chefs, a father-and-son team. I learned a lot from those two. Later I went to the Sorbonne in Paris and studied art history and French."

**EXPERIENCE** "While I was studying in France in the seventies, I met a lot of restaurant people, including chef Roger Vergé. I moved down to Moulin and worked for Vergé for four seasons, and after that he moved me all around France. Then I went to New York City and worked at Vienna 79, Le Cirque, La Côte Basque, Le Périgord and Brussels; I helped open Le Parker Meridien Hotel. I was traveling back and forth to France then, working for Paul Bocuse, Joël Robuchon, Frédy Girardet—the food scene in the United States was still so far behind France that I wasn't learning anything here. I settled back in New York in 1984, and the following year I became chef at Montrachet and proceeded to open my own restaurants—Bouley, Bouley Bakery and, in 1999, Danube."

**HOW HE FELL IN LOVE WITH FOOD** "I'm one of nine kids, but I was the only one who wanted to spend summers at our French grandparents' home in Rhode Island. They had a big farm where they raised pheasants and rabbits. They had a couple of hundred chickens and 20 acres of fruit trees. My grandmother made her own grape juice and vinegars and goat cheese."

**HOW HE FELL IN LOVE WITH AUSTRIAN CUISINE** "When I was living in France in the seventies, I had a friend who came from a Slavic family, and they'd invite me over to their house to eat. When I worked with the

**KEY TECHNIQUE** Slow cooking. "That's really the gist of the book. A lot of the food is braised and freezes well—it gets tender and the flavors evolve, so you can make it ahead."

group that owned Vienna 79, I fell in love with that kind of food all over again. I had really missed boiled beef and all those delicious things."

HOW AUSTRIAN CHEFS INSPIRED HIM "When I was working in New York in the late seventies and early eighties, French food was all about butter and cream, butter and cream. I thought, if I'm going to cook this food and make a career out of it, I have to get people to want to eat it. I have to create food that's lighter, that's more like the French food in France. At the same time, I heard about a bunch of young Austrian chefs—Vic Sigmund, Hans Winkler and Hans Hass—who'd gone to Germany to do the same thing for their restaurant, Tantris. They were using vegetables to thicken sauces, for instance. When I tried their food, I was excited to see the parallels between what we were doing."

**A REVITALIZING FOOD**
Goulash. "It has all those spices. It's just full of energy from the acids of the wine and the sugar of the caramelized onions. It warms you right up."

REDEFINING AUSTRIAN CUISINE "People always ask, 'What is Austrian food?' The food critic Jeffrey Steingarten came into Danube one day and said, 'So, David, what ocean in Austria are these scallops from?' And I said, 'They are from the same fields where the French get lemongrass.' French cuisine has evolved, and I don't see why other cuisines can't evolve, too, as long as they maintain their integrity."

ESSENTIAL AUSTRIAN INGREDIENT Paprika. "The problem in the United States is that we don't have really fresh paprika. Paprika in Austria has an expiration date on it. You rub it between your fingers and it leaves a stain like red lipstick. So you can imagine what that's like compared to the kind that's been in a can in an Oklahoma warehouse since the 17th century. There are so many different kinds of paprika: Austrian, Turkish, Hungarian, Spanish, Mediterranean, Mexican. In Austria they probably have 25 or 30 different kinds."

WHY HUMBLE INGREDIENTS ARE BEST "The success of a recipe hinges on finding good, fresh—not necessarily expensive—ingredients. I've never used a lot of caviar and truffles like some chefs do. People often seem happier to eat more rustic food with simple ingredients. Truffles and caviar are always pushed to the side of the plate, but I never see potato puree pushed aside."

# Salt-Crusted Lamb with Green Tomato Jam

**SERVES 4 AS A MAIN COURSE**

**Mario Lohninger:** This is a traditional dish from Salzburg, my hometown. Salzburg used to be famous for its salt; that's how it got its name. Salt was more powerful than gold—at one point it was a currency—and it made Salzburg a very rich town. So cooking things in salt is a common technique there.

You can put a salt crust on any meat. It's good with beef and venison, as well as lamb. First you surround the meat with herbs, pine needles, grape leaves, or hay, then you cover it in a salt crust. The salt makes the herb flavors sink into the meat and cooks it gently so it comes out perfect and tender. The thing is to make a very stiff dough, as stiff as you can work with. Anything too wet will oversalt the meat.

You can serve this lamb with anything, but the green tomato jam is especially good—a nice relish to make at the end of summer, when the last tomatoes are left on the vine.

Green tomato jam

½  teaspoon coriander seeds

1  teaspoon light corn syrup

¾  cup sugar

2  small onions, sliced

3  tablespoons extra-virgin olive oil

2  tablespoons sherry vinegar

2  pounds (about 5 large) green tomatoes, roughly chopped

½  lemon, peeled, white pith removed, sliced crosswise

4  bay leaves, preferably fresh

2  teaspoons fine sea salt, or to taste

Freshly ground black pepper

## on bouley's nightstand

One of my favorite books is **Michel Guérard's Cuisine Minceur.** He was one of the first chefs to do the lighter style French cuisine. And there's another wonderful book called **Japanese Cooking: A Simple Art** by **Shizuo Tsuji,** the founder of the Tsuji Culinary Institute in Japan and France. I've been working closely with Tsuji's son on some of my projects.

*food* & *wine* tip

The salt-crust dough
really sticks to
the baking pan—a
parchment-paper lining
will prevent a
cleanup headache.

Salt-crusted lamb

| | |
|---|---|
| 3⅔ | cups kosher salt |
| 1½ | cups all-purpose flour |
| 6 | large egg whites |
| 1 | tablespoon canola oil |
| 2 | racks of baby lamb, frenched, about 4 pounds |

Freshly ground black pepper

2   cups loosely packed mixed fresh herbs (any combination of basil, mint, thyme, rosemary, marjoram, sage—as great a variety as possible)

1. Prepare the tomato jam: Place the coriander seeds in a small skillet and toast them over medium-high heat until fragrant, about 2 minutes. Transfer them to a mortar or electric spice mill and grind coarsely. Set them aside.

2. Place ½ cup water in the bottom of a heavy saucepan. Add the corn syrup to this pool, and mound the sugar over it. Warm the mixture over low heat, stirring constantly, until all the sugar has dissolved, 3 to 5 minutes. Raise the heat to high and simmer, stirring and scraping around the sides of the pan, until the sugar begins to darken, 6 to 8 minutes. Cook, stirring, until the sugar is amber colored and caramelized, 7 minutes. Then add the onions and olive oil (stand back—the caramel will sputter). Reduce the heat to medium and cook, stirring, until the onions begin to soften, 3 to 5 minutes. Add the sherry vinegar and stir and scrape the sides of the pan, loosening any crystals that have hardened, stirring until the liquid is smooth. Add the green tomatoes, ground coriander seeds, lemon slices, and bay leaves. Season with the salt, and add pepper to taste. Raise the heat and bring the mixture to a simmer. Cook gently until the tomatoes begin to break down but have not completely lost their shape, 15 to 20 minutes.

3. Preheat the oven to 350°F.

**4.** Prepare the salt crust: In a small bowl, stir the kosher salt and flour together. In a separate bowl, whisk the egg whites until frothy; then whisk in the salt mixture. Work the mixture with your hands, adding water as necessary (about 2 tablespoons), until it resembles a crumbly dough.

**5.** Heat the canola oil in a large sauté pan over medium-high heat until it is very hot. Season the lamb with pepper, add it to the pan, and sear until brown, about 2 minutes on each side.

**6.** Spread a thin layer of the dough in a 9-by-13-inch metal pan. Sprinkle half of the fresh herbs over this, then arrange the racks of lamb on top. Cover with the rest of the fresh herbs, followed by the remaining dough, patting it around the lamb to form a crust (the crust should cover the meat completely, leaving only the rib bones exposed). Using an instant-read thermometer, make a hole in the crust over the center of one of the racks (so you can check the temperature of the meat as it cooks without breaking the crust).

**7.** Bake for 15 minutes, or until an internal temperature of 130°F has been reached. Break the lamb out of the salt crust by pulling upward on the rib bones. Let the meat rest for a few minutes before slicing it. Serve the meat with the green tomato jam.

# Beet Salad with Caraway Seeds and Walnut Oil

**SERVES 4 TO 6 AS AN APPETIZER OR SIDE DISH**

**David Bouley:** Many people associate beets with something they had when they were kids that was pickled or served out of a can. And many people don't understand that a good beet straight from the garden doesn't taste anything like that. A fresh beet, still with its greens attached, is tender and sweet, almost more like a fruit than a vegetable. It's not woody and tough, or dry like a potato. It's beautiful.

Beets are one of my favorite things—I've loved them since I was about eight or nine when I first realized what vegetables were supposed to taste like. I was on a farm helping out during the harvest. After gathering the produce, there was a big cookout, and all the root vegetables were wrapped in aluminum foil and roasted in an open fire. The beets got intensely sweet, and I thought they were the best vegetables I'd ever had.

This recipe shows off how simple and delicious a garden-fresh beet can be, so it's important to use baby beets that have been harvested within a few days of cooking.

1   pound baby red beets, trimmed but not peeled
1   tablespoon canola oil
2   sprigs fresh thyme
1   bay leaf, preferably fresh
Fine sea salt and freshly ground black pepper
1   teaspoon caraway seeds
¼   cup plus 2 teaspoons Champagne vinegar
1   tablespoon plus 2 teaspoons sugar, or to taste
6   tablespoons walnut oil
Micro cress, mâche, or watercress leaves, for garnish
Chopped walnuts, for garnish

*food* & *wine* tip

If you can't find
baby beets, use regular
beets and cut
them into quarters.

1. Preheat the oven to 425°F.

2. In an ovenproof dish, toss the beets with the canola oil, thyme, bay leaf, and salt and pepper to taste. Cover the dish with aluminum foil and roast until the beets are tender and cooked through, 45 minutes to 1 hour.

3. Meanwhile, make the dressing: Place 1 cup water in a saucepan, add the caraway seeds, and bring to a boil. Take the pan off the heat and stir in the vinegar and sugar. Whisk in the walnut oil, and season with salt and pepper.

4. When the beets are cool enough to handle, slip off their skins and place them in a bowl. Pour the dressing over them and let marinate for at least 1 hour. Serve garnished with the cress and walnuts.

NOTES FROM THE KITCHEN  The caraway here is a nice contrast to the beet's sweetness, as is the walnut oil, which has a slightly bitter note. This is a versatile salad that will go with practically anything as a side dish: meat, fish, pasta, or potatoes. For a substantial first course, you can add cheese: a goat cheese, fresh or aged, a nice granular aged Cheddar or Parmigiano-Reggiano, or even a blue cheese.

# Roast Chicken with Paprika Sauce

**SERVES 4 AS A MAIN COURSE**

4 tablespoons unsalted butter, softened

3 teaspoons sweet Hungarian paprika

Fine sea salt and freshly ground black pepper

One 3½-pound chicken

10 cipollini onions, blanched and peeled

1 large onion, cut crosswise into ½-inch-thick slices

1 head garlic, cloves separated but not peeled

2 bell peppers (preferably 1 red, 1 yellow), trimmed, seeded, and cut into ½-inch slices

1½ ounces (about 6) shiitake mushrooms, trimmed

2 sprigs fresh thyme

¼ cup dry white wine

Paprika sauce

2 tablespoons unsalted butter

1 cup chopped onion

1 garlic clove, minced

Fine sea salt and freshly ground white pepper

1 tablespoon sweet paprika

½ teaspoon hot paprika

¾ cup Chicken Stock (recipe follows) or canned low-sodium chicken broth

½ cup heavy cream

¼ cup dry white wine

2 tablespoons sour cream

2 tablespoons crème fraîche (or use 4 tablespoons sour cream or crème fraîche instead of 2 tablespoons of each)

Fresh juice of ½ lemon

1. Preheat the oven to 450°F.

2. Mix the softened butter with the paprika in a small bowl, and season generously with salt and pepper. Wash and dry the chicken inside and out, and season it generously with salt and pepper. Rub the paprika butter all over the chicken, going under the skin of the breast and trying to stretch your fingers down into the leg so that you can put butter there as well.

3. Lay the cipollini onions, sliced onion, garlic cloves, bell peppers, mushrooms, and thyme sprigs in the bottom of a roasting pan, and place the chicken, breast side down, on top. Drizzle the white wine around the chicken. Roast for 25 minutes. Then baste the chicken with the juices in the pan and turn the chicken over, breast side up. Roast, basting often, until the breast meat feels taut and the internal temperature is 165°F, 25 to 30 minutes. Let the chicken rest for 10 minutes.

4. Meanwhile, prepare the paprika sauce: Melt the butter in a saucepan over medium heat. Add the onion and cook, stirring frequently, until it is soft, brown, and caramelized, about 30 minutes. Add the garlic and cook for another minute. Season well with salt and white pepper. Stir in the paprikas, then pour in the chicken stock, heavy cream, and white wine. Cook over medium-low heat until the mixture has reduced by one-third, 10 minutes. Add the sour cream and crème fraîche, season to taste with drops of the lemon juice, and add more salt and pepper if needed. Puree the sauce in a blender or with an immersion blender.

5. Serve the chicken with a sauceboat of the paprika sauce alongside.

## bouley on paprika

Different types of paprika vary in terms of texture and taste as well as heat. Some paprika is smoked, rather than dried in the sun—this gives it a more distinct flavor. The varieties commonly found in the U.S. are usually limited to "sweet," which is mild, and "hot," which contains the same fiery chemical, capsaicin, that is found in cayenne, a related spice. The most important thing to look for in either is high quality and freshness. Good paprika should be deep red, with no hint of bitterness, and with a soft, silky-smooth texture that melts into a paste as soon as it's warmed.

# Chicken Stock

5   pounds chicken bones, trimmed of
    fat and skin, roughly chopped

1   leek, roughly chopped

1   carrot, roughly chopped

1   celery stalk, roughly chopped

½   head garlic

1   shallot, chopped

4   sprigs fresh parsley

1   sprig fresh thyme

½   teaspoon white peppercorns

1   bay leaf, preferably fresh

Fine sea salt, to taste

1. Rinse the chicken bones well and place them in a stockpot with cold water to cover (about 2½ quarts). Bring the liquid to a simmer and skim the surface.

2. Add the remaining ingredients, and cook at a gentle simmer for 2½ hours, skimming off the foam from time to time. Strain the stock through a fine-mesh sieve, discarding the solids, and let it cool completely. Cover and refrigerate for up to 4 days. Skim off the congealed fat before using.

# Rösti Potatoes with Smoked Salmon and Mustard Vinaigrette

**SERVES 4 AS AN APPETIZER OR LIGHT MAIN COURSE**

**Mario Lohninger:** There are two ways to make rösti potatoes. The first is my favorite. It's like a hash brown: You julienne the raw potato and season it with salt, pepper, and melted butter. Then you cook it in a cast-iron pan until golden brown, pressing down with the spatula to compress the potatoes into a cake. The idea is to have caramelization and crunch on the outside while the inside remains moist. You have to cook it slowly, though, so the inside cooks all the way through before it gets too brown on the surface. The other way to make rösti is to use grated cooked potatoes. The result is a little chewier and softer, and there's not as much contrast of texture. But it's good too, and a great way to use up leftover potatoes.

Here I put smoked salmon on top of the potatoes for a brunch or lunch dish; it's also good as an appetizer. You can use any smoked fish—sturgeon is popular in Austria. The caviar is nice with it, but you don't absolutely need it.

Mustard vinaigrette and lemon crème fraîche

2 ½ teaspoons German sweet whole-grain mustard or whole-grain honey mustard

1    teaspoon Dijon mustard

3    tablespoons fresh lemon juice

Fine sea salt and freshly ground white pepper

2    tablespoons extra-virgin olive oil

2    tablespoons canola oil

3    tablespoons chopped fresh chives

¼    cup crème fraîche or sour cream

Rösti potatoes

4    tablespoons unsalted butter

3    large or 6 small Yukon Gold potatoes (about 1 pound), peeled and grated

2    tablespoons canola oil, plus additional if needed

Fine sea salt and freshly ground black pepper

For serving

2 cups mixed micro greens or baby lettuces

¾ pound cold-smoked salmon, thinly sliced

Salmon roe or caviar (optional)

1. Prepare the mustard vinaigrette: In a small bowl, whisk together the mustards, 1½ tablespoons of the lemon juice, and salt and white pepper to taste. Gradually drizzle the olive oil, then the canola oil, into the mustard mixture, whisking constantly until well combined. Stir in the chives and add up to 3 tablespoons water, ½ tablespoon at a time, until thinned to the desired consistency (you should be able to drizzle the dressing). Set it aside.

2. In another small bowl, combine the crème fraîche with the remaining 1½ tablespoons lemon juice. Season with salt and white pepper, and set aside.

3. Prepare the potatoes: Melt the butter in an 11-inch cast-iron skillet over medium heat (see Note on next page). Place the grated potatoes in a large bowl and pour the melted butter over them. Toss to coat.

4. Add enough canola oil to the same pan to coat the bottom well (1 to 2 tablespoons), and warm it over medium heat. Add the potatoes and press them down to form a ½-inch-thick cake. Season well with salt and pepper, and cook until brown on the underside, 12 to 15 minutes—reduce the heat if the potatoes are browning too quickly. Slide the cake out onto a plate and flip it over back into the pan. Cook until brown on the other side, 8 to 10 minutes, adding another ½ tablespoon oil if necessary to keep the potatoes from sticking.

**5.** Gently toss the micro greens with 2 tablespoons of the mustard vinaigrette.

**6.** To serve, divide the rösti potatoes into 4 portions and place a portion on each plate. Spread a thin layer of lemon crème fraîche over the potatoes. Pile 3 or 4 slices of salmon on each piece. Arrange a few of the dressed greens on top, and scatter the rest around the potatoes. Drizzle the salmon and potatoes with mustard vinaigrette, and sprinkle a few beads of salmon roe or caviar over the top if desired. Serve at once.

N O T E  This recipe calls for an 11-inch cast-iron pan. If you don't have one, use a 10-inch pan, decreasing the heat and increasing the cooking time slightly. Or use an 8-inch pan to make 2 smaller röstis: Decrease the cooking time; transfer the first rösti to an ovenproof plate lined with paper towels and keep it warm in a 200°F oven; and add more oil to coat the bottom of the pan before cooking the second rösti.

# Everyday Greens

## ANNIE SOMERVILLE

### the book

*Everyday Greens: Home Cooking from Greens, the Celebrated Vegetarian Restaurant* by Annie Somerville (Scribner), $40, 396 pages, color illustrations.

### the gist

Delicious recipes for meatless meals from the famed San Francisco restaurant Greens.

### the ideal reader

The cook who is after exciting recipes for vegetables, grains and pastas.

### the extras

Beautiful watercolor illustrations and a concise, informative overview of what wines and beers work best with vegetarian dishes.

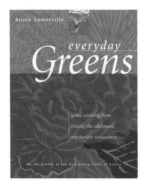

**BACKGROUND** Born outside Detroit, Michigan; lives in San Francisco.

**EDUCATION** Studied liberal arts at Humboldt State University in Arcata, California, and Zen meditation and practice at the San Francisco Zen Center.

**EXPERIENCE** "I started cooking when I first walked in the door at the Zen Center, in 1973. The Zen Center was often described as 'the food cult.' All of the cooking we did was definitely inspired by our meditation practice. At the Zen Center's monastery, Tassajara, a big part of life is feeding the monks, students and guests. We started the Tassajara Bakery as a means to support the Center and its growing community. So it seemed the next thing to do was to take a big risk and open a restaurant. The Zen Center opened Greens in 1979. I've been here since 1981."

**PREVIOUS BOOK** Somerville has authored one other book. "Writing *Fields of Greens,* in 1993, was really difficult. It's very hard to take restaurant recipes and make them accessible, and very challenging to determine when it's okay to sacrifice something in a dish or when we should say, forget this recipe, it just won't work at home. *Fields of Greens* focused on recipes that were a little easier to make at home, with fewer dairy products, because at that time everyone was looking at fat, so we lightened up. And there was a lot of information about gardening."

**IMPORTANCE OF EVERYDAY RECIPES** "The practical emphasis of the book, of course, is on an easy style of cooking. Also, these are recipes that we would make any day of the week at the restaurant. The title further recognizes the wonderful quality in life that comes from everyday moments. Buddhist practice is: This is your life, this is it, every day."

**SECRET TO SUCCESSFUL VEGETARIAN COOKING** "Our focus at the restaurant is always on great

### HEALTHY BALANCE

"We're never lacking protein because every menu has an abundance of beans, grains, tofu, nuts, cheese and other dairy products. We love dairy!"

ingredients—using the best, most seasonal produce we can get our hands on and making balanced dishes out of it. We're not looking for meat substitutes."

PERSONAL DIET "I'm not a strict vegetarian. I eat a tiny bit of chicken and fish—but not very often. The Greens menu, however, is based on 'No meat, no fish, no fowl.' And that's predominantly how I've been eating for so many years."

STRONGEST ETHNIC INFLUENCES ON THE GREENS MENU Southeast Asian, Mexican and Indian. "The influx of immigrants to the Bay Area has brought huge change to the culinary scene, and consequently our customers are craving spicier and hotter foods. Our dinner chef, Tai Do, is from a restaurant-owning family in Vietnam, and he's been a big influence on the kitchen. He's given us incredible curries, spring rolls, green papaya salad, squash soup."

ESSENTIAL EQUIPMENT A stainless steel Japanese vegetable knife or an eight-inch chef's knife, a good paring knife, a bread knife (also good for slicing tomatoes) and a really good zester—either a Microplane or five-hole Victorinox. "I also like using a hand-held reamer to juice citrus fruits."

MOST INTIMIDATING TOOL "The restaurant uses a mandoline, but I'm afraid of it."

FAVORITE SEASONAL INGREDIENT "These really great white beans we call *gigandes.* They produce a lot of starch and break down to help make the sauce, for instance, in the Fall Vegetable Ragoût recipe."

BEST RECIPE SHORTCUT "If you don't have time to roast your own tomatoes, you can always use the really good canned Muir Glen fire-roasted tomatoes."

FAVORITE BAY AREA RESTAURANTS "In San Francisco, inexpensive ethnic places that I can bike to, like La Tacqueria in the Mission or Rosa's Café, a simple California-Mediterranean spot on Union Street. The high-end places I admire most are The Slanted Door, Delfina and Boulevard, and in Berkeley, Chez Panisse."

RECOMMENDED FOOD SOURCE "Local farmers' markets. The quality and variety of food available today is truly amazing. And they're full of wonderful surprises."

**MAKE-AHEAD TIP** "Don't be afraid to prep vegetables a day ahead. Wash lettuces and refrigerate them in the salad spinner; wrap cut vegetables in damp towels and refrigerate; soak and cook beans."

# Orecchiette with Broccoli Rabe, Almonds, and Manchego

**SERVES 4 TO 6**

## somerville on nuts

**IN THE OVEN**
Toast in an ovenproof dish or on a rimmed baking sheet in a preheated 350°F oven until they smell nutty and begin to turn golden, 8 to 10 minutes, depending on the nut or seed. Give them a shake after 4 to 5 minutes, to redistribute them and keep their color even.

**IN A SMALL SKILLET**
Use a heavy-bottomed skillet—the little French ones or cast-iron skillets are ideal conductors of heat. Don't be tempted to walk away while toasting nuts or seeds on the stovetop. Toast them over very low heat, shaking the pan as needed, until they're golden and smell nutty.

1 large bunch of broccoli rabe, about ¾ pound

½ pound orecchiette

¼ cup extra-virgin olive oil

½ pound spring onions, sliced, about 2 cups

Salt and pepper

½ tablespoon minced garlic

Red pepper flakes

¼ cup unskinned almonds, toasted (instructions at left) and chopped

¼ pound Manchego cheese, grated, about 1 cup

Bring 2 large pots of water to a boil and salt lightly.

Trim the tough lower stems from the broccoli rabe and discard them. Chop the tops into 2-inch pieces; you should have about 8 cups of florets and stems. Drop the broccoli rabe into one of the pots and cook until tender, 2 to 3 minutes. Drain in a colander, rinse under cold water, and set aside.

Drop the orecchiette into the boiling water and cook until tender, 12 to 15 minutes. While the pasta is cooking, heat 2 tablespoons of the oil in a large sauté pan and add the onions, ½ teaspoon salt, and a pinch of pepper. Cook over medium heat until wilted, 2 to 3 minutes, add the garlic, and cook 1 minute more. Add 1½ cups of the pasta cooking water to the onions, along with the broccoli rabe, the remaining oil, ¼ teaspoon red pepper flakes, ¼ teaspoon salt, and a pinch of pepper.

Drain the pasta, add the pasta to the sauté pan, and cook for 1 to 2 minutes, tossing it gently to coat with the sauce. There will be a lot of liquid at first, but the pasta will absorb it. Toss in a pinch of red pepper flakes, the almonds, and half of the cheese and season to taste with salt and additional red pepper flakes. Divide the pasta into warm bowls and sprinkle with the remaining Manchego.

# Couscous Salad with Cherry Tomatoes, Lemon, and Pine Nuts

**SERVES 4**

Crunchy bites of toasted pine nuts contrast with juicy cherry tomatoes and the fresh taste of parsley and mint in this lemony, lively salad. We use a flat-bottomed dish to prepare the couscous, so the individual grains absorb the hot dressing evenly. Make this for a picnic or party—have the couscous ready in advance, and just toss in the cherry tomatoes, pine nuts, and herbs right before serving.

| | |
|---|---|
| 1 | cup instant couscous |
| 1 | teaspoon minced lemon zest |
| 1 | cup water |
| 2 | tablespoons fresh lemon juice |
| 1 | tablespoon Champagne vinegar |
| 3 | tablespoons olive oil |
| ¾ | teaspoon salt |

Pinch of pepper

| | |
|---|---|
| 3 | tablespoons pine nuts, toasted (see Somerville on Nuts on previous page) |
| 1 | scallion, both white and green parts, thinly sliced on the diagonal |
| 1 | cup ripe, little cherry tomatoes, cut in half |
| 2 | tablespoons chopped flat-leaf parsley |
| 2 | tablespoons chopped fresh mint |

Pour the couscous grains into a small baking dish. Set the lemon zest aside to toss with the salad later. Combine the water, lemon juice, vinegar, olive oil, salt, and pepper in a small saucepan. Bring to a boil, pour over the couscous, and give it a quick stir. Cover the dish and set aside for 20 minutes.

When the couscous is ready, gently fluff it with a fork to separate the grains. Transfer to a serving bowl and toss with the reserved lemon zest and remaining ingredients.

## on somerville's nightstand

Any of the books from **Chez Panisse** are influential—they get to the heart of the matter. **Deborah Madison's** books, certainly, and **Paula Wolfert's** are other favorites. Of course, **Julia Child's** books were early inspirations at the restaurant. And I never miss the Wednesday food sections of the *San Francisco Chronicle* and *The New York Times.*

# Potato, Spring Onion, and Sorrel Soup

**MAKES ABOUT 2 QUARTS**

**somerville's variation**

If sorrel isn't available, use thinly sliced spinach instead, but the tart sorrel flavor will be missed. You can also try thin ribbons of chard or kale, but allow extra time to cook the greens, particularly if using kale.

7 to 8 cups Vegetable Stock (recipe follows)

3  pounds Yellow Finn potatoes, peeled

Salt and pepper

1  tablespoon olive oil

1  tablespoon unsalted butter

1  bunch of spring onions, about ½ pound, sliced, including the firm part of the green, about 3 cups

1  tablespoon minced garlic

½  cup white wine

⅓  cup heavy cream

¼  pound sorrel, stems removed and leaves thinly sliced, about 2 cups

Grated Gruyère cheese

2 to 3 tablespoons chopped flat-leaf parsley

Make the Vegetable Stock and keep it warm over low heat.

Dice enough of the potatoes into ½-inch cubes to make 2 cups and set aside. Slice the remaining potatoes and place them in a soup pot, along with 6 cups of the stock, ½ teaspoon salt, and a pinch of pepper. Bring to a boil, lower the heat, and cook over medium heat until the potatoes begin to break apart, about 30 minutes. Pass through a food mill or quickly puree in a blender and return to the pot over low heat.

Heat the oil and butter in a large sauté pan and add the onions, ¼ teaspoon salt, and a pinch of pepper and cook over medium heat until soft and translucent, about 5 minutes. Add the garlic and cook 1 minute more. Pour in the wine and cook until the pan is nearly dry, about 3 minutes.

Stir in the diced potatoes, 1 cup of the stock, ¼ teaspoon salt, and a pinch of pepper. Cover the pan and simmer until the potatoes are tender, about 10 minutes. Add to the potato puree, adding stock, if needed, to thin. Stir in the cream and the sorrel and cook over low heat for 5 minutes. Season to taste with salt and pepper. Garnish each serving with a spoonful of Gruyère and a sprinkling of parsley.

## Vegetable Stock

**MAKES ABOUT 2 QUARTS**

Double the recipe and freeze half of it for later. It keeps nearly indefinitely in the freezer, but only a day or two in the refrigerator.

1   large yellow onion, sliced

2 to 3 leek tops, chopped and washed

3   celery ribs, sliced

2   large carrots, sliced

½   pound white mushrooms, sliced

1   large potato, sliced

6   garlic cloves, smashed with the flat side of a knife, skins left on

1   teaspoon salt

½   teaspoon peppercorns

6   parsley sprigs

3 to 4 fresh thyme sprigs

2   fresh oregano or marjoram sprigs

5   fresh sage leaves

1   bay leaf

10   cups cold water

Combine all the ingredients in a stockpot and bring to a boil. Lower the heat and simmer, uncovered, for about 45 minutes, stirring as needed. Pour the stock through a strainer, pressing as much liquid from the vegetables as possible, then discard them.

# Food Network Kitchens Cookbook

**FOOD NETWORK KITCHENS**

INTERVIEW BELOW WITH SUSAN STOCKTON

**BACKGROUND** Susan Stockton oversees culinary production at Food Network in New York City. "There are 10 of us in the kitchen, and the rest of the people who helped with the book are editors, writers, researchers and shoppers. We're a very eclectic group: I was a graphic designer, and we also have a sculptor, a photographer and a cabaret singer. Cooking is a visual and tactile business, which is probably why so many of us have fine arts training."

**WHAT FOOD NETWORK'S KITCHEN STAFF DOES** "The talent, meaning the on-air personalities, comes up with the recipes and delivers them to us, and we figure out how many should go into every individual segment. Then we actually write a detailed script of how each recipe will be performed. The kitchen staff also preps, cooks and styles all the food for every show."

**WHY THEY WROTE THE BOOK** "Food Network is celebrating its tenth anniversary, and we realized how much the test kitchen informs the production of the shows. It seemed natural for us to share with our viewers all the trial-and-error knowledge that we've acquired in a decade. We've received tons of viewer mail over the years, so we thought we had a good sense of what people are interested in and what their concerns are. We also thought that while there are a lot of excellent ethnic cookbooks, there aren't many about basic American homestyle cooking that has evolved from various ethnic cuisines."

**HOW THEY DEVELOPED THE RECIPES** "It was an ongoing process. First Katharine Alford, the test kitchen director, sent out an e-mail to everyone in the culinary department asking them to contribute their favorite food memories. Then we saw which of those overlapped and where there were holes. For example, people are always clamoring for chicken recipes, so we made sure to have a lot of poultry dishes; and we know there's a trend toward Spanish food, so we made sure to include plenty of those recipes as well."

## BANNED INGREDIENT
Foie gras. "A lot of people think it's too la-di-da."

VIEWERS' EVOLVING TASTES "A lot of viewers wrote to us about their favorite comfort-food recipes from childhood—pineapple upside-down cake, Cobb salad—and asked us if we could somehow make these dishes more modern. Tastes and expectations evolve over time in this way. In fact, menus in restaurants are a good barometer, often reflecting the changing attitudes of the day."

FOOD TREND "I think people are really interested in baking, which is pretty ironic because of the low-carb trend. But they still want to reward themselves."

THE MOVE TOWARD BOLDER FLAVORS "Our viewers want bigger, bolder flavors than what we were all used to in the seventies. That is why, for our Southwestern Cobb Salad with Chili-Rubbed Steak, we used sirloin instead of the traditional chicken, and a buttermilk-chipotle dressing instead of the standard blue cheese vinaigrette. In general, our palates are able to take more spice and more heat. And we balance that with the right amount of sweetness."

DEFINING MODERN AMERICAN COMFORT CUISINE "We found that the range of foods that are meaningful to us is pretty broad, so we labeled it Modern American, which is a new kind of comfort cuisine. It's not meat loaf and potatoes anymore. It's a mix, a melding of different American cuisines. In the book, we were trying to replicate familiar flavors and add little twists, like the surprising addition of ginger and rum to a coconut cake. We tweak our recipes so that they'll be different from the ones that your mom made."

FAVORITE STAFF RECIPE "One of our food stylists, Santos Loo, who grew up in Peru and has a Peruvian mother and a Chinese father, developed the Peruvian Roast Chicken with Aji Verde, a family dish with both Peruvian and Chinese influences. He phoned home to get the recipe."

ESSENTIAL EQUIPMENT A good set of knives, tongs, a rasp zester, an instant-read thermometer, a cast-iron skillet and nonstick silicone baking mats.

MOST POPULAR FOOD NETWORK SHOWS Rachael Ray's *30 Minute Meals* and Giada De Laurentiis's *Everyday Italian,* "because the recipes are so simple. We used to focus on high-end chef-type recipes, but now we've reached a middle point where there's a balance between recipes from chefs and recipes from home cooks."

# Shrimp Phad Thai

**6 SERVINGS**

Thailand's most famous noodle dish is often most people's introduction to
Thai food. A little sweet, a little hot, and very fresh, one bite is all you need to
become a devotee.

4    ounces medium-thick flat rice noodles (see Cook's Note, page 126)

2    tablespoons plus 1 teaspoon sugar

2    tablespoons plus 1 teaspoon fish sauce (see Food Network Kitchens on
     Sauces, at right)

2    tablespoons rice vinegar

¼    cup peanut oil

2    large eggs, beaten with a pinch salt

12   ounces peeled and deveined medium shrimp (see Deveining Shrimp, page 127)

¾    teaspoon crushed red pepper flakes

Kosher salt

4    cloves garlic, chopped

2    shallots, thinly sliced

1    cup cubed firm tofu (about 6 ounces)

5    scallions (white and green parts), 3 cut into ½-inch pieces, 2 chopped

1¼ cups mung bean sprouts

⅓    cup salted roasted peanuts, chopped, plus additional for garnish

Lime wedges

Sriracha sauce (see Food Network Kitchens on Sauces, at right)

## food network kitchens on sauces

**FISH SAUCE**
This pungent sauce
made from the liquid
from salted and
fermented fish is what
distinguishes much
Southeast Asian
cooking from other
Asian cuisines.

**SRIRACHA SAUCE**
This is the red-orange
sauce you see in
those squeeze bottles
on the tables of
Thai restaurants.
A moderately hot chili
sauce, it's used
widely in Thai cooking
as a condiment.

1. Put the noodles in a medium bowl and add enough hot water to cover.
Soak until tender, about 30 minutes. Drain and set aside. Whisk the sugar with
the fish sauce and vinegar in a small bowl.

2. Heat a large skillet over medium heat until hot and add 1 tablespoon of the
peanut oil. Pour in the eggs, tilting the skillet as you pour to make a thin, even

*food & wine tip*

After you soak and drain
the rice noodles, set
them aside wrapped in
damp paper towels.
This will keep them from
drying out before you
are ready to use them.

coating of egg. Cook until just set, about 45 seconds. Invert the eggs onto a cutting board and cut into ½-inch pieces. Set aside.

3. Add another 1 tablespoon peanut oil to the same skillet and heat over high heat. Add the shrimp, ½ teaspoon of the pepper flakes, and salt to taste. Stir-fry until the shrimp are pink and just cooked through, about 1½ minutes. Transfer to a plate.

4. Heat the remaining 2 tablespoons peanut oil over high heat. Add the garlic, shallots, and remaining ¼ teaspoon red pepper flakes and stir-fry until lightly browned, about 1 minute. Add the tofu and cook about 2 minutes more. Add the noodles and cook, tossing, until lightly coated with the garlic mixture, about 1 minute. Add the fish sauce mixture and large scallion pieces and heat through. Stir in the cooked egg and shrimp, 1 cup of the sprouts, and the ⅓ cup peanuts and toss until hot. Divide the phad Thai among plates and top with the remaining ¼ cup sprouts, additional peanuts, and chopped scallions. Serve immediately with the lime wedges and Sriracha.

COOK'S NOTE Rice noodles for phad Thai are about the same thickness as linguine. They're available in supermarkets and Asian food stores.

## deveining shrimp

1. Shrimp can be deveined in the shell or out. To devein through the shell, make a cut along the back of the shrimp just deep enough to expose the vein.

2. Gently remove the vein with the tip of the knife or your fingers.

3. Peel the shells off, starting at the head end.

## in food network's library

Our favorites include anything by **Julia Child,** but especially *The Way to Cook.* We also love the *Joy of Cooking, Cookwise* by **Shirley Corriher** and *Vegetables from Amaranth to Zucchini* by **Elizabeth Schneider.** And of course we adore the books from all of our talent, like **Emeril Lagasse, Wolfgang Puck, Rachael Ray** and **Mario Batali.**

# Chicken Ragù with Farfalle

4 TO 6 SERVINGS

2    tablespoons extra-virgin olive oil

4    whole chicken legs (about 2 pounds)

2    teaspoons kosher salt, plus additional for seasoning

Freshly ground black pepper

1    medium red onion, diced

1    large carrot, peeled and diced

1    rib celery, diced

1    clove garlic, minced

½    cup dry white wine

4    canned plum tomatoes, chopped

1    tablespoon tomato paste

1    teaspoon dried thyme

1    teaspoon dried sage

1    teaspoon dried rosemary

2    sprigs fresh flat-leaf parsley, plus 2 tablespoons chopped

About 1 ½ cups chicken broth, homemade (recipe follows), or low-sodium canned

1    pound farfalle pasta (bow ties)

2    tablespoons freshly grated Pecorino Romano cheese, plus more for serving

1. Heat a large skillet over medium heat, add the olive oil, and heat until shimmering. Season the chicken with some salt and pepper to taste, and cook until brown on all sides, about 20 minutes. Remove the chicken to a platter. Add the onion, carrot, celery, and the 2 teaspoons salt to the skillet and cook, stirring occasionally, until the vegetables begin to soften, about 5 minutes. Add the garlic and cook until the vegetables are just tender, about 5 minutes more. Add the wine, tomatoes, tomato paste, thyme, sage, rosemary, and the parsley sprigs. Cook, stirring occasionally, until the tomatoes break down and the mixture is saucy, about 5 minutes.

2. Slip the chicken with any juices into the tomato sauce. Add enough chicken broth to cover about ⅔ of the chicken. Simmer the ragù with the lid slightly ajar until the meat pulls easily from the bone, turning the chicken halfway through, about 30 minutes. Remove the chicken and when cool enough to handle, pull the meat from the bones, discarding the skin and bones. Skim off any fat that has collected on the top of the sauce and stir in the chicken. (The dish can be prepared up to this point 1 day ahead and refrigerated in a tightly sealed container.)

3. When ready to serve, heat the ragù over low heat. Bring a large pot of cold water to a boil over high heat and salt it generously. Add the farfalle and cook, stirring occasionally, until al dente, about 10 minutes. Ladle out about 1 cup of cooking water and set aside. Drain the pasta, add it to the ragù, and toss over low heat, adding about ¼ cup of the reserved pasta-cooking liquid at a time until the sauce coats the farfalle. Add the chopped parsley and the Pecorino Romano cheese and toss again. Serve in warm bowls with additional cheese.

*food & wine tip*

This delicious recipe is even better when made with fresh herbs. Instead of 1 teaspoon each of dried thyme, sage and rosemary, use 1 tablespoon each of chopped fresh herbs.

# Chicken Broth

ABOUT 3 QUARTS OF BROTH,
PLUS 3 TO 4 CUPS POACHED
CHICKEN

1    4-pound whole chicken

1    onion, peeled and quartered

2    carrots, quartered

2    ribs celery, quartered

1 to 2 dark green leek tops
     (optional)

1    medium parsnip, quartered
     (optional)

3    generous sprigs fresh thyme or
     1 teaspoon dried

3    generous sprigs fresh
     flat-leaf parsley

5    black peppercorns

1    bay leaf

About 4 quarts water

1. Combine the chicken, vegetables, fresh herbs, peppercorns, and bay leaf in a stockpot. Pour in enough water to cover the chicken completely. Heat the water to just under a boil over medium-high heat.

Reduce the heat to a very low simmer. Skim any fat and scum from the surface with a ladle or large spoon. Cook until the chicken is cooked through but not dry, about 1 hour.

2. Remove the chicken from the pot and cool. Continue to simmer the broth while you cut the chicken meat from the bone. Use the meat for salad, soups, or other recipes. Return the bones to the pot and simmer for another hour.

3. Strain the broth into another pot, a large bowl, or a plastic container. Fill the sink up with ice water to come about halfway up the sides of the container. Nestle the broth in the ice bath and stir it periodically to cool it down. Cover and refrigerate for up to 5 days or freeze up to 3 months.

# Hoisin-Glazed Beef Tenderloin with Shiitake Mushrooms

**6 SERVINGS**

Go mushroom-hunting at your market. Button mushrooms may abound, but also look for the slightly exotic, dried or fresh: chanterelles, morels, porcini, shiitake, and wood ear.

| | |
|---|---|
| 2 | pounds center-cut beef tenderloin roast |
| 1½ | teaspoons kosher salt, plus additional for seasoning |
| | Freshly ground black pepper |
| 2 | tablespoons vegetable oil |
| ⅓ | cup hoisin sauce (see Food Network Kitchens on Hoisin Sauce, at right) |
| 1 | pound fresh shiitake mushrooms, stems removed, caps quartered |
| 3 | bunches scallions (white and green parts separate), cut into 2-inch pieces |
| 4 | cloves garlic, minced |
| 1 | ½-inch piece peeled fresh ginger, very thinly sliced |
| ½ | teaspoon crushed red pepper flakes |
| ½ | cup dry sherry |

### food network kitchens on hoisin sauce

We count Chinese hoisin sauce—a sweet and spicy blend of fermented soybeans, garlic, chile peppers, and spices—as one of the Condiments We Love. It's fabulous as a glaze for roasted and grilled meats and as a flavoring in other sauces.

1. Preheat the oven to 400°F. Heat a large skillet over medium-high heat. Season the beef all over with salt and a generous amount of pepper. Add the oil to the skillet and heat until shimmering, then sear the beef until it is a mahogany brown on all sides, about 8 minutes in all. Transfer the tenderloin to a shallow roasting pan, reserving the skillet. Brush the beef all over with the hoisin sauce and roast until an instant-read thermometer inserted in the center registers 125°F for medium-rare, about 30 minutes. Transfer the roast to a cutting board, tent it very loosely with aluminum foil, and let it rest while you cook the mushrooms.

2. Heat the skillet over medium-high heat. Add the mushrooms, scallion whites, garlic, ginger, the 1½ teaspoons salt, and red pepper flakes and cook until soft, about 8 minutes. Add the scallion greens and sherry and cook until almost all the liquid has evaporated, about 2 minutes. Slice the roast and serve with the vegetables.

# Veal Scaloppini with Greens & Radicchio

**2 SERVINGS**

The perfect date food—romantic, just right for two, and simple to do. Dazzle with wit. Charm with your smile. Then seduce with your scaloppini.

5   slices white bread

3   cloves garlic, minced

2   tablespoons minced fresh flat-leaf parsley

2   teaspoons minced fresh rosemary

2   teaspoons minced fresh thyme

1   teaspoon finely grated lemon zest

Kosher salt and freshly ground black pepper

2   large eggs, beaten

2   veal scaloppini, top-round center cuts preferred (about 8 ounces each)

1½ cups torn arugula

1½ cups torn frisée

1   cup torn radicchio

2   tablespoons unsalted butter

2   tablespoons extra-virgin olive oil

1   lemon, halved

Small chunk Parmigiano-Reggiano or Pecorino Romano cheese

1. Pulse the bread into coarse crumbs in a food processor; then spread them on a microwave-safe plate and microwave on high for 1 minute. (Alternatively, spread the crumbs on a baking sheet and dry in a 200°F oven for 10 minutes.) Toss the bread crumbs with the garlic, parsley, rosemary, thyme, lemon zest, and salt and pepper to taste.

2. Put the bread crumbs in one shallow dish and the eggs in another. Pat the veal dry and season both sides with salt and pepper. Dip each piece into

**food & wine tip**

As you cook the veal,
you may need to add
extra butter and olive oil
to the skillet because
the bread crumbs tend
to soak them up quickly.

the egg, shaking off excess, and then press both sides into the breading to coat. Place on a baking sheet, cover, and refrigerate for at least 20 minutes or up to 2 hours to set the breading.

**3.** Toss the arugula, frisée, and radicchio in a bowl. Heat a medium nonstick skillet over medium heat and add 1 tablespoon each of the butter and olive oil. When the butter stops foaming, add 1 piece of veal and cook (press down lightly with a spatula to help keep it from curling), turning once, until golden brown, about 2½ minutes per side. Repeat. After the veal is cooked, add the greens to the skillet, season with salt and pepper, and toss just until they begin to wilt, about 30 seconds. Squeeze the lemon over the greens and toss again. Pile some greens on top of each piece of veal and shave the cheese over the greens.

# Forever Summer

### NIGELLA LAWSON

**BACKGROUND** Born and lives in London.

**EDUCATION** "I studied modern and medieval languages at Oxford and planned to write a doctoral thesis on 14th-century Italian poetry, but instead I ended up in publishing and journalism."

**EXPERIENCE** "In London I was the deputy literary editor at *The Sunday Times* when I was 26, and I was also an arts interviewer, a book reviewer, the restaurant critic for *The Spectator* and an op-ed columnist for *The Times* and *The Observer*. Soon after my first child was born, in 1993, I started writing the food column for British *Vogue*. That segued into becoming a full-time food journalist, cookbook author and TV personality."

**HOW SHE CAME TO LOVE FOOD** "My mother's father started the Lyons Corner Houses chain of tea rooms, and my father's father was a tea merchant. We were all always talking about food, which is unusual in England."

**HOW SHE LEARNED TO COOK** "My mother would get us all to help—having us whisk eggs for mayonnaise, or setting us up by the stove and showing us how to make white sauce. That was how we learned—cooking real meals rather than kids' stuff."

**MENTOR** Anna Del Conte, who wrote *The Classic Food of Northern Italy* and *Gastronomy of Italy*. "I sought her out when I was in my twenties. I love her practical recipes, and also the way she relates food to the history of a country, like Claudia Roden and Jane Grigson do. Food in their books is shown to be a very important part of life, and their recipes are more than just formulas."

**PREVIOUS BOOKS** "*How to Eat: The Pleasures and Principles of Good Food*, which came out in 1998, was a personal story: my life in food. It was really about remembering my mother and

**HOW TO GAIN KITCHEN CONFIDENCE** Cook for yourself. "If you don't cook day to day, you don't want to be cooking a dinner party for ten. It's like having just passed a driver's test and thinking that you'll do a bit of Formula One racing this weekend."

sister, who died young, by writing about what the three of us cooked together. After that book came *How to Be a Domestic Goddess* and *Nigella Bites.*"

**WHY "FOREVER SUMMER" IS DIFFERENT** "The food in my prior books was very cocooning. There's a psychological change in this one. It's sunnier."

**FAVORITE RECIPE IN THE BOOK** The Slow-Roasted Garlic and Lemon Chicken. "This dish is easy to do when people are coming over, but it also works well in small quantities. My mother used to roast a chicken with half a lemon in the cavity, and that smell has always made me feel like I'm at home."

**CREATING A SUMMER MENU** "I like cold and hot on the table. Like Za'atar Chicken with Fattoush—the chicken is hot, in both spices and temperature, with that wonderfully cold fattoush salad. It's all about contrast and balance."

**INDOOR VERSUS OUTDOOR GRILLING** "I usually use the griddle inside rather than the grill outside. I used to have a cast-iron griddle, but it was so heavy. Now I have an All-Clad one that looks like cast-iron but is lighter and has a nonstick surface. It goes across two burners."

**FAVORITE SUMMER FLAVOR** Mint. "Mint is an ancient herb and it has such a depth and pungency but also a coolness. It works with both sweet and savory—parsley, scallions, white wine and salty cheeses like French goat cheese and feta. Everyone cooks with cilantro, but mint should be used just as much."

**USING OUT-OF-SEASON PRODUCE** "Poaching peaches brings out their flavor. And balsamic vinegar on strawberries—that's a trick I learned from Anna Del Conte. I find a squeeze of lemon or lime on fruit makes it taste sweeter. And I never put tomatoes anywhere near the fridge. I put them on the windowsill to soak up any sun, as I find that then they start smelling like they were fresh picked."

**FOOD TRENDS** "I'm so bad at predicting trends. As a home cook, I don't need to be aware of trends. Chefs are the ones who need to know what's in fashion."

**FUTURE PROJECT** "I'm writing a new book with the working title 'Feast.' But what's really important is the subtitle: 'Food to Celebrate Life.'"

## WHY SUMMER IS SIMPLE

"In summer I'm in the mood for food that just needs a quick stir on the stove. In fact, when they shot my *Forever Summer* TV series, there was so little to do they taped me going in and out of the house to fill time."

# Squid Salad with Lime, Cilantro, Mint and Mizuna

**SERVES 6**

OK. First off, don't worry if the word mizuna means nothing to you. It's a tenderly peppery Japanese salad leaf, which some greengrocers, and even supermarkets, stock these days, but you can easily use arugula instead.

In this seafood salad, tender, pink-tinged baby squid are quickly fried, and then coated in a pungent dressing made simply by puréeing a peeled lime along with some cilantro, mint, fish sauce, garlic and sugar in the processor. It makes a wonderful starter to a full-blown summer dinner party, but I love it, with nothing before or after, except perhaps a bit of fruit, when I've got a couple of friends coming over for lunch.

For the dressing

1    (approximately 4 ounces) bunch fresh cilantro or mint, or a mixture of both

1    clove garlic, peeled

1 to 2 tablespoons fish sauce

½    teaspoon granulated sugar

1    green finger or jalapeño chilli, seeded (optional)

1    lime

6    tablespoons peanut oil

For the salad

7    ounces mizuna (or arugula) leaves

1    small red onion

18    ounces baby squid (cleaned weight)

2 to 3 tablespoons peanut oil for frying

Salt

## on lawson's nightstand

I just read a fabulous book that's not really a cookbook; it's a memoir about food called *Toast: The Story of a Boy's Hunger* by **Nigel Slater.** I like cookbooks that are big and old-fashioned and make you feel comfortable, like *The King Arthur Flour Baker's Companion.* Reading that makes you feel better. I like **Anna Del Conte's** books— *Gastronomy of Italy* and *The Classic Food of Northern Italy.* I know her recipes will turn out well. It's like having a conversation and knowing that it's going great.

Tear the cilantro and mint leaves from the stalks, not worrying if a few stalky bits are attached, and throw into the food processor along with the garlic, fish sauce and sugar, plus the chilli if you are using it; this is completely up to you and simply depends on whether you want any heat or not. Peel the lime by first cutting off a slice at the ends so that you can make the lime sit on a wooden board and then just cut strips downward so that peel, and pith, come off cleanly. Add the peeled lime, halved and with the seeds removed, to the bowl and process everything until it is a smooth pulp, then drizzle the oil in, down the funnel, with the motor running, to emulsify the sauce. Scrape into a bowl to use later.

Arrange the salad leaves—mizuna or arugula, whichever you're using—in a bowl or on a large plate. Peel the onion, cut it in half and then slice into very thin half-moons and sprinkle them over the greenery.

Slice the baby squid, leaving the tentacles whole, and fry in a large pan with a little oil; you will have to do this in a couple of batches. Remove the cooked squid to a bowl, sprinkle with salt, then, once you've got all cooked and cooled a little, toss in the lime and herb dressing and arrange over the waiting leaves and onions.

# Slow-Roasted Garlic and Lemon Chicken

**SERVES 4 TO 6**

| | |
|---|---|
| 1 | chicken (approximately 3½ to 4 pounds), cut into 10 pieces |
| 1 | head garlic, separated into unpeeled cloves |
| 2 | unwaxed lemons, cut into chunky eighths |

Small handful fresh thyme

| | |
|---|---|
| 3 | tablespoons olive oil |
| 10 | tablespoons white wine |

Black pepper

*food & wine* **tip**

Use a roasting pan that fits all of the chicken pieces snugly in one layer. Select a pan without handles so the foil cover fits most tightly.

Preheat the oven to 300°F.

Put the chicken pieces into a roasting pan and add the garlic cloves, lemon chunks and the thyme; just roughly pull the leaves off the stalks, leaving some intact for strewing over later. Add the oil and using your hands mix everything together, then spread the mixture out, making sure all the chicken pieces are skin-side up.

Sprinkle over the white wine and grind on some pepper, then cover tightly with foil and put in the oven to cook, at flavor-intensifyingly low heat, for 2 hours.

Remove the foil from the roasting pan, and turn up the oven to 400°F. Cook the uncovered chicken for another 30–45 minutes, by which time the skin on the meat will have turned golden brown and the lemons will have begun to scorch and caramelize at the edges.

I like to serve this as it is, straight from the roasting pan: so just strew with your remaining thyme and dole out.

# Baked Ricotta with Broiled Radicchio

**SERVES 4 TO 6**

For all that you need to clatter about with springform pans and baking sheets, this is remarkably easy to make. I always seem to have spare egg white knocking around, which also inclines me to cook it. But it's worth making the—slight—effort even if you have to put aside the yolks for use elsewhere. This makes a wonderful summer starter or light lunch, the latter either by itself or rustled up as a vegetarian-pleaser.

For the baked ricotta

18 ounces (2¼ cups) ricotta cheese

2 egg whites, lightly beaten

1 tablespoon chopped fresh thyme

Zest of 1 lemon

Salt and pepper

2 tablespoons olive oil

For the radicchio

Approximately 6 tablespoons olive oil

2 tablespoons chopped fresh thyme

1 large head radicchio, cut into eighths lengthwise

1 lemon to serve

Preheat the oven to 350°F.

Mix the ricotta with the beaten egg whites and add most of the chopped thyme, the lemon zest and salt and pepper.

Brush an 8-inch springform pan with oil and pour in the ricotta mixture, then drizzle with olive oil and scatter a little more chopped thyme over the top. Don't be alarmed at how shallow this is; it is not intended to be other than a slim disk.

*food & wine tip*
_____

Don't trim off the root
end of the radicchio
when you slice it
lengthwise. This will
make it easier to turn
as it cooks.

Place on a baking sheet and cook in the oven for about 30 minutes. The baked ricotta will rise a little and set dry on top, but will not turn a golden color like a cake.

Let the pan cool a little before springing open and removing to a plate. Leave to cool a little longer, then cut into wedges and eat, still warm, with the radicchio.

Talking of which, you should get on with this just before serving, which really means preheating the broiler while the ricotta-cake is cooling. Mix the olive oil and thyme in a shallow bowl, and then wipe the radicchio slices in the herby oil before broiling them for a few minutes, turning them as necessary, until slightly wilted and golden at the edges.

Add a squeeze of lemon at the end before serving with the baked ricotta.

# Chocolate Raspberry Pavlova

**SERVES 8 TO 10**

For the chocolate meringue base

6    egg whites

1    cup granulated sugar

3    tablespoons unsweetened cocoa powder, sifted

1    teaspoon balsamic or red wine vinegar

2    ounces bittersweet chocolate, finely chopped

For the topping

2¼  cups heavy cream

1    very full pint raspberries

2 to 3 tablespoons coarsely grated bittersweet chocolate

*food* & *wine* **tip**

If you prefer, just slide the meringue disk onto a plate instead of inverting it. The fallen center will hold the cream and raspberries perfectly.

Preheat the oven to 350°F and line a baking sheet with baking parchment. Beat the egg whites until satiny peaks form, and then beat in the sugar a spoonful at a time until the meringue is stiff and shiny. Sprinkle over the cocoa and vinegar, and the chopped chocolate. Then gently fold everything until the cocoa is thoroughly mixed in. Mound onto the baking sheet in a fat circle approximately 9 inches in diameter, smoothing the sides and top. Place in the oven, then immediately turn the temperature down to 300°F and cook for about one to one and a quarter hours. When it's ready it should look crisp around the edges and on the sides and be dry on top, but when you prod the center you should feel the promise of squidginess beneath your fingers. Turn off the oven and open the door slightly, and let the chocolate meringue disk cool completely.

When you're ready to serve, invert onto a big, flat-bottomed plate. Whisk the cream till thick but still soft and pile it on top of the meringue, then scatter over the raspberries. Coarsely grate the chocolate so that you get curls rather than rubble, as you don't want the raspberries' luscious color and form to be obscured, and sprinkle haphazardly over the top, letting some fall, as it will, on the plate's rim.

# French Food at Home

## LAURA CALDER

**BACKGROUND** Born in Long Reach, New Brunswick, Canada; lives in Paris.

**EDUCATION** Western civilization, linguistics, psychology and cross-cultural studies are among the subjects Calder studied at Canadian and English universities. She graduated from the Dubrulle Culinary Institute in Vancouver and La Varenne cooking school in Paris.

**EXPERIENCE** "After cooking school, I went to Napa Valley for five or six months to work for a master of wine named Tim Hanni. I helped him develop a food-and-wine pairing course for college-level students. Then I went to Burgundy to work on various projects for Anne Willan of La Varenne."

**HOW SHE CAME TO LOVE FOOD** "My parents are Canadian, but we ate Anglo-Irish-Scottish food: oatmeal, buckwheat pancakes, pickles. We were a baking family in the English tradition rather than a cooking family in the French way. Homemade bread and cakes and cookies and jams and all that. Everything was very organic and wholesome and back-to-the-land. I mean, my mother made butter, for God's sake. On the cooking side we were very meat and vegetables. Mind you, the meat was probably some neighbor's chicken and the veggies were from our own gardens. It was basic English cooking. It wasn't extraordinary, but the ingredients were really good. I knew what a carrot ripped out of the ground tasted like."

**FAVORITE CHILDHOOD FOOD** Skins of organic potatoes fried in butter.

**HOW SHE CAME TO LOVE COOKING** "I started off my career as a journalist, but then I found myself in a public relations job, sitting in front of a computer going raving mad. I think I finally went into cooking because I was so desperate for reality. All the time I was in that cubicle I'd be listing the things I wanted to do before I died, and one was to become a really good cook. So I quit my job and went to cooking school. It's been five years since I first made that list."

**WHY SHE LOVES FRENCH FOOD** "It's more playful and less rule-ridden than people imagine."

# featured recipes

**WHY SHE WROTE THE BOOK** "The whole purpose of the book is to show how people eat in France. They don't eat just traditional French food. I mean, when we say American food, we include pizza and burritos, right? They weren't American originally, but they are what people eat in America now, so they've become American. The same is true in France. People eat pasta there, and you can't say, 'Oh, that's Italian.' What I'm trying to show in my book is that the French don't only eat foods that have been simmered for three days."

**HOW TO MAKE SIMPLE FOOD LOOK LUXURIOUS** "You can cook something really basic and make it look like a million bucks. To feed some friends recently, I made a chickpea soup with maybe two and a half ingredients. I served it in beautiful bowls with an elegant swirl of olive oil on top, and everyone kept asking, 'What is this?' They thought they were getting some three-star thing. I bet that whole pot of soup cost me 30 cents to make."

**FAVORITE PLACE TO EAT**
"I'm not really very interested in restaurants. People always ask me where I like to eat in Paris, and I always say, 'My place.'"

**EATING-AT-HOME MOTTO** "Make food as nice for yourself as you would for guests."

**ESSENTIAL FRENCH INGREDIENTS** "Crème fraîche is at the top of the list. Also butter, olive oil, eggs, capers and bacon. I always have nuts—walnuts, pine nuts, almonds—because they are so versatile: You can put them in salads, you can use them in cakes. I also always have honey on hand."

**ESSENTIAL EQUIPMENT** "My top tool is my hands. I put them in everything. And I do everything in a large 10-inch sauté pan. I think you really need only three knives in life: a chef's knife, a paring knife and a bread knife. Another interesting tool I have is a pastry scraper. I've got this great stainless steel one about the size of an index card that I use for lifting stuff and moving things around. The only electric tool I have, without exaggeration, is an immersion blender. I do almost everything by hand. I whisk egg whites by hand, I whip cream by hand."

**IDEAL COAUTHOR** Rita Konig. "She wrote *Domestic Bliss* and has a column in British *Vogue* on house-y stuff like vacuuming and cleaning and how to install your whatever. She'd be fun to write a book with."

# Bacon and Hazelnut Leeks

**SERVES 4**

*food & wine tip*

You'll need only
1 to 2 teaspoons of
bacon fat for this recipe.
Pour out any excess
before deglazing
the pan with vinegar.

Now this is one of those recipes that should never be corseted by recipe form, because leeks come in all sizes and this means that you may need more or less bacon, more or fewer nuts, plus or minus a glug or two of cream. So toy with the amounts: they're not absolute. To help with your planning: in the case of baby leeks, estimate two to three per person; with medium narrow leeks, as I indicate below, one per person is fine; and if you should find yourself facing leeks of thug-like thickness, peel off a few outer layers to narrow them down, and then halve lengthwise once cooked, planning one-half per person.

4    medium leeks

4    tablespoons coarsely chopped hazelnuts

4 to 6 strips bacon, cut into pieces

1    tablespoon white wine vinegar

1    cup heavy cream (250 ml)

Salt and pepper

Bring a large pot of salted water to a boil. Trim all but an inch of green from the leeks. Wash them thoroughly, tie them in a bunch with string, and plunge them into the boiling water. Cook until tender when pierced with a fork, about 20 minutes. Drain and quickly rinse in cold water to stop the cooking. Drain, remove the string, pat dry, and keep warm.

Meanwhile, toast the hazelnuts in a dry frying pan; set aside. In the same pan, fry the bacon until crisp; set aside. Deglaze the pan with the vinegar, scraping up any good stick-to-the-pan bits. Pour in the cream and boil for a minute or so to reduce to sauce consistency. Season with salt and pepper. Stir in the bacon and nuts.

Place 1 leek on each serving plate, spoon around the sauce, and serve hot.

# Pistou Zucchini Ribbons

**SERVES 4**

This is zucchini masquerading as pasta and tossed in the elements of *pistou,* or pesto (garlic, basil, pine nuts, olive oil, and Parmigiano-Reggiano). To get the best "pasta" slices, choose skinny, young zucchini with few seeds. For larger zucchini, halve them lengthwise and peel the ribbons down the narrow side.

4    small zucchini

2 to 3 tablespoons olive oil, more if needed

2    garlic cloves, chopped fine

½    cup pine nuts (80 g), toasted

½    cup freshly grated Parmigiano-Reggiano (60 g)

1    large bunch basil, stemmed and chopped

Salt and pepper

Bring a pot of salted water to boil. Peel the zucchini into long strips with a vegetable peeler, or use a mandoline. You'll finish with a pile of vegetable "pasta." Cook the zucchini in the boiling water until just al dente, 1 to 2 minutes. Drain and immediately rinse under ice-cold water to stop the cooking and to preserve the bright color.

Heat the oil gently in a large frying pan. Add the garlic and sauté about a minute. Add the zucchini ribbons, with the pine nuts, cheese, and basil, tossing to coat. Season with salt and pepper. Twist a stack of zucchini onto the center of each serving plate. Garnish, if you like, with additional curls of Parmigiano-Reggiano and a few extra basil leaves. Serve immediately.

## on calder's nightstand

*"Times" Cookbook* by **Frances Bissell,** a compilation of recipes from *The Times of London,* is my favorite classic. *Larousse Gastronomique* is encyclopedic; I always find the basic template for a recipe and then play with it. **Elizabeth David's** *Italian Food* must have 500 classic recipes in it! They are all written simply, the way someone talks. Another useful book is **Anne Willan's** *La Varenne Practique.* I think *How to Eat* by **Nigella Lawson** is a terrific read. She inspires people and makes them less afraid of food.

# Parmesan Flatfish

**SERVES 4**

Better than bread crumbs alone, the grated cheese adds a slightly tangy note, freckled with herbs and fluffed around the fillet. It's ready in no time, and good with a squirt of lemon. Serve with steamed snow peas or broccoli on the side.

½    cup milk (125 ml)

1    cup freshly grated Parmigiano-Reggiano (3 to 4 ounces/about 100 g)

¼    cup fine bread crumbs (20 g)

1    tablespoon *herbes de Provence*

4    sole, flounder, or other flatfish fillets (about ¼ pound/125 g each)

Salt and pepper

3 to 4 tablespoons unsalted butter

Preheat the oven to broil, with the rack near the top. Pour the milk into a wide bowl. Mix the grated cheese, bread crumbs, and herbs together on a plate.

Dip each fish fillet into the milk to coat, then dip into the cheese mixture to enrobe well. Lay on a greased baking sheet or dish. Sprinkle over any remaining crumb mixture. Season with salt and pepper. Broil until the fish is cooked through and the top is golden and crispy, about 5 minutes.

Meanwhile, heat the butter in a small pan until foaming and turning hazelnut color. When the fish is cooked, remove to plates and drizzle with the foaming brown butter.

## *food & wine tip*

If the flavor of *herbes de Provence*—a blend of dried thyme, rosemary, bay leaf, basil, lavender and savory—is too strong for you, add an equivalent amount of any dried herbs to the bread crumb coating. Thyme, rosemary and sage are particularly nice.

# Tarragon Chicken

**SERVES 4**

Some recipes are a relief. That's how I felt about this one, one night when people I was too tired to have over were coming anyway. It's a bistro dish in its simple execution and appearance, but somehow tarragon, with its refreshing anise scent, raises the whole thing to a higher level.

1  tablespoon unsalted butter
1  tablespoon olive oil
1  chicken (about 3 pounds/1.4 kg), cut into 8 pieces
Salt and pepper
About ¾ cup white wine (175 ml)
1  shallot, finely chopped
About 1 cup heavy cream (250 ml)
2 to 3 tablespoons chopped fresh tarragon
Lemon juice to taste

Melt the butter with the oil in a large skillet over quite high heat. Season the chicken pieces with salt and pepper and fry in batches until well browned, about 5 minutes per side. Put all the chicken back in the pan, reduce the heat to medium, cover, and cook until tender, about 30 minutes. Remove the chicken to a plate and keep warm.

Deglaze the pan with the wine, scraping up the good bits on the bottom with a wooden spoon. Add the shallot, and boil until the wine has reduced with the cooking juices to make a thickish sauce, about 5 minutes. Add the cream and half the tarragon. Boil down again to thick sauce consistency, 3 to 5 minutes.

Season the sauce with salt and pepper. Squeeze in lemon juice to taste. Put the chicken pieces back in and turn to coat, then transfer to a platter, scraping the sauce over the chicken. Scatter over the remaining tarragon, and serve.

# From Emeril's Kitchens

## EMERIL LAGASSE

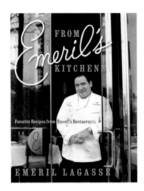

**BACKGROUND** Born in Fall River, Massachusetts; lives in New Orleans.

**EDUCATION** Lagasse turned down a scholarship to the New England Conservatory of Music to study cooking at Johnson & Wales University in Providence, Rhode Island.

**EXPERIENCE** Began his career as a teenager working in a Portuguese bakery, where he learned to bake bread and make pastry. After cooking school, he traveled to Paris and Lyon and then to New York, Boston and Philadelphia to gain professional kitchen experience. In 1983 he took a job as the executive chef at Commander's Palace in New Orleans, and received many accolades during his seven and a half years there. In 1990 Lagasse went out on his own and opened Emeril's Restaurant in New Orleans, followed two years later by Nola Restaurant. Lagasse now has nine restaurants across the country. In 1993 Lagasse joined the Food Network, where he now hosts two popular cooking shows, *Essence of Emeril* and *Emeril Live*.

**MENTORS** Ella and Dick Brennan of Commander's Palace, Roger Vergé of Le Moulin de Mougins in Mougins, France, Charlie Trotter of Charlie Trotter's restaurant in Chicago and Larry Forgione of New York's An American Place restaurant and American Spoon Foods, the gourmet food–products company.

**COOKING PHILOSOPHY** "If you don't learn something new every day, you're wasting time. Life is too short. And it's easy to learn when it comes to food—it's so complex and there's so much room to grow."

**PREVIOUS BOOKS** Lagasse has written eight—most recently *Emeril's There's a Chef in My Family! Recipes to Get Everybody Cooking.*

**WHY HE WROTE "FROM EMERIL'S KITCHENS"** "The book includes some of my most requested recipes. My goal was to work with my chefs in order to give my customers what they've been wanting. But I didn't want to write a 'shelf'

**IDEAL COAUTHOR**
Julia Child. "I've done some work with her in the past, on a book and on TV. She's the real deal."

book—I wanted a book people would cook with, one that would get dirty and bent."

**RECIPES THAT DIDN'T MAKE THE BOOK** "Some great restaurant dishes aren't really meant for home cooking. Recipes with 40 or 50 ingredients are very intimidating, so those types of dishes didn't make it. Other recipes that didn't make the book call for ingredients most home cooks aren't ready to tackle, or ingredients that are difficult to find, like partridge, grouse and squab. It's one thing to cook them on television, and another to put them in a book."

**BIGGEST COOKING MISTAKE PEOPLE MAKE** "So many people don't take the time to read the recipe. Then they go shopping, and it's already starting to be a bad experience because they get home and find that they forgot something. You have to read the recipe—you need a road map. I mean, if I was driving from New York to New Orleans, I wouldn't just get in the car and drive. You need to prepare, and you have to allow yourself enough time."

**SECOND BIGGEST COOKING MISTAKE PEOPLE MAKE** "They don't evaluate the heat when they're cooking. They jack the stove up, and then they wonder why things are overcooked or burned or scorched. That's why stoves have that knob thing."

**FAVORITE RESTAURANTS** "In New York City my favorite restaurant right now is probably Café Boulud. Also Teodora. And of course I love Charlie Trotter's in Chicago. I also love Norman Van Aken's food at Norman's in Coral Gables, Florida."

**SEMI-RETIREMENT PLANS** "Ten to fifteen years from now I see myself, hopefully, spending a lot more time on the golf course."

**ON PASSING HIS COOKING LEGACY ON TO HIS CHILDREN** "I have two daughters, who are 22 and 24, and the older one said to me, 'Dad, I've seen how much you've sacrificed in your life for your career, and I don't want to be in the business.' My year-old son, E. J., will have to make that decision for himself one day."

**FUTURE PROJECTS** "I have a book coming out in the fall about potluck recipes, 'Emeril's Potluck.' I'm also working on a restaurant book right now for next year, which is a look at the history of the 109-year-old Delmonico Restaurant in New Orleans, which I reopened in 1998."

**IF HE WEREN'T A CHEF**
"Boy, that would be disastrous. But if I had to do something else, it would probably be music-related."

# Shrimp and Coconut Milk Risotto with Summer Squash, Peas, and Roasted Red Pepper Sauce

**MAKES 6 TO 8 SERVINGS**

Chef Chris [Chris Wilson, the executive chef at Emeril's New Orleans] devised this dish for a recipe contest a few years back and now it appears periodically on the menu at Emeril's New Orleans. The flavors of the coconut milk and red pepper sauce together make this version of risotto one you won't soon forget. Chef Chris won that contest—make this, and you'll see why!

1   pound medium shrimp in their shells

4   cups water

2   cloves garlic, peeled and smashed, plus 2 teaspoons minced garlic

½   cup dry white wine

¼   cup fresh lime juice

One 14-ounce can unsweetened coconut milk

3   tablespoons olive oil

1   cup finely chopped yellow onions

¾   cup finely chopped leeks, well rinsed (white parts only)

2   cups Arborio rice

2   teaspoons salt

1   teaspoon freshly ground white pepper

½   teaspoon freshly ground black pepper

2   cups fresh or thawed frozen green peas

2   cups cubed yellow summer squash

1   cup freshly grated Parmigiano-Reggiano

4   tablespoons unsalted butter, cut into pieces

¼   cup chopped fresh cilantro

1   recipe Roasted Red Pepper Sauce (recipe follows)

1. To make the stock, peel the shrimp and set aside. Place the shells in a medium saucepan. Add the water, smashed garlic cloves, white wine, and lime juice and bring to a boil. Reduce the heat to medium-low and simmer until reduced by half.

2. Remove the stock from the heat and add the coconut milk. Strain through a fine-mesh strainer into a clean saucepan, cover, and keep warm over very low heat.

3. Heat the oil in a medium saucepan over medium heat. Add the onions and leeks and cook, stirring, until soft, about 3 minutes. Add the 2 teaspoons minced garlic and cook, stirring, for 30 seconds. Add the rice, stir to coat with the oil, and cook for 1 minute. Add enough of the shrimp stock just to cover the rice, about 2 cups, then add the salt, white pepper, and black pepper and stir well. Simmer, stirring constantly, adding more stock as it is absorbed by the rice.

4. When the rice is almost completely cooked but still retains a slight crunch, about 12 minutes, add the peas, squash, and shrimp. Simmer, adding more stock as necessary, until the shrimp are cooked through and the vegetables are tender, about 6 minutes. Add the cheese, butter, and cilantro and stir to combine. Cook, stirring, until all the liquid has been absorbed and the rice is tender but not mushy, about 10 minutes longer.

5. Remove from the heat and adjust the seasoning to taste. Spoon the risotto into six or eight serving bowls, drizzle the red pepper sauce around it, and serve.

## on lagasse's nightstand

There are a lot of good books out there. One that I'm reading right now is not by a well-known author: *Gulf Coast Kitchens* by **Constance Snow.** **John Ash** is coming out with an interesting book called *John Ash: Cooking One on One.* I always use *Joy of Cooking* and *Larousse Gastronomique* in the restaurants.

# Roasted Red Pepper Sauce

**MAKES 1¾ CUPS**

| | |
|---|---|
| 2 | large red bell peppers (about 1 pound) |
| 1 | cup extra-virgin olive oil |
| 3 | tablespoons minced shallots |
| 10 | fresh cilantro leaves |
| 4 | fresh basil leaves |
| ¼ | teaspoon balsamic vinegar |
| ½ | teaspoon salt |
| ¼ | teaspoon freshly ground white pepper |

1. Roast the peppers over an open gas flame, turning them frequently with tongs until all sides are charred black, 7 to 10 minutes. (Alternatively, the peppers can be roasted under a broiler, or on a gas or charcoal grill.) Place the blackened peppers in a plastic or paper bag, seal tightly, and let stand until cool enough to handle, about 15 minutes.

2. Peel the peppers, remove the seeds and stems, and coarsely chop.

3. Heat 2 tablespoons of the oil in a small skillet over medium heat. Add the shallots and cook, stirring, for 1 minute. Add the peppers and cook for 5 minutes. Transfer to a food processor or blender.

4. Add the cilantro, basil, vinegar, salt, and pepper to the peppers and process for 20 seconds. With the machine running, add the remaining ¾ cup plus 2 tablespoons oil in a slow, steady stream, processing until thick and smooth. Serve warm, or transfer to a bowl or other container, cover, and refrigerate for up to 3 days. Reheat gently before serving.

# Kick-Butt Gumbo

**MAKES 8 SERVINGS**

Traditional Louisiana gumbos are usually made with seafood, or chicken and sausage, and some have okra—but hey, everyone has his own recipe for gumbo. Over the years, I've had the privilege of eating and making thousands and thousands of gumbos. Taste this one, and you'll know how it got its name! It will send you reeling! (Note that the pork must marinate overnight.)

1 pound boneless pork butt, cut into ½-inch cubes

2 teaspoons Emeril's Original Essence or Creole Seasoning (recipe follows)

1 teaspoon Worcestershire sauce

1 teaspoon Emeril's Kick It Up Red Pepper Sauce or other hot pepper sauce

1 cup vegetable oil

1 cup all-purpose flour

1 pound andouille sausage, cut into ¼-inch slices

¼ pound tasso, diced

1½ cups chopped yellow onions

1 cup chopped celery

1 cup chopped green bell peppers

6 cups Rich Chicken Stock (page 158)

One 12-ounce bottle dark beer

1½ teaspoons salt

¼ teaspoon cayenne

3 bay leaves

1 recipe White Rice (recipe follows), for serving

½ cup chopped green onions (green parts only), for garnish

¼ cup chopped fresh parsley, for garnish

*food & wine* **tip**

If you can't find tasso, a special smoked, spiced pork or beef from Louisiana, replace it with an equal amount of andouille sausage.

*food* & *wine* tip

Roux, essential to all gumbos, is a thickener made by cooking equal parts flour and fat. It can take up to 50 minutes to turn a nice chocolate color.

1. Put the pork in a bowl and season with the Essence, Worcestershire, and hot sauce. Cover with plastic wrap and refrigerate overnight.

2. Heat the oil in a Dutch oven or other large heavy pot over medium heat. Add the flour and cook, stirring constantly with a large wooden spoon, to make a dark chocolate brown roux, 30 to 35 minutes.

3. Add the pork, sausage, and tasso and cook, stirring, until caramelized, 6 to 7 minutes. Add the onions, celery, and bell peppers and cook, stirring constantly, until soft, 7 to 10 minutes. Add the stock, stirring constantly to prevent lumps from forming, and bring to a boil. Add the beer, salt, cayenne, and bay leaves and stir to blend. Reduce the heat and simmer, uncovered, stirring occasionally, until the pork is tender, 1½ to 2 hours. Remove from the heat and remove the bay leaves.

4. Ladle the gumbo into eight large soup bowls. Spoon the rice into the center of the gumbo, and sprinkle each serving with the green onions and parsley. Serve immediately.

## Creole Seasoning

**MAKES ⅔ CUP**

2½ tablespoons paprika

2   tablespoons salt

2   tablespoons garlic powder

1   tablespoon freshly ground
    black pepper

1   tablespoon onion powder

1   tablespoon cayenne

1   tablespoon dried oregano

1   tablespoon dried thyme

Combine all the ingredients in a
bowl and mix thoroughly. Store in
an airtight container for up to
3 months at room temperature.

## White Rice

**MAKES 7 CUPS**

We use rice as a component in a lot
of different restaurant dishes—from
gumbo to red beans and rice. Here's
a quick refresher recipe for basic rice
that's great every time. Just don't stir
it until it's had a chance to rest after
cooking!

2   cups long-grain white rice

4   cups water, Rich Chicken Stock
    (recipe follows), or canned
    low-sodium chicken broth

1½  teaspoons salt

2   bay leaves

1. In a 2-quart saucepan, combine
the rice, water, salt, and bay leaves
and bring to a boil over high heat.
Reduce the heat to low, cover, and
simmer until all the liquid is
absorbed, about 20 minutes. Remove
the pan from the heat and let sit,
covered, for 10 minutes.

2. Fluff the rice with a fork, and
remove the bay leaves before serving.

# Rich Chicken Stock

**MAKES 2 QUARTS**

| | |
|---|---|
| 4 | pounds chicken bones (backs, necks, wings, etc.) |
| 1 | cup coarsely chopped yellow onions |
| ½ | cup coarsely chopped carrots |
| ½ | cup coarsely chopped celery |
| 5 | garlic cloves, peeled and smashed |

One 6-ounce can tomato paste

| | |
|---|---|
| 1 | cup dry red wine |
| 5 | sprigs fresh parsley |
| 5 | sprigs fresh thyme |
| 2 | bay leaves |
| 1 | teaspoon black peppercorns |

1. Preheat the oven to 375°F.

2. Spread the chicken bones evenly in a large roasting pan. Roast for 2 hours, stirring after 1 hour.

3. Remove from the oven and add the onions, carrots, celery, garlic, and tomato paste, stirring to mix. Roast for 45 minutes longer.

4. Transfer the hot vegetables and bones to a large heavy stockpot. Place the roasting pan over two burners on medium-high heat, add the wine, and stir with a wooden spoon to deglaze and dislodge any browned bits from the bottom of the pan. Pour the hot wine mixture into the stockpot. Add the parsley, thyme, bay leaves, peppercorns, and enough water to cover by 1 inch.

5. Bring to a boil over medium-high heat. Reduce the heat to medium-low and simmer, uncovered, for 4 hours, skimming frequently to remove the foam that forms on the surface.

6. Remove from the heat and strain through a fine-mesh strainer into a clean container, and let cool completely. The stock can be stored in the refrigerator for up to 3 days, or frozen in airtight containers for up to 2 months.

# Homemade English Muffins

**MAKES 8 MUFFINS**

1    teaspoon vegetable oil

1¼ cups water, at room temperature

One ¼-ounce envelope (2¼ teaspoons) active dry yeast

½    teaspoon sugar

3½ cups bread flour, or more if needed

2    teaspoons salt

3    tablespoons nonfat dry milk

2    teaspoons solid vegetable shortening

¼    cup yellow cornmeal

*food & wine tip*

After you finish making
this recipe, split
the muffins in half and
toast them as you
would store-bought
English muffins.

1. Lightly grease a large bowl with the oil, and set aside.

2. Combine the water, yeast, and sugar in a large bowl, stir well, and let sit
until foamy, about 5 minutes. Add the remaining ingredients except the
cornmeal and mix with a large wooden spoon until well blended, about
3 minutes. Turn the dough out onto a lightly floured surface, and knead for
15 minutes, or until smooth, adding more flour 1 teaspoon at a time if the
dough is too sticky. Place in the prepared bowl, cover with plastic wrap, and
set aside in a warm, draft-free place until doubled in size, 1½ to 2 hours.

3. Dust a baking sheet with the cornmeal.

4. Turn the dough out onto a lightly floured surface and divide into 8 equal
portions. Roll into smooth balls and place evenly spaced on the prepared
baking sheet. Cover with a slightly damp kitchen cloth and let rise until
doubled in size, about 30 minutes.

5. Heat a large skillet over medium heat. Add the dough balls, non-cornmeal-
coated side first, in batches, and cook until golden brown on the bottom,
about 5 minutes. Turn the muffins over, press down on them with a large
spatula to flatten slightly, and cook until golden brown on the second side,
about 5 minutes longer.

# Sliced Tomato Salad with Herb Vinaigrette, Red Onions, and Maytag Blue Cheese

**MAKES 4 SERVINGS**

*food & wine tip*

Buy onions that are about the same size as your tomatoes. If the onions are too large, trim off a couple of outer layers so the rings aren't too unwieldy to eat.

This is a great way to start your meal if you're diving into a big hearty steak, like folks do at the Steakhouse [Emeril's Delmonico in New Orleans]. Use sweet onions, such as Vidalia, Maui, or Walla Walla, when they are in season.

3  large ripe tomatoes, each cut into 4 thick slices

1  teaspoon salt

1  teaspoon freshly ground black pepper

½  recipe Herb Vinaigrette (recipe follows)

Twelve ⅛-inch-thick slices red onion or sweet onion

½  cup crumbled Maytag blue cheese (about 3 ounces)

1. Place the tomatoes in a large shallow bowl and season on both sides with the salt and pepper. Add 2 tablespoons of the vinaigrette and toss lightly to coat.

2. Place 1 tomato slice on each of four salad plates and top with an onion slice. Repeat to make 3 layers each of tomatoes and onions, ending with onions. Crumble 2 tablespoons of the cheese on top of each stack, drizzle with the remaining vinaigrette, and serve.

## Herb Vinaigrette

**MAKES 1¼ CUPS**

Serve with any tomato salad or mixed greens.

1    tablespoon champagne vinegar

1½  teaspoons fresh orange juice

¾    teaspoon fresh lemon juice

¾    teaspoon fresh lime juice

¾    teaspoon fresh grapefruit juice

½    cup vegetable oil

½    cup extra-virgin olive oil

½    cup chopped mixed fresh thyme, parsley, chives, and basil

¼    teaspoon salt

¼    teaspoon freshly ground black pepper

Combine the vinegar and citrus juices in a medium bowl and whisk together. Add the vegetable and olive oils in a slow stream, whisking constantly to form an emulsion. Add the herbs, salt, and pepper and whisk well to incorporate. (The dressing keeps refrigerated for up to 2 days.)

# Good Food No Fuss

## ANNE WILLAN

### the book

*Good Food No Fuss: 150 Recipes and Ideas for Easy-to-Cook Dishes* by Anne Willan (Stewart, Tabori & Chang), $27.50, 168 pages, color photos.

### the gist

A collection of straightforward recipes that are simple but not dumbed down, from the founder of La Varenne cooking school.

### the ideal reader

The busy yet ambitious home cook who wants to make good food every night of the week.

### the extras

Shortcuts and "Getting Ahead" tips for each recipe that make it easy to save time in the kitchen.

**BACKGROUND** Born in Yorkshire, England; splits her time currently between France and the United States.

**EDUCATION** "I went to Cambridge University in England, where I was one of only two women studying economics. After I got my degree, I spent a year teaching dressmaking and then went to learn how to cook at the Cordon Bleu in London."

**EXPERIENCE** "I stayed on to teach at the Cordon Bleu and then lived in France for some time. Then I moved to the States, where I worked for *Gourmet* and became food editor for *The Washington Star*. That was when I started writing and editing cookbooks. In the early seventies I went back to France, and in 1975 I founded La Varenne cooking school in Paris."

**MENTOR** "It's very obvious, but Julia Child, for certain. We've been in close contact for over 30 years. She's a wonderful communicator, with a gift for going to the heart of a question. That's very rare. And she expresses herself in these amazingly quotable quotes. She's exactly the same no matter who you are or what the situation is, very down-to-earth. And her energy is astonishing. She might be slowing down a little bit now, but even so, she never thinks of herself as being from another generation. She lives in the present."

**PREVIOUS BOOKS** "I wrote a 17-book series, called *Look & Cook,* which was kind of like a video on the page. It covered just about everything—soup, chicken, fish, chocolate, pasta. Including those, I've written over 30 books."

**HOW "GOOD FOOD NO FUSS" CAME ABOUT** "For a long time I've been collecting any good, simple recipes that I do at home. Then one day an editor at BBC books said that I should put them all together. People always want tasty traditional cooking that is done in a minimum of time."

**PET PEEVE** "I don't like the trend of sprinkling everything with sea salt and cracked black pepper."

# featured recipes

**LESSON LEARNED FROM CHEFS** To taste food at every step of the cooking process. "A chef will taste the salted water for vegetables before putting them in. It's especially important to taste sauces or braises as they cook to see if salt or pepper or a spice is missing. And those should be added during cooking, as well as during a check at the end, so they blend with the other flavors. For my final exam at the Cordon Bleu I added salt at the end and the chef said, 'I can taste the salt.'"

**BEST COOKING TIMESAVERS** "When you go into the kitchen, immediately put a pot of water on to boil and switch on the oven, then think of what you're going to make. If you don't use them it doesn't matter, but you could save yourself five or ten minutes."

**FAVORITE INGREDIENT** Spice mixes. "We were in Morocco recently, and since then I can't get enough of *ras el-hanout*. Using spice mixes is a very easy way to add complexity. But don't just sprinkle them on. I usually cook them in oil over a low heat for a minute or so to mellow the flavor."

**COOKING WITH WINE** "When you heat wine, don't just bring it to the boil; make sure it reduces by at least half. This softens the tannins, which can be very harsh, and rounds out the wine's roughness on the tongue."

**PANTRY STAPLES** Grated cheese (Parmesan and Gruyère), Dijon mustard, garlic, onion and shallots. "I also feel uncomfortable if I don't have half a pound of butter in the fridge and stock in the freezer."

**FOOD TRENDS** "We're all going to continue to want reassurance: familiar, friendly food. There's going to be a reaction against foods out of season, and mysterious foods coming from far and wide that no one knows how to cook, like peculiar tropical fruits that don't taste of anything."

**FUTURE PROJECT** A history of cookbooks. "It's fascinating, because food has changed enormously in the last 15 years. It's a huge project. I'm writing it with my husband, Mark Cherniavsky. He studied politics, philosophy and economics at Oxford, and for 20 years he was an economist and a writer for the World Bank. He provides the academic side—and he collects cookbooks. I always say that he collects them and I use them."

# Goats' Cheese Gougère

**SERVES 6**

*Gougères* are the savory version of cream puffs, flavored with cheese, and we love them so much at home that I've developed several versions over the years. This one is flat, resembling a light pizza, and you can add any herb to the topping and a bit of garlic, too, if you like.

4 ½ ounces Gruyère cheese

1   cup flour

¾   cup milk

½   teaspoon salt

5   tablespoons unsalted butter, cut in pieces

4   eggs

For the topping

4 ½ ounces goats' cheese (about ¾ log)

1   tablespoon chopped thyme, rosemary, sage, or tarragon

1   garlic clove, crushed (optional)

1   tablespoon olive oil (for brushing), more for the pan

Equipment 10- to 11-inch tart tin with removable base (optional)

1. Heat the oven to 375°F. Brush the tart pan with oil. Cut the Gruyère cheese in small dice and the goats' cheese in 6–8 slices.

2. For the cream puff pastry: Sift the flour onto a sheet of paper. In a small saucepan heat the milk, salt, and butter until the butter is melted. Bring to a boil, take from the heat, and immediately add all the flour. Beat vigorously with a wooden spoon for a few moments until the mixture pulls away from the sides of the pan to form a ball. Beat for ½–1 minute over low heat to dry the dough slightly, just until it starts to stick to the base of the pan. Take the dough from the heat and let it cool 2–3 minutes.

## on willan's nightstand

One favorite book was written at the end of the 20th century and will still be around at the end of the 21st: **Alan Davidson's** *The Oxford Companion to Food.* It's brilliant—authoritative and a good read—and paints a fascinating picture of food. I also like **Elizabeth Schneider's** *Vegetables from Amaranth to Zucchini.* When you see strange ingredients in the supermarket and wonder what the hell to do with them, she tells you. I would also recommend **Julia Child's** and **Jacques Pépin's** *Cooking at Home.* It's a lovely book, with a strong personal voice.

3. Beat the eggs one by one into the dough, using the wooden spoon or a hand-held electric mixer. Adding just the right amount of egg is the key to cream puff pastry, so break the last egg into a small bowl, whisk it with a fork to mix, and add it a little at a time—you may not need all of it. At the end the dough will be shiny and should just fall from the spoon. Beat in the diced Gruyère cheese.

4. Spread the dough evenly in the tart pan, using the back of a spoon (for a more rustic effect, simply spread the dough in a round on an oiled baking sheet). Sprinkle with the herbs, and garlic if using, leaving a ¾-inch border of dough. Top the herbs with rounds of goats' cheese—the dough will show between them. Brush the cheese rounds with olive oil.

5. Bake the *gougère* in the oven until the dough is crusty and brown and the goats' cheese is toasted, 45–50 minutes. The *gougère* will puff, then deflate slightly as it cools. Serve it warm, cut in wedges.

Shortcut Individual *gougères*, each topped with a round of goats' cheese, will take 10–15 minutes less to cook.

Getting ahead *Gougère* is best eaten at once, but it can be baked 2–3 hours ahead and reheated.

In the glass *Gougère* is Burgundian in origin, customary accompaniment to a chilled glass of Kir (dry white wine with a teaspoon of Cassis blackcurrant liqueur), or a fruity red Beaujolais.

# Vodka and Sesame Salmon with Parsley Salad

**SERVES 4**

I've a weakness for the smoky flavors of toasted sesame, a perfect match for salmon sharpened with a sprinkling of lime, then flamed with vodka. With the salmon comes a salad of fresh parsley, dressed with oil and lime juice; it's delicious too with other fish and chicken.

1½ pound salmon fillet, skinned

5 to 6 tablespoons vodka

Salt and pepper

2    tablespoons sesame seeds

¼    cup butter

2    garlic cloves, finely chopped

1    teaspoon dark sesame oil

1    lime, cut in wedges, for serving

For the parsley salad

Juice of 1 lime

3    tablespoons vegetable oil

Large bunch of flatleaf parsley (about 3 ounces)

### food & wine tip

Have your fishmonger skin the salmon and cut it into four equal portions to shorten the prep time.

1. Cut the salmon into four equal pieces so they take the same time to cook. Lay them in a non-metallic dish and sprinkle with 2 tablespoons of the vodka and some salt and pepper. Turn and sprinkle the other sides with a tablespoon of vodka and more salt and pepper. Leave them to marinate for 10–15 minutes so they pickle slightly and pick up taste.

2. Meanwhile, toast the sesame seeds in a dry non-stick frying pan over medium heat, stirring often, until they are brown and fragrant, 4–5 minutes.

3. Make the parsley salad: reserve 2 tablespoons of lime juice. Whisk the remaining juice in a small bowl with the oil, and a little salt and pepper.

Pull the parsley sprigs from the stems and discard the stems. Rinse the sprigs in cold water and dry on paper towels or in a salad spinner. Add the parsley to the lime dressing and toss to mix. Taste and adjust the seasoning.

**4.** Drain the salmon and pat it dry on paper towels. Melt the butter in a frying pan. Sauté the salmon until browned, 2–3 minutes. For an attractive golden brown it's best to heat the butter until spluttering stops, then put in the salmon with the cut- or backbone-side downwards. When brown, sprinkle it with the chopped garlic, then turn and continue cooking. Depending on the thickness of the fillets, this should take 2–3 minutes for medium done salmon that is still translucent in the center, or 4–5 minutes if you prefer it well done.

**5.** Pour the remaining vodka into the pan, bring just to a boil, then set it alight, standing well back. Take the pan from the heat and sprinkle the salmon with the reserved lime juice, sesame oil, and sesame seeds. Arrange the salmon on warm plates and spoon over the pan juices. Garnish the plates with parsley salad and lime wedges.

In the glass A lemon-tinged Sauvignon Blanc, or just possibly a tot of ice-cold vodka.

# Winter Salad of Country Ham with Beets, Endive, and Lamb's Lettuce

**SERVES 4 FOR SUPPER**

Endive and lamb's lettuce are among the treats of winter, a glimpse of green among the seasonal roots on the vegetable stand. Teamed with beets for color and hazelnuts for crunch, they are a classic French combination, delicious with thinly sliced Virginia or Smithfield ham, or some imported prosciutto.

½   cup hazelnuts

1   pound cooked baby beets

2   heads (about ½ pound) Belgian endive

6   ounces lamb's lettuce

¾   pound thinly sliced country ham

For the dressing

2   tablespoons red wine vinegar

Salt and pepper

1   teaspoon Dijon mustard

⅓   cup walnut oil

1. Toast and peel the hazelnuts. Trim the beets and slip off the skins with your fingers. Cut the beets in quarters or leave them whole depending on size. Trim the Belgian endive, discarding any browned outer leaves. Cut the heads diagonally into ¼-inch slices.

2. Trim the roots of the lamb's lettuce and discard any wilted leaves, leaving them in bunches. Soak them in a sink of water for 15 minutes, shaking to loosen grit between the leaves—even the cleanest lamb's lettuce seems to trap earth in the crevices. Lift out the bunches, rinsing each one under running water to remove grit, and drain thoroughly. Combine the lamb's lettuce and endive in a bowl.

## willan on hazelnuts

**TOASTING AND PEELING HAZELNUTS**
Heat the oven to 350°F. Spread the nuts in a single layer on a shallow pan or baking sheet with edges and toast them in the oven until browned, 12 to 15 minutes. Let them cool slightly and, if not already peeled, rub them with a rough cloth to remove the skins.

**3.** For the dressing: whisk the vinegar, salt, pepper, and mustard in a bowl. Gradually whisk in the oil so the dressing emulsifies and thickens slightly. Taste it, adjust the seasoning, and pour about half over the greens. Toss them and taste again for seasoning.

**4.** Pile the greens on four plates and sprinkle with the hazelnuts. Curl the ham slices and arrange them on top with beets around the edge. Spoon the remaining dressing over the beets and serve the salad within 15 minutes so the greens do not wilt.

Shortcut You'll gain a bit of time by buying hazelnuts already peeled.

Getting ahead Make the dressing and prepare all the ingredients ready to go and store them in the refrigerator for up to 8 hours. Dress the greens and assemble the salad just before serving.

On the side A hearty slice of country bread, or possibly a fluffy southern biscuit.

In the glass Red wine, robust and warming. Go for a Shiraz or a Zinfandel.

# Vanilla Roasted Pineapple

**SERVES 4 TO 6**

A whole pineapple spiked with sticks of vanilla bean, then roasted until it is caramelized, will fill your kitchen with fragrance. If you come across little individual pineapples, allow one per person—a treat indeed!

1    large ripe pineapple

4    vanilla beans, each cut into 2 or 3 sticks

½    cup light brown sugar

½    cup water

About 1 tablespoon grated fresh root ginger

Grated zest and juice of 1 orange

Grated zest and juice of 1 lemon

1. Heat the oven to 325°F. Cut the plume and base from the pineapple and set it upright. Following the curve of the fruit, cut away the skin and hollow out the eyes with the point of a knife. Cut out the core with an apple corer. Spear the fruit with pieces of vanilla. Stand the pineapple upright in a baking dish.

2. Heat the sugar, water, ginger, and orange and lemon zest and juice in a small pan, stirring gently until the sugar dissolves. Pour the syrup over the pineapple and roast it in the oven, basting often until the pineapple browns and the syrup starts to caramelize, 1¼–1½ hours. Toward the end of cooking, keep a close watch as the syrup will scorch rapidly once it cooks to a glaze.

3. Slice the pineapple into thick rings and serve warm, basted with the cooking syrup and topped with a scoop of ice cream. I often leave the pieces of vanilla for decoration, though I'm afraid you cannot eat them. (If you like you can wash them after use, dry them, and store in the sugar jar to make vanilla sugar.)

Shortcut Buy a whole pineapple that has already been peeled and cored.

*food & wine* tip

We find that the easiest way to remove the "eyes" of a pineapple is to scoop them out with the small side of a melon baller.

*food & wine*
*on vanilla*

**BOURBON BEANS**
The premium vanilla bean variety, from Madagascar. Characterized by a thick and oily skin, an abundance of tiny seeds and a sweet aroma.

**MEXICAN BEANS**
From Mexico, the original source of *Vanilla planifolia*, the tropical orchid plant that produces the vanilla pod. Characterized by a spicy or woody aroma.

**TAHITIAN BEANS**
Shorter and plumper than other beans, with more oil and water, fewer seeds and a soft, flowery flavor reminiscent of cherries, prunes or wine.

Getting ahead Roast the pineapple ahead and store it for up to three days in the refrigerator. For serving, it is delicious at room temperature, or you can warm it gently in the oven.

On the side I like to serve it with coconut ice cream or any nut ice cream.

In the glass Perhaps a fruity Sauvignon Blanc—the citrus notes will complement the pineapple's glaze.

# I Am Almost Always Hungry

## LORA ZARUBIN

**BACKGROUND** Born in San Francisco; lives in New York City.

**EDUCATION** Studied painting at the San Francisco Art Institute.

**EXPERIENCE** Zarubin founded Good Food Catering in San Francisco in 1982 and opened Lora restaurant in New York City 10 years later. She has been the food and wine editor at *House & Garden* since 1996.

**HOW SHE CAME TO LOVE FOOD** "I've been cooking since I was four years old. I'd cook with both my grandmothers. They taught me to focus on ingredients. I learned to be honest with myself about what I know and what I like, and to use my instincts."

**CHEF SHE MOST ADMIRES** "Alice Waters, especially when I was growing up in San Francisco. What's truly inspirational is that she and her staff always work as a team; although she's the leader, it's a group effort. Eating at her restaurant, Chez Panisse, is different from eating at any other restaurant."

**WHY SHE WROTE THE BOOK** "I wanted to create recipes that would make people want to cook. I like telling a personal story about the dish to get people engaged in making the recipe. As for the title of the book, it isn't necessarily about being hungry for food—it's a metaphor. I'm always hungry for new experiences, new tastes. I'm a very curious person."

**WHY SHE ESPECIALLY LOVES SALADS** "One of the things I adore about salads is the idea of layering, of discovering different flavors in every bite. There's something so fantastic about combining the freshness of asparagus with the saltiness of Parmesan and the tang of vinaigrette. Or of having the sweetness of ripe avocado with the nuttiness of sesame seeds and the bitterness of watercress."

**RECIPE TRIUMPH** Halibut Fillet Baked in Parchment with Salsa Verde. "I always grill fish because I can't stand the way it smells

## ESSENTIAL EQUIPMENT
A good knife. "My Japanese Kyocera ceramic knife is great. It's all I need."

when it's sautéed. But I wanted to figure out a way to cook fish indoors without stinking up the house. I was especially interested in halibut, which is a profound fish, delicate yet with a lot of texture and body. But it's tricky to cook: If it's underdone you can't cut through it, and if it's overdone it's too dry. I discovered that wrapping halibut in parchment before cooking it is the foolproof way. And salsa verde is a gorgeous complement."

**HER FASCINATION WITH FOOD-AND-WINE PAIRINGS** "My job has given me travel assignments to amazing locations that I probably would never have been able to visit on my own. I've met with winemakers all over the world and had so many great meals at their homes, which has been a privilege. Learning what foods winemakers serve with their wines and what their favorite foods are has always fascinated me. Wherever I happen to be—the south of France, Bordeaux, Alsace, Chile, Argentina— I'm interested in what inspires that marriage. And that is reflected in my book."

**RESTAURANT TREND** "I think the trend is toward smaller restaurants where the head chefs are actually cooking, as opposed to places owned by chefs who have 10 restaurants and are never in any of the kitchens."

**DISHES THAT DIDN'T MAKE IT INTO THE BOOK** "One is called *oeuf en meurette,* which I can't even translate. I haven't been able to track down a recipe, but it's an egg dish baked in a red wine and shallot sauce. Another dish that I loved is a barley risotto made with some kind of fresh salami that's more like pork—it has the most incredible texture. It's from the Italian region of Friuli, near the Slovenian border, where there's a lot of cross-cultural cooking. I tasted it and tried to find the recipe for it, without success. A lot of the recipes in the book are like that: I'd taste something, and then I'd just do whatever it took to find the recipe."

**WHAT MAKES A GOOD COOKBOOK** "A lot of people look at cookbooks because they enjoy being voyeurs. I love reading about how Paula Wolfert traveled all over southwest France, say, with the goal of tasting every different kind of cassoulet so she could write about them. I love Elizabeth David's funny stories about finding the perfect omelet, or Richard Olney's stories about obsessively seeking out perfect foods. The books I admire the most are narrative-driven; they tell you all about the experience of food rather than just instructing you how to make it."

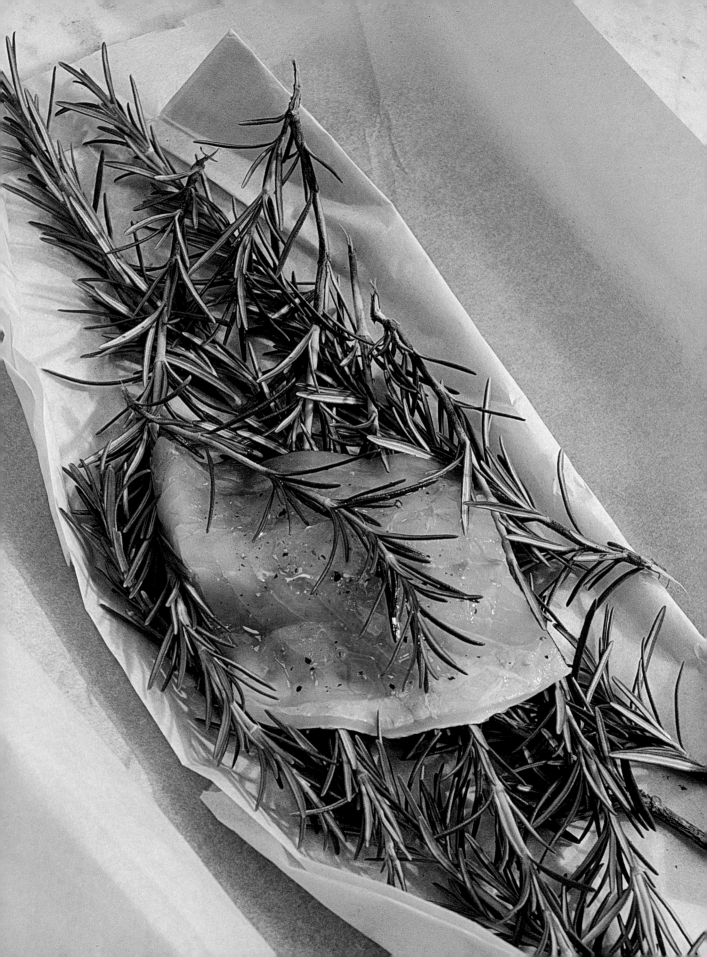

# Halibut Fillet Baked in Parchment with Salsa Verde

**SERVES 6**

Halibut is a firm, white-fleshed fish. If undercooked it is tough and chewy and if overcooked can be very dry. I have found that cooking it in parchment is foolproof. Most fishmongers cut halibut steaks, but I prefer a fillet because it is more flaky when cooked. If halibut is not available, substitute striped bass or cod. When using parchment paper, select unbleached, which is free of chemicals.

Salsa verde

1   slice ½-inch-thick hearty white bread, about 4 inches by 2 inches

1   tablespoon red wine vinegar

2   anchovy fillets, packed in salt

2   cloves garlic, peeled

2   tablespoons capers in brine or vinegar, drained and rinsed

1   cup loosely packed flat-leaf parsley leaves, washed and dried

1   cup extra-virgin olive oil

Sea salt, to taste

Halibut

12   3-inch sprigs fresh rosemary

6   halibut fillets, ½ pound each

Olive oil

**Make the salsa verde** Slice the crusts off the bread and discard. Place the bread on a small plate and drizzle both sides with the red wine vinegar.

Soak the anchovies in a bowl of cold water for 30 minutes. Remove the bones and reserve the fillets.

In a marble mortar, combine the anchovies, garlic, and capers. Pound the mixture into a paste. Add the bread and parsley and pound to a fine paste.

Slowly pour in the olive oil, stirring constantly until all the oil is incorporated. Add salt to taste, if necessary.

Prepare the halibut Preheat the oven to 360 degrees. Cut 4 sheets of parchment paper into 6 12-inch squares on a work surface. Place 2 sprigs of rosemary in the center of each piece of parchment, then place a halibut fillet on top of the rosemary sprigs. Drizzle with a little olive oil. Bring the front and back of each piece of parchment together over the center of each fillet. Gently fold together three times and then fold the ends of the paper under the packets. Place the packets in a heavy-duty baking pan and bake for 25 minutes. Remove the fish from the oven and let it rest for 5 minutes before serving.

To serve, unfold the parchment papers and gently slide a spatula under the fillets, lifting each one onto an individual serving plate. Spoon several tablespoons of salsa verde on top.

# Watercress and Avocado Salad with Toasted Sesame Vinaigrette

**SERVES 6 TO 8**

I find this salad a good course before cheese to clean the palate. The bitter watercress, the nuttiness of the toasted sesame seeds, and the creaminess of the avocado are a wonderful combination of flavors and textures.

| | |
|---|---|
| 2 | bunches watercress (about 1 pound) |
| 2 | tablespoons raw sesame seeds |
| 1 | tablespoon Spanish sherry vinegar |
| ¼ | cup extra-virgin olive oil |
| ½ | teaspoon sea salt |

Freshly ground black pepper

| | |
|---|---|
| 1 | avocado, peeled, quartered, and sliced lengthwise into ½-inch slices |

Trim off and discard 3 inches from the stems of the watercress. Wash and dry well. Refrigerate until ready to use.

Heat a small skillet over medium heat. Add the sesame seeds and toast for 1 minute or until they are light golden brown. Shake the skillet constantly so the seeds cook evenly and don't stick. Immediately scrape them into a small bowl. While the seeds are still warm, mix them with the sherry vinegar. Whisk in the olive oil gradually and season with the salt and pepper to taste.

To assemble the salad, place the watercress in a salad bowl. Add half the dressing and toss well. In a small bowl, gently toss the remaining dressing with the avocado. Add the dressed avocado to the salad and serve.

## on zarubin's nightstand

I see a million cookbooks, but the ones I go back to over and over again are those by **Elizabeth David,** such as *French Provincial Cooking,* **Richard Olney's** *Simple French Food* and **M.F.K. Fisher's** books (I've read them all because I love reading about her experiences). Another great book is *Adventures on the Wine Route* by **Kermit Lynch**. He tells a lot of anecdotes, and food plays such a big role.

# Risotto Verde

**SERVES 4**

On my first visit to Rome, I stumbled across a small trattoria near Campo dei Fiori whose kitchen emitted wonderful aromas—a sure sign that the food would be delicious. I ordered a risotto verde, never having had one before, and out came a mound of rice in a mélange of beautiful green shades. At home I immediately tried to re-create what I had eaten in Rome.

6   cups spinach leaves firmly packed with stems removed

3   cups arugula leaves firmly packed

1   cup lightly packed flat-leaf parsley leaves (about ½ ounce)

4½ cups chicken or vegetable stock

3   tablespoons extra-virgin olive oil

1   tablespoon unsalted butter

2   shallots, finely minced (about ¼ cup)

1   clove garlic, peeled and crushed

1¼ cups Arborio rice

1   cup dry white wine

1   teaspoon sea salt, plus more for seasoning

½   cup fresh shelled peas, chilled in ice water

¼   cup heavy cream

1   cup grated Parmigiano

½   teaspoon freshly ground red pepper (optional)

Freshly ground black pepper to taste

Soak the spinach and arugula leaves separately in water for 30 minutes to remove all the grit and sand.

Heat a 10- to 12-inch skillet and add the washed spinach leaves. Sauté for several minutes, stirring, until wilted. Place the spinach in a colander and drain well, then finely chop.

**zarubin on
rice for risotto**

Even rice has a shelf
life. Buy quality rice for
risotto—I prefer Italian
Arborio or Canaroli—
with an expiration date
on the bag or box.
Always store rice in a
cool dark location in an
airtight container.

Drain the arugula leaves and roughly chop. Wash and drain the parsley leaves
and roughly chop.

Place the stock in a saucepan and bring to a boil. Reduce the heat to a high
simmer. Skim off any scum that rises to the surface.

In a 6-quart nonreactive saucepan, melt the olive oil and butter. Add the
shallots and garlic and stir over low heat for 2 minutes. Add the rice and
continue stirring for another minute or until the rice is translucent. Add the
white wine and cook over medium heat until all the liquid has been
absorbed. Add 1 teaspoon salt. Then, using a ladle, begin adding the warm
stock approximately 1 cup at a time, stirring with a wooden spoon several
times after each addition. Wait until the stock has been absorbed before
adding more. Repeat this until almost all the stock has been absorbed and the
rice is al dente. The cooking time for the risotto is approximately 35 minutes.

Stir in the chopped spinach, chopped arugula, chopped parsley, and peas.
Cook for 4 minutes, stirring occasionally. Remove from the heat and stir in
the heavy cream and ½ cup of the Parmigiano. Season with the red pepper
and add salt and black pepper. Serve immediately, passing the remaining
Parmigiano separately.

# Asparagus with Eggs, Parmigiano, and Shallot Vinaigrette

**SERVES 4**

There are many different ways to enjoy asparagus in season. The combination of these ingredients is not only delicious, but the way they are layered makes a gorgeous presentation. For me this dish is often a meal in itself.

Asparagus

1   pound thin asparagus

1   tablespoon olive oil

1   teaspoon sea salt, plus more for sprinkling

1   hard-boiled egg, chopped

½   cup shaved Parmigiano

2   tablespoons chopped fresh parsley

Freshly ground black pepper to taste

Shallot vinaigrette

1   shallot, peeled and finely minced (approximately 2 tablespoons)

2   tablespoons sherry vinegar

1   tablespoon red wine vinegar

6   tablespoons extra-virgin olive oil

¾   teaspoon sea salt

Freshly ground black pepper to taste

Preheat the oven to 400 degrees.

Prepare the asparagus If thin asparagus are not available, peel the bottom half of each asparagus with a vegetable peeler and trim 1 inch off the end of each stalk. Place the asparagus in a nonreactive baking dish with enough water to barely cover them. Drizzle the olive oil over the asparagus and season with the 1 teaspoon sea salt. Cover tightly with aluminum foil or a lid and bake for 20 minutes or until tender when pierced with a sharp knife.

LORA ZARUBIN IN FRONT OF THE POLICE
BUILDING IN DOWNTOWN MANHATTAN.

*food & wine* tip

Sprinkle coarse sea salt
over the asparagus
before serving. It adds
nice flavor and texture
to the finished dish.

**Meanwhile, prepare the shallot vinaigrette** Mix the shallots and vinegars in a small bowl. Let the mixture sit for 15 minutes. Slowly whisk in the extra-virgin olive oil, and then the salt and pepper to taste.

Remove the pan from the oven, take the asparagus out of the water, and place them on a large serving platter or divide them among 4 individual plates. Sprinkle the chopped egg over the asparagus, then drizzle the shallot vinaigrette over the eggs and asparagus. Sprinkle with the Parmigiano, parsley, sea salt, and pepper. Serve slightly warm.

# It's *All* American Food

## DAVID ROSENGARTEN

### the book
*It's* All *American Food: The Best Recipes for More Than 400 New American Classics* by David Rosengarten (Little, Brown), $29.95, 494 pages, black-and-white illustrations.

### the gist
A thorough cross-country tour of America's favorite foods, from regional to classic to ethnic.

### the ideal reader
The cook who appreciates the melting pot of American cooking.

### the extras
An entertaining narrative on American culinary history and the origins of recipes.

**BACKGROUND** Born in Brooklyn, New York; lives in Manhattan.

**EDUCATION** Studied English and theater at Colgate University; got a doctorate from Cornell University in theater. "I always wanted to work in food, but I was scared about going into the restaurant business. I also always loved the theater, so I became a director and a drama professor at Cornell and then at Skidmore College, always doing some job in food on the side."

**EXPERIENCE** "About 20 years ago I had the chance to take a little time off from academia. I came back to New York City and started to write articles about food, and lo and behold, editors started buying them. In the late eighties I published my first book, *Red Wine with Fish: The New Art of Matching Wine with Food*. Later I began working with the Food Network, which changed everything in my life, and then I wrote *The Dean & DeLuca Cookbook*. It was a big success and sold a lot of copies. I've written three cookbooks since then."

**HOW HE CAME TO LOVE FOOD** "My dad was an insane foodie. We'd sit down on Friday night and talk about what we were going to cook that weekend and where we'd shop for the ingredients, making sure to get in at least one restaurant meal. While other kids were helping Dad fix the car, I was helping Dad fix lobster fra diavolo."

**IDEAL COAUTHORS** "Without a doubt it would be my kids, who are 12 and 14. They have the most unbelievable palates I've come across. Their favorite food is sushi, specifically sea urchin. One time we ate 21 pieces in a sitting. It just goes to show you that if you treat children like real people, they will respond."

**CONCEPT BEHIND "IT'S *ALL* AMERICAN FOOD"** "My idea was to include all-American recipes like the BLT, but also regional dishes like gumbo and ethnic foods like Shanghai soup dumplings that Americans are beginning to embrace and call their own."

### PANTRY ESSENTIALS
"Olive oil and salt, obviously. And mayonnaise. And let's add tuna to the list; I make lots of tuna salad."

HOW HE DEVELOPED HIS RECIPES "My method was to take as a starting point all of the things I learned from talking to people and tasting food across the country. I have what I call a chameleon palate: I can taste something and pretty easily reproduce it in my kitchen. I worked with a team of developers, and together we created about 600 recipes. This is not a compilation; these are all original recipes. Some got cut at the last moment because the book was too long. It was a herculean effort."

WHY AMERICANS SHOULD FEEL MORE PRIDE IN AMERICAN FOOD "In the book I tell stories about going for barbecue with superchef Alain Ducasse and watching him freak out about how good it was, and about accompanying star French pastry chef Pierre Hermé as he bought Hellman's mayonnaise by the case to take back to Paris."

**FAVORITE ITALIAN-AMERICAN DISH** Linguine with white clam sauce from the now-defunct Angelo's in Brooklyn. "It's very, very rare that I find one that tastes as good as the one I had there in 1964."

WHY HE'S ESPECIALLY PASSIONATE ABOUT ITALIAN-AMERICAN CUISINE "No great Italian chef wants to cook that kind of food; they're too busy building mountains of radicchio. So I say, if you take that cuisine seriously and make great linguine with white clam sauce, you'll have some of the best food on the planet. In fact, linguine with white clam sauce is sort of my holy grail in Italian-American restaurants."

LEFTOVERS TRICK "When I'm making a dinner, I buy really good bread and freeze what's left over so that I can always have a great sandwich on the spot."

COOKBOOK TRENDS "This year I was amazed to see lots of other books about saving America's endangered recipes and getting back to things we used to eat."

FOOD TRENDS "Certainly the whole world of fancy, trendy, stupid, creative-for-the-sake-of-being-creative food is not going away immediately. But our notion of what's good has changed. Now we care about the intrinsic quality of ingredients and presenting them in a way that won't hide that quality. I think that's what people are doing at parties. If you're giving a tapas party, you might think about getting yourself an incredible ham from Spain and presenting it as a compliment to your guests: 'I know you know what's good.' I see that spirit at restaurants as well."

FUTURE PROJECT A book about entertaining.

# Pasta Primavera

YIELDS 6 PASTA-COURSE SERVINGS

In the 1970s the Italian-American restaurant dish that announced "We have moved beyond red-sauce Italian" was Pasta Primavera, a combination of pasta, cream, and vegetables. It was when your local Italian restaurant became a "ristorante." Le Cirque in New York City made the dish famous, but it became a nationwide menu staple soon after that. Oddly, the dish may have had less to do with real Italian food than the red-sauce stuff did. As the myth of some "northern Italian" food spread, many Americans assumed the cuisine was rich in cream—which it never had been. Nevertheless, Pasta Primavera usually featured not only cream but lots of cream—for this was still the era when pasta in America carried too much sauce, no matter what the sauce was. The following version certainly has its fair share of cream, to be true to its Upper East Side roots—but you will find, I hope, a much more up-to-date sensibility in it, which I think makes the dish much better.

Salt

8 medium asparagus spears, ends trimmed and sliced on the bias in ½-inch lengths (about 1 cup)

1 bunch of broccoli, bite-size florets only (about 1 cup)

2 small zucchini, quartered lengthwise and cut into ⅓-inch-wide pieces (about 1½ cups)

½ pound string beans, trimmed and cut into ½-inch lengths

1 pound fresh green peas in the pod, shelled (about 1 cup), or 1 cup frozen peas

6 tablespoons pine nuts

2 tablespoons olive oil

½ pound small white mushrooms, thinly sliced (about 2 cups)

1¾ cups whipping cream

2 medium shallots, minced (about 2 tablespoons)

2 large garlic cloves, minced

Finely grated zest of 1 lemon

⅛ teaspoon cayenne

Black pepper

5 tablespoons unsalted butter, cut into small pieces

2 tablespoons lemon juice

1 pound spaghetti

½ cup grated Parmigiano-Reggiano cheese

1 cup firmly packed shredded basil leaves, plus 6 sprigs for garnish

### food & wine tip

The list of vegetables in this recipe is somewhat long. Feel free to simplify by using just the vegetables you want.

1. Bring a large stockpot of very well salted water to a boil. (Add enough salt to the pot so it tastes almost as salty as seawater.) Have ready a medium-size strainer and a large bowl of ice water. Cook the asparagus, broccoli, zucchini, and green beans, one group of vegetables at a time, in the boiling water until each group is tender but still a bit crisp, about 3 to 4 minutes for each one. As each group of vegetables finishes cooking, collect the pieces in the strainer and immediately immerse the strainer in the bowl of ice water to stop the cooking and set the color. Once the vegetables are cool (about a minute), transfer them to a bowl lined with paper towels (to absorb excess water). Cook the peas for about 30 seconds and cool in the same way. Combine the cooked vegetables and set aside. Cover the pot and the water and set it aside for cooking the pasta.

2. In a large sauté pan over medium heat, add the pine nuts and, shaking the pan occasionally, allow them to toast lightly, taking care not to let them burn. When they become golden brown in spots, about 3 to 5 minutes, remove them from the pan and set aside.

3. Add the olive oil to the pan. When the oil shimmers and slides easily in the pan, add the mushrooms and stir them to coat with the oil. Cook until the mushrooms are just tender and cooked through, about 5 minutes. Salt the mushrooms to taste, remove from the heat, and drain on paper towels. Let cool, then combine with the other vegetables.

**4.** In a small saucepan over medium-high heat, bring the cream to a boil, reduce to a brisk simmer, and cook until reduced by about half and slightly thickened. Be careful not to let the cream boil over. Add the shallots, garlic, lemon zest, cayenne, and a few grinds of black pepper. Whisk in the butter until the sauce is well blended and creamy. It should easily coat the back of a spoon. Whisk in the lemon juice and add salt to taste. Simmer and whisk for another minute or so to rethicken slightly. Remove from the heat and set aside on a warm part of the stove. Check frequently to make sure the sauce is holding; whisk it together if it isn't.

**5.** Return the large pot of water to a boil and add the spaghetti, stirring occasionally to prevent sticking. When the pasta is tender but still firm (al dente), reserve a cup of the pasta water, drain the pasta, and return the pasta to the pot. Add the reserved vegetables, the cream sauce, pine nuts, cheese, and shredded basil and toss thoroughly over low heat. If the sauce seems a bit thick—each strand of pasta should glisten with a little medium-runny sauce—add some of the reserved cooking water and toss again. Taste for seasoning. Serve in warmed bowls, garnished with basil sprigs.

# Green Goddess Dressing

**YIELDS ENOUGH FOR 6 MEDIUM-SIZE SALADS**

This American restaurant classic—a creamy, bright green friend for your salads, bursting with the flavor of fresh herbs—was invented in San Francisco in the 1920s. An actor named George Arliss, staying at the Palace Hotel, was appearing locally in a play named *The Green Goddess*, and the hotel chef created this dressing to honor the actor and the play. Good PR, even then!

¼  cup white vinegar

Juice of ½ lemon

1  garlic clove, peeled

1  shallot, peeled

5  anchovy fillets

1  cup parsley leaves, loosely packed

¼  cup tarragon leaves

¼  cup dill leaves

¼  cup chopped chives

1  scallion, white and green parts, chopped

¾  cup mayonnaise

½  cup plain yogurt

Salt and freshly ground pepper

**1.** In a blender combine the vinegar, lemon juice, garlic, shallot, and anchovies. Blend until you have a puree.

**2.** If the herbs are at all sandy or gritty, wash them thoroughly and dry on paper towels or in a salad spinner. Add the parsley, tarragon, dill, chives, and scallion to the blender and puree until the mixture becomes bright green. Add the mayonnaise and yogurt and puree until smooth. Season to taste with salt and pepper.

## rosengarten on green goddess dressing

The lower quantity of mayonnaise and the addition of yogurt make this version of Green Goddess even more celestial. It works best on hearty lettuces such as romaine; in one old tradition, a wooden salad bowl is rubbed with cut garlic, and the dressing is tossed therein with romaine, Boston lettuce, and chicory. Green Goddess is also heavenly with cold fish and shellfish.

# Chilaquiles with Chicken and Green Sauce

YIELDS 4 MAIN-COURSE SERVINGS

Happily, chilaquiles—the great Mexican next-day casserole of leftover corn tortillas—is finally finding its way onto menus in Mexican-American restaurants. It is my favorite Mexican comfort food.

2 chipotle chilies plus 2 tablespoons adobo sauce (from canned chipotle chilies in adobo sauce)

¼ cup tomato sauce (canned is fine)

2 boneless, skinless chicken breast halves, flattened to ½ inch thick

2 small white onions, peeled

12 ounces tomatillos, husked and rinsed

3 large jalapeño peppers

5 garlic cloves, unpeeled

1 cup cilantro leaves

2 teaspoons sugar, plus extra for seasoning

½ teaspoon salt, plus extra for seasoning

¼ cup water

Canola oil for frying tortillas, plus 1 tablespoon extra

10 (6-inch) corn tortillas, each cut into 8 wedges

Freshly ground pepper

1½ cups chicken stock

1 cup crumbled queso fresco cheese, for garnish

½ cup grated cotija cheese, for garnish (optional)

½ cup sour cream, thinned with 2 tablespoons milk, for garnish

1. Place the chipotles, the adobo sauce, and the tomato sauce in a blender. Puree. Place chicken breasts in a baking dish and pour the sauce over them, coating all sides of the chicken with the sauce. Cover and refrigerate for at least 4 hours or overnight.

**2.** Cut 1 of the onions into thick rings. Heat a large skillet, preferably cast-iron, over medium heat. Place the onion rings, tomatillos, jalapeño peppers, and garlic in the skillet. Blacken on all sides. As tomatillos char and soften, place in a blender. Once jalapeños are blackened on all sides, place in a plastic bag and seal. Once garlic is charred and softened, squeeze from skin into blender container. Once onion is charred on all sides, add to the blender as well. Once jalapeños are cooled, peel skin off, remove stems and discard. Add the jalapeño flesh to the blender.

**3.** To the blender, add ½ cup of the cilantro, the sugar, and the salt. Blend on medium speed until smooth (though there will still be seeds from the tomatillos). Add the water, blend again just to combine. Set sauce aside.

**4.** In a large saucepan, heat 2 inches of canola oil to 365 degrees. Fry tortilla wedges a few handfuls at a time until crispy and golden, about 2 minutes per batch. Drain on paper towels and season with salt.

**5.** Remove chicken from marinade and pat dry. Season with salt and pepper. In the same skillet used to char the tomatillos, heat 1 tablespoon canola oil over high heat. Cook chicken until browned and cooked through, about 2 minutes per side. Remove from skillet and set aside.

**6.** In the same skillet over medium-high heat, add reserved tomatillo sauce. Bring to a simmer and cook for 5 minutes. Add chicken stock and return to a simmer. Add fried tortillas and stir to combine with sauce. Simmer on low heat until tortillas are softened but still chewy in some places, about 5 minutes.

**7.** To serve, cut chicken into bite-size shreds. Chop the remaining 1 onion coarsely. Divide tortillas and sauce among four wide, shallow soup bowls (the kind of bowl you'd serve pasta in). Top chilaquiles with chicken, chopped onion, the remaining ½ cup of cilantro leaves, queso fresco, cotija, and sour cream. Serve immediately.

### *food & wine* tip

To save time, use good-quality salted tortilla chips instead of frying your own.

# Pennsylvania Dutch Chicken Corn Soup

**YIELDS 6 SERVINGS AS A MAIN-COURSE SOUP**

For chicken stock

1   (4-pound) roasting chicken, cut into pieces and skin removed

2   pounds chicken backs and necks

1   medium onion, peeled and cut into 4 pieces

1   medium carrot, scraped and roughly chopped

1   stalk celery, roughly chopped

1   sprig thyme

1   sprig parsley

1   bay leaf

¼   teaspoon whole black peppercorns

4   corncobs, cut in half lengthwise (from corn used for soup, below)

For egg noodles

2   eggs

1   egg yolk

½   teaspoon salt

1¼ cups all-purpose flour, plus extra for dusting

Cornmeal for dusting

For the soup

8   cups chicken stock (from above)

½   teaspoon saffron threads

1   cup carrot, cut into ½-inch dice

1   cup celery, cut into ½-inch dice

2   cups uncooked corn kernels, removed from the cob (reserve cobs for chicken stock, above)

2 to 3 cups cubed cooked chicken (from chicken used for stock, above)

2   tablespoons chopped parsley

1   recipe egg noodles (above) or 2 cups wide, dried egg noodles

Salt and freshly ground pepper

1. To make stock, place all ingredients for stock in a large pot and add water
to cover. Bring to a boil, then simmer until chicken is tender, about 1½ hours.
Skim foam that accumulates during simmering and discard.

2. Remove chicken pieces and cool, but simmer stock (with backs and necks
still in it) for another hour. Cut chicken meat into ½-inch cubes and reserve.
Discard bones. After the additional hour, strain stock and discard the rest of
the solids. You should have about 8 cups stock.

3. Make noodle dough: In a medium bowl, beat eggs and egg yolk with salt.
Add 1 cup of the flour and stir with a fork to combine. Add additional flour,
1 tablespoon at a time, until you have a dough that comes together and
is no longer wet and sticky. Turn onto a floured surface and knead for only
1 to 2 minutes, until the dough is no longer lumpy. Wrap in plastic and let
rest in the refrigerator for at least a half hour.

4. Roll noodles: Divide noodle dough into 4 pieces. Using a rolling pin, roll
dough out as thin as you can on a well-floured surface. Cut dough into
noodles that are 2 inches long by ⅓ inch wide. Place noodles on a sheet pan
dusted with cornmeal and dry, uncovered, for an hour. While still pliable,
twist each noodle once at the center and return to sheet pan. Dry, uncovered,
in the refrigerator, until ready to use.

5. Make soup: Bring stock to a simmer. Add saffron, carrot, and celery
and simmer until vegetables are tender, about 15 minutes. Add corn, chicken,
parsley, and noodles. Continue to simmer until noodles are cooked, about
5 minutes (longer for dried noodles). Season with salt and pepper to taste.
Serve hot.

# Jamie's Kitchen

**JAMIE OLIVER**

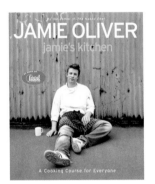

**BACKGROUND** Born in Clavering, Essex, England; lives in London.

**EDUCATION** Attended Westminster Catering College.

**EXPERIENCE** Oliver was working at London's River Cafe when he was discovered by the BBC. He was then given his own cooking show, *The Naked Chef,* by Optimum Television. He is currently chef and owner of Fifteen restaurant, in East London, where each year 15 disadvantaged youths train to become chefs.

**HOW HE FELL IN LOVE WITH COOKING** "I grew up in my parents' pub, The Cricketers, in Clavering. The focus there was on organic local ingredients. I never sat still and was always looking for pocket money, so my dad put me to work podding peas and washing up. When I was eight I started cooking."

**PREVIOUS BOOKS** *The Naked Chef, Happy Days with the Naked Chef* and *The Naked Chef Takes Off.* "I call *Jamie's Kitchen* 'Book Four' because there are so many different names for it in the 35 different countries where it's published."

**WHY HE WROTE "JAMIE'S KITCHEN"** "In my other books, I just share my favorite recipes. Book Four is all about techniques: chopping, sautéeing and a bunch of others. So far, I am most proud of this book, because it really teaches cooking."

**MENTOR** "My mate Gennaro Contaldo, who runs the genius restaurant Passione here in London. He taught me to make bread and pasta and helps my students and takes me to Italy to show me things. We've gone on trips where he's made me pull the car over to grab some wild fennel growing by the side of the road."

**MOST INSPIRING MOMENT** "About a year ago, I was filming in London outside a chocolate shop, and there on the street was a homeless guy eating a bag of Poilâne bread, which is made in Paris and is, like, the most expensive bread in the world. I asked him how he'd gotten the bread, and he told me that he'd used his begging money to buy it. It was amazing. That day changed my whole year. I wrote a story about it."

**COOKING TIP** "Before you start, be sure to get your pans really hot."

**FAVORITE HOME-COOKING TECHNIQUE** Roasting. "I like to cook the meat, vegetables and potatoes in one pan. You just put it in the oven—it cooks, and you know it's just getting better and better. Then you can go to the pub for a few pints with your mates. Finally, you put the pan right on the table. It's no work at all."

**HOME-COOKING TECHNIQUE THAT REQUIRES THE MOST PATIENCE** Bread baking. "It's a science, and learning about it can be an absolute bore. My book makes the process really fun and easy."

**ULTIMATE COMFORT FOOD** A bacon sarnie (sandwich).

**ULTIMATE DISCOMFORT FOOD** Cods' ballocks (testes). "I ate them once in Japan—never again."

**INGREDIENT OBSESSION** "I am a chile freak. I keep creating more and more spiced-up dishes just so I can experiment with them."

**MUSIC HE LIKES TO LISTEN TO WHILE COOKING** Coldplay, Red Hot Chili Peppers, The White Stripes. "All my old stuff, mainly."

**FAVORITE U.K. RESTAURANTS** "In London, they're St. John, Passione and River Cafe. Also, near Cambridge, there's a restaurant called the Fat Duck that just got its third Michelin star. The chef, Heston Blumenthal, does these combinations like egg-and-bacon ice cream that actually work."

**FAVORITE U.S. RESTAURANTS** "Anything that Alice Waters does, or Mario Batali. And Jean-Georges Vongerichten's restaurants are always pretty special. Nobu Matsuhisa is really good; I've been to a few of his places, and they're so consistent."

**FOOD TREND** "I think people in the States are going to see more North African food and Asian street food, like the spicy stuff that Jean-Georges Vongerichten is doing at Spice Market, his new restaurant in New York City. Soon you're going to see that type of cuisine here, there and everywhere."

**COOKBOOK TREND** Collections of chefs' home recipes. "People want to know what kind of burger Charlie Trotter makes for his dinner and what type of pasta Mario Batali cooks at home. In the early nineties, chefs were doing loads of pretentious cookbooks, but people don't really want that now."

## DINNER-PARTY STRATEGIES

"Make a list of everything you need to do. Get rid of the keys, the cookie jars, all the sweet, lovely family clutter, and put it in a cabinet so you have room to lay out your plates."

# The Proper French Side Salad

**SERVES 4**

*food* & *wine* tip

If you can't find chervil, substitute about a handful or so of fresh parsley leaves and 1 teaspoon of fresh chopped tarragon.

You know what I'm like—I'm the world's biggest lover of salads! When I worked in France, we used to have brilliant cheap French salads, but on my last trip to Paris all I kept getting in restaurants were some miserable leaves served with bits of overcooked hard-boiled egg and big clumsy chunks of plain old tomato. I'm sure this was just bad luck, but it made me think about the good salads I'd had over there, with a cracking French dressing that didn't have any added sugar. I even saw a chef add some raw egg whites to a French dressing once to help it emulsify—a sackable offense.

2    banana shallots or 6 normal-sized ones, peeled

White wine vinegar

1    large frisée (curly endive)

1    bunch of fresh chives

1    handful of fresh chervil, leaves picked

2    handfuls of slender green beans

2    heads of Boston lettuce

For the ultimate French dressing

1    tablespoon Dijon mustard

1 to 2 cloves of garlic, peeled and finely chopped

9    tablespoons extra virgin olive oil

Sea salt and freshly ground black pepper

Finely slice the shallots and put them into a small dish. Cover them with vinegar and let them sit for about 10–15 minutes. Pull off all the dark green frisée leaves and throw them away, as they are bitter. Then cut off all the yellow-white leaves down to the stalk. Wash these in ice-cold water with the chives and chervil, then dry them in a salad spinner and place them in a large salad bowl. Cook your green beans in salted boiling water until tender, then drain and allow to cool. I'm not a great fan of fridge-cold beans, but

beans at room temperature or warm are fantastic in this salad, so add them to the bowl. Remove any sad-looking outer leaves from the Boston lettuces and then cut them into 8 pieces (wash them if necessary, but they probably won't need it as the inner leaves will have been protected). Add to the salad bowl.

To make the dressing, first remove the shallots from the vinegar and sprinkle them over the salad leaves. Put 4 tablespoons of the leftover vinegar in a separate bowl, add the mustard and garlic with a small pinch of salt, then whisk in the oil until the dressing emulsifies. Taste and correct the seasoning. Dress the salad, give it a good toss and divide between 4 bowls. Serve immediately.

# Chinese Chicken Parcels

**SERVES 4**

1    Savoy or Chinese cabbage

2    cloves of garlic, peeled

1    thumb-sized piece of fresh ginger, peeled

1    bunch of scallions, trimmed

1    handful of fresh cilantro

1 to 2 fresh red chillies

1    tablespoon fish sauce

Sea salt

4    trimmed boneless chicken thighs, skin removed, roughly chopped

1    handful of water chestnuts

Zest and juice of 2 limes

1    teaspoon sesame oil

Extra virgin olive oil

Sweet chilli jam, jelly or sauce

Soy sauce

1    tablespoon toasted sesame seeds

Remove and discard the core and outer leaves from the cabbage, undo the remaining cabbage leaves and place them in a pan of salted boiling water for 2 minutes to soften. Cool them in a bowl of cold water, drain and put to one side.

In a food processor, whiz up your garlic, ginger, scallions, cilantro, chilli and fish sauce with a good pinch of salt. Then add the chicken, water chestnuts, lime zest and juice and sesame oil and pulse until you have a ground-meat consistency.

Place a heaped dessertspoonful of the flavored chicken on to one end of each cabbage leaf. Fold it up and tuck in the sides, then roll up. Rub a bamboo steamer, colander or normal steamer with a little olive oil and place in the

cabbage parcels. They may try to unfold themselves, but once you start putting them next to each other they will hold in place. When they're all in, sit the steamer over a pan of boiling water, making sure the water doesn't touch the parcels and that it's just the steam that's cooking them. Put a lid on top and steam for about 6 minutes, until cooked. If you're worried about the cooking time, take one of the parcels out and cut it in half to make sure that the heat has penetrated and that they're cooked.

When they're done, I like to serve them in the bamboo steamer. I move a couple of the parcels out of the way and put in a dish of sweet chilli jam, jelly or sauce—you can get these in supermarkets and specialty shops. The parcels are also good dipped in soy sauce and sprinkled with the sesame seeds.

# Crispy Fried Salmon with Spring Vegetable Broth

**SERVES 4**

## food & wine tip

The recipe calls for lightly seasoned stock, but to give the vegetables a real boost of flavor, we suggest using plenty of salt and pepper.

1 Aïoli recipe (recipe follows)

3 cups chicken or vegetable stock, lightly seasoned

8 baby bulbs of fennel, stalks removed and herby tops reserved

4 6- to 8-ounce salmon steaks, scored

Extra virgin olive oil

Sea salt and freshly ground black pepper

Around 3½ ounces green beans, tops removed

Around 3½ ounces shelled fava beans

Around 3½ ounces shelled peas

1 small handful of fresh mint, ripped

1 small handful of basil, leaves picked

First, make the Aïoli. When you've done that, bring your stock to a boil in a large pan, then add your fennel and allow this to boil for 4 minutes while you heat up a nonstick frying pan. Take your salmon steaks and, if you fancy it, you could finely slice a little of your mint and basil and push this into the score marks. Pat the salmon steaks with a little olive oil, season with salt and pepper and place skin-side down in the frying pan. Leave them for 2 minutes to get really crispy, then check how they're doing. They'll want around 4 minutes on the skin side and 1 minute on the other. You'll get an idea of how they're cooking as you'll see the salmon change color.

When the fennel has had 4 minutes, add the green beans and the fava beans. Give them a further 2 minutes. By this time you will probably want to turn over the salmon steaks for their last minute. Add the peas to the other veg and cook for a final 2 minutes. Don't be tempted to overcook the salmon—remove it from the heat. Divide the vegetables between 4 bowls, rip over the mint and basil, ladle over some of your hot cooking stock and place the salmon on top. Serve with a dollop of Aïoli. Fantastic!

## Aïoli

**SERVES 8**

Aïoli is a lovely fragrant and pungent type of mayonnaise—and the great thing is that you can take the flavor in any direction—try adding some pounded or chopped basil, fennel tops, dill or roasted nuts. Also great flavored with lemon zest and juice. It's normally seasoned well and is used to enhance things like fish stew in order to give them a real kick. You might wonder why I suggest using two types of olive oil to make this. By blending a strong peppery one with a mellower one, you achieve a lovely rounded flavor.

½ a small clove of garlic, peeled

Sea salt and freshly ground
    black pepper

1 large egg yolk

1 teaspoon Dijon mustard

1 cup extra virgin olive oil

1 cup olive oil

Lemon juice, to taste

Smash up the garlic with 1 teaspoon of salt with a mortar and pestle (or use the end of a rolling pin and a metal bowl). Place the egg yolk and mustard in a bowl and whisk together, then start to add your olive oils bit by bit. Once you've blended in a quarter of the oil, you can start to add the rest in larger amounts. When it's all gone in, add the garlic and lemon juice and any extra flavors. To finish it off, season to taste with salt, pepper and a bit more lemon juice if needed.

**TRY THIS** Lemon- or basil-flavored aïoli is good with salads, all types of fish and in seafood soups. Also great with roasted fish, chicken or pork, and classic with salmon.

# The King Arthur Flour Baker's Companion

## THE KING ARTHUR FLOUR COMPANY

INTERVIEW BELOW WITH P. J. HAMEL

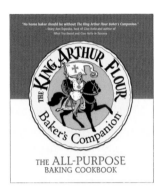

**BACKGROUND** P. J. Hamel, a former food journalist who started working at King Arthur Flour in 1990, collaborated on the book with Brinna Sands (the wife of a former owner of King Arthur Flour and, Hamel says, "the premier grandmotherly baker in this country") and the bakers at the King Arthur Flour kitchens in Norwich, Vermont.

**RECIPE ORIGINS** "The five members of our kitchen staff and several other employees are constantly developing recipes. We publish them in our catalog and our e-mail and print newsletters. We also attach recipes to almost all our products—nearly every ingredient we sell comes with a recipe."

**MOST LABORED-OVER RECIPE IN THE BOOK** The chocolate chip cookies. "We worked and worked and *worked* on those because everyone had a slightly different idea of what the best one was. Chocolate chip is the classic American cookie, so the recipe had to be perfect! We tested it 60 or 70 times to get it exactly right. And in the end we came up with a chewy one *and* a crisp one."

**BAKING: ART OR SCIENCE?** "Baking is as much art as science, but it is definitely science because there are rules you need to follow. You can't throw in a little of this or that. Still, when you're baking you shouldn't just follow a recipe blindly. You need to look at the dough, for instance, and say, 'Gee, this seems wet; I better adjust the amount of flour.' You have to be flexible."

**ESSENTIAL BAKING INGREDIENTS** A good flour and instant yeast (not to be confused with rapid-rise dry yeast). "We use instant yeast because it has more live yeast cells than active dry yeast. When you use active dry yeast you need to proof it—which means you have to dissolve it in water to slough away the dead cells. On the other hand, you can just throw instant yeast right into the flour. It's truly wonderful stuff."

### ESSENTIAL EQUIPMENT
Your hands. "You can tell so much by touch. A well-kneaded dough feels like a baby's bottom."

BEST FLOUR-STORAGE TIPS "Freeze whole wheat, pumpernickel and other whole-grain flours that still contain the germ of the grain. This prevents them from going rancid. Wrapped tightly in a plastic bag, the flour keeps for up to four months. You can keep all-purpose white flour in your pantry for up to a year. If you have bugs, stick two or three bay leaves in the flour. This will keep the bugs away, and no, it won't affect flavor."

BEST FLOUR-MEASURING METHOD "Use a baker's scale. It's so much more accurate to measure dry ingredients by weight than by volume."

**BAKING ON A RAINY DAY** "In bad weather, bread rises very well because of the low atmospheric pressure. But because flour's like a sponge, in rainy or humid weather, you'll want to add a little less liquid."

TOP PIE DOUGH TIPS "Roll out your dough from the center outward, never back and forth (which toughens the gluten). Make it about 4 inches larger than your pie pan so it will set easily into the pan without stretching (a 9-inch pie pan calls for a 13-inch dough round)."

MOST UNEXPECTED BAKING TIP "There are never any mistakes in baking because there are always birds who will eat what you don't want."

BIGGEST BAKING MISTAKES "One, to make a sweet yeast bread, people think they need to add a ton of sugar to the dough—not true. Two, when baking cookies, people will use old, darkened cookie sheets, the ones they've had forever. The problem with this is that the darker the sheet, the hotter it gets, and the more likely it is that the cookies will burn on the bottom."

BAKING TRENDS "Scones are still going strong—the craze started about five years ago and it hasn't let up. Also, people are more and more interested in making their own pizza. They get very involved with deciding between a crunchy crust versus a chewy crust (thin or thick), putting the cheese on first or last, cooking the vegetables or not before adding them."

FADING BAKING TREND Sourdough bread. "It was such a big thing, but I'm just not hearing the phenomenal buzz about it that I used to."

FUTURE PROJECT A King Arthur Flour cookie book. "I think that 98 percent of the people in this country who bake are making cookies."

# Chewy Chocolate Chip Cookies

**3 DOZEN 2½-INCH COOKIES**

Invented at the Toll House Restaurant (thus the cookie's alternate name,
Toll House), in Whitman, Massachusetts, back in the 1930s, the chocolate chip
cookie has become an American icon, right up there with apple pie and
birthday cake. Everyone has a favorite recipe, from back-of-the-Nestlé's-bag to
Mom's to the supposed Neiman Marcus recipe that made the rounds years ago.

The following recipe yields a soft and chewy cookie: get ready to pour a big,
frosty glass of milk.

| | |
|---|---|
| 12 | tablespoons (1½ sticks, 6 ounces) butter |
| 1¼ | cups (10 ounces) light brown sugar, firmly packed |
| ¼ | cup (2½ ounces) light corn syrup |
| 2 | teaspoons vanilla extract |
| ¾ | teaspoon baking powder |
| ¾ | teaspoon salt |
| ¼ | teaspoon baking soda |
| 1 | large egg |
| 2¼ | cups (9½ ounces) unbleached all-purpose flour |
| 1 | cup (4 ounces) chopped nuts (toasted, optional) |
| 2 | cups (12 ounces) semisweet or bittersweet chocolate chips |

Preheat the oven to 375°F.

Beat the butter, light brown sugar, and corn syrup together until fluffy. Beat
in the vanilla, baking powder, salt, and baking soda, and then mix in the egg.
Beat well. Beat in the flour, then stir in the nuts and chocolate chips. Drop
cookie dough by the rounded tablespoon onto lightly greased or parchment-
lined sheet pans. Bake for 12 to 14 minutes, just until lightly browned at the
edges. For the chewiest cookies, do not overbake. The cookies will look slightly

## on hamel's nightstand

I just love any of **Carol Field's** books, especially *The Italian Baker* and *Celebrating Italy.* I happen to like Italian baking, so **Mary Ann Esposito** is another favorite. And **Lora Brody's** books are so well written and funny. *Bernard Clayton's New Complete Book of Breads*—that's a classic. Other good ones are **Peter Reinhart's** gorgeous *The Bread Baker's Apprentice* and *Baking Illustrated* by the *Cook's Illustrated* magazine staff.

underdone in the middle, but will set up as they cool. Cool on the baking sheet for 5 minutes, and then remove to a wire rack to cool completely. To maintain the chewiest texture, store in an airtight container with a slice of apple or a sugar softener.

To be sure you have the amount of spread you like in a cookie, we recommend baking one cookie to test it. Then if it does not spread enough, simply flatten the cookie before baking. If it spreads more than you would like, mix in an extra ¼ cup of flour.

# Lemon-Glazed Pound Cake

**I CAKE, ABOUT I6 SERVINGS**

A subset of butter cakes, pound cakes were originally made from a pound each of flour, sugar, butter, and eggs. Over the years the proportions have changed somewhat and flavors have been added; but the result is still a very fine-textured, moderately heavy moist cake, perfect for slicing and serving as a base for fruit or ice cream.

One of our very favorite ways to serve pound cake is to brush both sides with a slice of butter, then sauté it, as you would a grilled cheese sandwich. When it's golden brown, remove it from the heat and top with ice cream, choosing a flavor that's complementary to the cake. Add fudge sauce and whipped cream and you've reached cake nirvana.

The sunny taste of citrus highlights this buttery pound cake.

Cake

14   tablespoons (1¾ sticks, 7 ounces) butter

1    package (3 ounces) cream cheese

½    teaspoon salt

1½   cups (10½ ounces) sugar

1    teaspoon baking powder

2    teaspoons vanilla extract

½    teaspoon lemon oil, or 1 tablespoon lemon zest

1¾   cups (7¼ ounces) unbleached all-purpose flour

5    large eggs

Glaze

¼    cup (2 ounces) fresh lemon juice

½    cup (3½ ounces) sugar

Preheat the oven to 350°F and grease two 8½ x 4½-inch loaf pans or a
9- to 10-cup tube or bundt-style pan.

**For the cake**  In a medium-sized mixing bowl, beat together the butter and
cream cheese until soft and fluffy. Add the salt, sugar, baking powder, vanilla,
lemon, and flour and beat for 5 minutes; the batter will be stiff.

Add 1 egg, beating until well combined. Continue to add the eggs, one at a
time, beating well and scraping the sides and bottom of the bowl after
each addition. When done, the batter will be very fluffy. Spoon the batter
into the prepared pan(s).

Bake the cake for 55 to 60 minutes (for the tube or bundt-style pans) or
35 to 40 minutes (for the two loaf pans), or until a cake tester inserted into
the center comes out clean.

**For the glaze**  Just before the cake is done, combine the lemon juice and sugar
and heat over low heat (or in the microwave) until the sugar has dissolved;
don't let the mixture boil.

Remove the cake from the oven and let it cool for 10 minutes in the pan. Turn
it out onto a wire rack or serving platter. Poke the top all over with a cake
tester or toothpick and gradually drizzle the glaze over it, pausing occasionally
to let it sink in. Let the cake cool for several hours before slicing.

*food & wine tip*

Make sure the butter
and cream cheese are
at room temperature.
When you beat them,
they'll get fluffy quickly.

# S'more Granola Bars

SIXTEEN 2¼-INCH SQUARES

S'mores. If you can read that word without immediately conjuring up memories of smoky campfires when you were ten years old—then you were never a Scout. Granola Bars. If you can read those words without immediately thinking of a green, leafy canopy overhead; the good feeling of a heavy pack resting on your hips; the cool mountain air—then you've never been hiking. Even if you weren't a Scout and have never been hiking, don't let that stop you from enjoying these delicious, simple-to-make snack bars.

6    tablespoons (¾ stick, 3 ounces) unsalted butter

¼    cup (2 ounces) firmly packed light brown sugar

6    tablespoons (4 ounces) golden syrup, maple syrup, or dark corn syrup

2¼   cups (7¾ ounces) rolled oats

½    cup (2 ounces) unbleached all-purpose flour

½    teaspoon salt

1    cup (3½ ounces) graham cracker crumbs

1    cup (6 ounces) semisweet or bittersweet chocolate chips

1¼   cups (5½ ounces) mini marshmallows, or 1 cup (6 ounces) marshmallow creme


In a medium-sized saucepan set over medium heat, melt and stir together the butter, sugar, and syrup, cooking until the sugar has dissolved. Stir in the oats, flour, salt, and graham cracker crumbs.

Press slightly more than half of the mixture into a lightly greased 9 x 9-inch pan. Let cool completely. Preheat the oven to 350°F. Sprinkle the chocolate chips evenly over the top, then the marshmallows. If using marshmallow creme, oil your fingers and a spoon and drop by teaspoonfuls evenly over the chocolate chips. Top with the remaining crust mixture. Bake the bars for 15 to 20 minutes. Remove from the oven and let them rest for 20 minutes, then cut into squares while still slightly warm.

# Open-Faced Rustic Berry Pie

**6 SERVINGS**

The "rustic" in the recipe title refers to the method of shaping the crust. All you have to do is roll out a big circle, pile the sugared berries in the middle, and gently fold the edges of the crust in toward the center, leaving about a 4-inch-wide circle of berries showing (that's the open-faced part). The number-one goal is to bring the crust over the berries without tearing it; a crust with holes will allow leakage of the bubbling berry syrup.

One 9-inch single piecrust (recipe follows)

⅔ cup (4¾ ounces) sugar

3 tablespoons (¾ ounce) pie filling thickener of your choice (tapioca or cornstarch)

3 cups (15 ounces) berries, fresh or frozen and thawed

Preheat the oven to 425°F.

Roll the crust into a 12- to 13-inch round and transfer the round to a pizza pan or baking sheet; if you use a baking sheet, the crust may (temporarily) hang off the edges, which is okay. (Instructions for rolling out dough are given on page 211.)

In a medium-sized bowl, blend together the sugar and thickener. Add the berries, tossing to coat.

Mound the sugared berries in the center of the crust, leaving about a 3½-inch margin of bare crust all the way around; the mound of fruit will be quite high. Using a pancake turner or a giant spatula, fold the edges of the crust up over the fruit, leaving 4 to 5 inches of fruit exposed in the center.

Bake the pie for about 35 minutes, or until the filling is beginning to bubble and the edges of the crust are brown. Remove it from the oven and let it cool for 15 to 30 minutes before cutting wedges.

*food & wine* **tip**

If your berries are very sweet, be sure to cut back the quantity of sugar in this recipe.

## Basic Piecrust

### food & wine tip

The pie on the previous page uses only half the dough this recipe yields. Save the remaining pie dough by wrapping it tightly in plastic and freezing it for up to one month.

**ONE 9-INCH DOUBLE PIECRUST**

2½ cups (10½ ounces) unbleached all-purpose flour, pastry flour, or a combination of both

1    teaspoon salt

1    cup cold shortening (6½ ounces), or lard (8 ounces), or butter (2 sticks, 8 ounces)*

¼ to ½ cup (2 to 4 ounces) ice water

*We like a combination of ½ cup (3¼ ounces) of shortening (for the texture it lends), and 1 stick (4 ounces) of butter (for its flavor).

**Mix dry ingredients** Whisk together the flour and salt in a bowl large enough that you'll be able to plunge both hands in to work with the dough.

**Cut in half of the fat, combining thoroughly** The mixture should form very small, very even crumbs. If using a single type of fat, cut half the fat into the flour. If using our recommended combination of shortening and butter, cut all the shortening into the flour and reserve the butter.

"Cutting the fat into the flour" simply means combining them. The degree to which you combine them defines the final texture of the crust. Barely combining will yield a flaky crust, thoroughly combining, a crisp, nonflaky crust. This can be done by plunging your hands into the bowl and working the pieces of fat with the flour. Or you can use a pastry fork or pastry blender. Combining flour with half the fat thoroughly, then combining with the remaining fat and leaving large chunks (pea-sized, or even larger) will yield a medium-flake crust.

**Cut in remaining fat** Cut or pinch the remaining fat into small bits. If using butter, cut the stick into 4 lengthwise slices one way, flip it on its side, cut 4 slices the other way, then cut across the strips into ¼ inch pats. Toss the tiny bits of fat (butter or shortening) into the flour mixture, mixing just enough to coat them with flour.

**Add water** Add the water, a tablespoon at a time, and toss with a fork to moisten the dough evenly. To test for the right amount of liquid, use your hands to squeeze a chunk of it together. If it sticks together easily, it's moist enough. If it falls apart, add a bit more water. When you're sprinkling water on the flour and fat mixture and tossing it around, keep grabbing small handfuls; when the dough barely sticks together, add 1 more tablespoon of water. This should be just the right amount to yield a dough that's soft enough to roll nicely, but not so soft that it sticks to the counter and rolling pin.

**Turn out dough and refrigerate** Turn out the dough onto a lightly floured surface. Divide the ball of dough in half, pat into flat disks about an inch thick, wrap both halves in plastic wrap, and refrigerate for at least 30 minutes.

**Roll out the dough** Flour your work surface—counter, tabletop, pastry board, or marble slab. Unwrap one piece of dough and put it on the floured surface. Whatever size pie you're making, you'll want to roll the crust to a diameter that's about 3 to 4 inches greater than the inside diameter of the pan, for example, for a 9-inch pie pan, roll the crust to a 12- to 13-inch diameter. When rolling piecrust, be forceful but make it brief; the best piecrust is rolled from the center outward (to make an evenly round crust), with as few strokes as possible being used to stretch the crust to its necessary size. Don't roll back and forth over the dough endlessly. Roll in one direction only (so as not to "confuse" the developing gluten). Don't whack the dough with the rolling pin, but be assertive enough to flatten it quickly. A crust that's fussed over too long develops a toughness that is none too appealing.

Use a spatula (a giant spatula is a big help) to lift the crust from the well-floured work surface every few strokes, adding more flour to the work surface if the crust starts to stick.

Transfer the rolled-out crust to a pizza pan or baking sheet and proceed with the Open-Faced Rustic Berry Pie recipe.

# Land of Plenty

## FUCHSIA DUNLOP

**BACKGROUND** Born and raised in Oxford, England; lives in London.

**EDUCATION** "I studied English literature at Cambridge University, and then had a scholarship to study in China, where I went to Sichuan University and the Sichuan Institute of Higher Cuisine. After that I did a master's in Chinese studies at the School of Oriental and African Studies at London University."

**EARLIEST INTEREST IN FOOD** "As a small child I loved cooking, really from the age of five or six. I think when I was ten or eleven I actually wanted to be a chef."

**HOW SHE CAME TO LOVE CHINESE FOOD** "I was editing lots of news reports about China for the BBC and first went there on a trip for work. Later I again found myself in this place with the most extraordinarily good food. And it was totally cheap. My friends and I used to go to these small, insignificant restaurants and eat the most sublime dishes. I started asking questions and learning a few things, and that's how it started. It was greed and curiosity."

**ON ATTENDING PROFESSIONAL COOKING SCHOOL IN CHINA** "They had never had any foreign students, and they didn't quite know what to do with me and my German friend. But they agreed to give us some private classes. Later I asked if I might pop in on the odd cooking demonstration, and they said, 'We've got a course starting just about now; why don't you join in?' It was a three-month chef's training course. I was one of only three women in a class of 48 and the first foreigner to study full-time at the school. It was hard because the language was all Sichuan dialect, and of course I had studied Mandarin—I knew only a bit of Sichuan. It was challenging, yes, but great fun."

**ABOUT THE BOOK'S TITLE** "'Land of Plenty'—*tian fu zhi guo*—is what the

## APPEAL OF SICHUAN FOOD

"It's amazingly diverse in flavor—you taste the spiciness of chiles, you have ginger, garlic, onion, a bit of sourness, saltiness, all in the same dish."

Chinese call Sichuan because the region has a very nice climate that produces excellent local fruits and vegetables. Also, because of the comfortable climate, the Sichuanese developed a reputation for being sort of idle and pleasure-loving—enjoying the finer things in life, including, of course, food."

**WHY SHE WROTE THE BOOK** "People have researched regional cuisines in France and Italy, but not in China. So it was partly this sense of mission and partly the excitement of doing something quite new. Also, the book sort of wrote itself because I've always kept travel diaries. When I came back to England, I had all these notebooks, which were just recipes and lyrical descriptions of meals."

**GUIDING PRINCIPLES OF SICHUAN COOKING** "The combination of flavors is absolutely fundamental. The way things are cut is pretty important, too. For some dishes all the ingredients may be sliced into fine slivers, so the evenness of it, the mouth-feel of it, is part of the dish's quality."

**ESSENTIAL EQUIPMENT** "A wok for stir-frying. And it's nice to do the cutting with a Chinese knife, although it's not essential. Only the basics are needed. In fact, most of my Chinese friends don't even have an oven in their kitchens. They have gas hot plates, a wok, a rice cooker, a few pans and bowls, a cleaver and chopsticks. I was struck by the complete simplicity of it all. Very impressive."

**ESSENTIAL SICHUAN INGREDIENTS** Sichuan chiles and broad bean paste—"this wonderful, mellow paste. You cook with it by sizzling it first in some oil. It stains the oil a beautiful red color and becomes marvelously aromatic."

**FAVORITE LONDON RESTAURANTS** "I love the dim sum at Hakkasan and Royal China. A recent favorite is St. John Bread and Wine, a wonderful place to eat traditional English food."

**FOOD TREND** "I expect to see more regional Chinese cooking. There have been some signs of that, certainly at British restaurants, because there are new immigrants from different areas within China."

**CREATING A PERFECT SICHUAN MENU** "You don't want all the dishes to be very spicy and you don't want them all to be stir-fries. It's just putting together some cold dishes, some hot dishes, some slow dishes."

# Dry-Fried Green Beans

*gan bian si ji dou*

**SERVES 4 WITH THREE OTHER DISHES**

This is one of Sichuan's most famous vegetable dishes. The green beans are traditionally dry-fried over a medium heat until they are tender and slightly wrinkled, although these days most restaurants deep-fry them.

10   ounces haricots verts or green beans

Peanut oil

3   ounces ground pork (about ⅔ cup)

2   teaspoons Shaoxing rice wine or medium-dry sherry

2   teaspoons soy sauce

2   tablespoons Sichuanese *ya cai* or Tianjin preserved vegetable, finely chopped

Salt to taste

1   teaspoon sesame oil

1. Remove any strings from the edges of the beans and trim off the tops and tails. Break them into short sections (about 2 inches long).

2. Heat 2 tablespoons of oil in a wok, add the beans, and stir-fry over a medium flame for about 6 minutes, until they are tender and their skins are a little puckered. Remove from the wok and set aside. (If you want to save time, deep-fry the beans at about 350°F until they are tender and puckered.)

3. Heat another 2 tablespoons of oil in the wok over a high flame, add the pork, and stir-fry for 30 seconds or so until it's cooked, splashing in the Shaoxing rice wine and the soy sauce as you go.

4. Add the *ya cai* or Tianjin preserved vegetable and stir-fry briefly until hot, then toss in the beans. Stir and toss, adding salt to taste (remember that the *ya cai* is already very salty).

5. Remove from the heat, stir in the sesame oil, and serve.

## dunlop's variation

One restaurant I know in Chengdu cooks a similar dish with bitter melon, which is sensational. The melon is deseeded and cut into thin strips and then fried in the same way as the beans, until the strips are tender and slightly wrinkly. The final frying is exactly the same as in the recipe, although they do add a few dried chiles and a couple of lengths of scallion, white and green parts.

# Fish-Fragrant Eggplants

*yu xiang qie zi*

**SERVES 4 WITH THREE OTHER DISHES**

## dunlop's variations

The fish-fragrant sauce made according to the second method can be poured over seafood such as prawns or squid. The seafood can be simply boiled or steamed, or deep-fried, perhaps with a light tempura-style batter. Some restaurants serve the sauce in a bowl as a dip for deep-fried prawns. These variations are recent innovations—they have only been served in upscale restaurants since fresh seafood began to be flown in from the coast.

The following recipe is a Sichuan classic and one of my personal favorites. More than any other dish, for me it sums up the luxuriant pleasures of Sichuan eating: the warmth of its colors and tastes, the rich subtlety of its complex flavors. Like other fish-fragrant dishes, it is prepared with the flavorings used in traditional Sichuanese fish cooking: pickled chiles, garlic, ginger, and scallion. But unlike the more illustrious fish-fragrant pork slivers, this dish derives its color not from pickled chiles alone, but from pickled chiles mixed with fava beans in the famous Pixian chili bean paste.

1⅓ to 1⅔ pounds eggplants (2 decent-sized eggplants or a generous handful of slender Asian eggplants)

Salt

Peanut or corn oil for deep-frying

1½ tablespoons Sichuanese chili bean paste

3 teaspoons finely chopped fresh ginger

3 teaspoons finely chopped garlic

½ cup Everyday Stock (see page 221) or chicken stock

1½ teaspoons white sugar

½ teaspoon light soy sauce

1⅓ teaspoons cornstarch mixed with 1 tablespoon cold water

1½ teaspoons Chinkiang or Chinese black vinegar

4 scallions, green parts only, sliced into fine rings

1 teaspoon sesame oil

METHOD I

1. Cut the eggplants in half lengthwise and then crosswise. Chop each quarter lengthwise into 3 or 4 evenly sliced chunks. Sprinkle with 1½ teaspoons of salt and leave for at least 30 minutes to draw out some of the juices. If you are using Asian eggplants, simply slice them in half lengthwise and then into 3-inch sections—there is no need to salt them.

2. In your wok, heat oil for deep-frying to 350–400°F (at this temperature it will just be beginning to smoke). Add the eggplants in batches and deep-fry for 3–4 minutes until slightly golden on the outside and soft and buttery within. Remove and drain on paper towels.

3. Drain off the deep-frying oil, rinse the wok if necessary, and then return it to a high flame with 2–3 tablespoons of oil. Add the chili bean paste and stir-fry for about 20 seconds until the oil is red and fragrant; then add the ginger and garlic and continue to stir-fry for another 20–30 seconds until they are fragrant. Take care not to burn the flavorings—remove the wok from the heat for a few seconds or turn down the heat if necessary.

4. Add the stock, sugar, and soy sauce and mix well. Season with salt to taste if necessary.

5. Add the fried eggplants to the sauce and let them simmer gently for a few minutes to absorb some of the flavors. Then sprinkle the cornstarch mixture over the eggplants and stir in gently to thicken the sauce. Next, stir in the vinegar and scallions and leave for a few seconds until the onions have lost their rawness. Finally, remove the pan from the heat, stir in the sesame oil, and serve.

METHOD 2

1. Follow steps 1–4 of the recipe above, but lay the fried eggplants neatly onto a warmed serving dish.

2. When the sauce has returned to a boil, add the cornstarch mixture and stir as it thickens. Throw in the vinegar and scallions and stir until the scallions have just lost their rawness. Remove from the heat, stir in the sesame oil, and pour over the waiting eggplants.

The advantage of the first method is that you can, if you wish, fry the eggplants some time in advance, because they will be warmed up by the final braising in the sauce.

## on dunlop's nightstand

Among my favorite cookbooks are **Claudia Roden's** books on Middle Eastern food. There's also a very traditional English book by **Pru Leith** and **Caroline Waldegrave** called *Leith's Cookery Course,* which I was given when I was eleven years old. It was with this book that I learned to make classic pastries—profiteroles and crème brûlée. That book is very close to my heart because I've used it for so long.

# Pock-Marked Mother Chen's Bean Curd

*ma po dou fu*

**SERVES 4 WITH THREE OTHER DISHES**

*food & wine* on
sichuan
peppercorns
_____

The last ingredient
here is ground roasted
Sichuan pepper.
Sichuan peppercorns are
illegal in the United
States, but they can still
be found in certain Asian
markets. If you can't
get them, substitute
black peppercorns.
To roast them, add them
to a dry wok over
low heat and stir until
fragrant. Then grind
them to a powder in
a spice grinder or with a
mortar and pestle.

*Ma po dou fu* is named after the smallpox-scarred wife of a Qing Dynasty restaurateur. She is said to have prepared this spicy, aromatic, oily dish for laborers who laid down their loads of cooking oil to eat lunch on their way to the city's markets. It's one of the most famous Sichuan dishes and epitomizes Sichuan's culinary culture, with its fiery peasant cooking and bustling private restaurants. Many unrecognizable imitations are served in Chinese restaurants worldwide, but this is the real thing, as taught at the Sichuan provincial cooking school and served in the Chengdu restaurants named after Old Mother Chen. The Sichuan pepper will make your lips tingle pleasantly, and the tender bean curd will slip down your throat. It's rich and warming, a perfect winter dish.

This recipe traditionally uses a scattering of ground beef, which is unusual in Sichuan cooking, where pork is the most common meat. Sometimes the beef is precooked and added to the main dish at the last minute to preserve its crispness. Vegetarians may omit the meat altogether and still enjoy the dish. The traditional vegetable ingredient is *suan miao*, the long, narrow Chinese leeks, but scallions are often used as a substitute if no leeks are available. You can reduce the amount of cooking oil if you wish (as little as 3 tablespoons will work), although it's traditional to serve this dish with a good layer of chile-red oil on top. For the deepest ruby-red color, use real Sichuan chili bean paste and ground Sichuanese chiles. *Ma po dou fu* is usually served heartily in a bowl, rather than on a plate.

| | |
|---|---|
| 1 | block bean curd (about 1 pound) |
| 4 | baby leeks or 2 leeks |
| ½ | cup peanut oil |
| 6 | ounces ground beef |
| 2½ | tablespoons Sichuanese chili bean paste |
| 1 | tablespoon fermented black beans |
| 2 | teaspoons ground Sichuanese chiles (only for chile fiends) |

The Chinese have been fermenting soybeans, wheat, and other grains into sauces since at least the third century B.C., and these condiments have long been regarded as an essential part of people's diets. These days two types of soy sauce are in common use—thinner, saltier, light soy sauce and heavier, richer, dark soy sauce. The light soy is used mainly as a salty seasoning, the darker one for adding color to sauces and marinades. Sichuanese cooks also make their own sweet, aromatic soy sauce by simmering dark soy with brown sugar and spices—this is used in cold dishes and sauces for various snacks. The finest soy sauce is allowed to ferment naturally, but most versions rely on added yeast.

1  cup Everyday Stock (recipe follows) or chicken stock

1  teaspoon white sugar

2  teaspoons light soy sauce

Salt to taste

4  tablespoons cornstarch mixed with 6 tablespoons cold water

½  teaspoon ground roasted Sichuan pepper

1. Cut the bean curd into 1-inch cubes and leave to steep in very hot or gently simmering water that you have lightly salted. Slice the leeks at a steep angle into thin "horse ear" slices 1½ inches long.

2. Season the wok, then add the peanut oil and heat over a high flame until smoking. Add the minced beef and stir-fry until it is crispy and a little brown, but not yet dry.

3. Turn the heat down to medium, add the chili bean paste, and stir-fry for about 30 seconds, until the oil is a rich red color. Add the fermented black beans and ground chiles and stir-fry for another 20–30 seconds until they are both fragrant and the chiles have added their color to the oil.

4. Pour in the stock, stir well, and add the drained bean curd. Mix it in gently by pushing the back of your ladle or wok scoop gently from the edges to the center of the wok—do not stir or the bean curd may break up. Season with the sugar, a couple of teaspoons of soy sauce, and salt to taste. Simmer for about 5 minutes, until the bean curd has absorbed the flavors of the sauce.

5. Add the leeks or scallions and gently stir in. When they are just cooked, add the cornstarch mixture in two or three stages, mixing well, until the sauce has thickened enough to cling glossily to the meat and bean curd. Don't add more than you need. Finally, pour everything into a deep bowl, scatter with the ground Sichuan pepper, and serve.

## Everyday Stock

*xian tang*

This is the Sichuanese all-purpose stock, used for all kinds of soups and sauces. It's not good enough for banquet cooking, but it is inexpensive, nourishing, and easy to make. If you use good bones, from traditionally reared or organically produced animals and fowl, all the better. Good butchers will probably give you the bones free of charge or for a nominal fee. Make the stock in large quantities and then freeze it in smaller batches, which can be quickly defrosted when you wish to use them. In restaurants a whole chicken is often used, but I generally just toss in what's left of the carcass when I've removed the breast and leg meat to use in other dishes. You can add some duck or duck bones too if you have them.

About 2 pounds of pork bones

About 1 pound of chicken parts (wings, backs)

A 2-inch piece of fresh ginger, with peel, crushed

A couple of scallions

Smash the chicken carcass and larger bones. Put all the meat and bones into a large pot. Fill with enough water to cover, bring to a rapid boil, and skim. Then add the ginger and scallions, turn down the heat, and simmer gently for 2–3 hours. Strain the liquid and let cool. Cover, keep refrigerated, and use it within a few days, or freeze. Skim off the fat each time you use it.

# Fish with Chiles and Sichuan Pepper

*la zi yu*

**SERVES 4 WITH THREE OTHER DISHES**

1   pound filleted carp, sea bass, or other white-fleshed fish

For the marinade

A 1-inch piece of fresh ginger, unpeeled

1   scallion, white and green parts

½   teaspoon salt

2   teaspoons Shaoxing rice wine or medium-dry sherry

4   tablespoons cornstarch mixed with 3 tablespoons cold water

For the base flavorings

6   dried Sichuanese chiles

A 1-inch piece of fresh ginger

3   cloves of garlic

5   scallions, white and green parts

3   tablespoons peanut or corn oil

1   tablespoon Sichuanese chili bean paste

½   teaspoon Sichuan pepper (see *Food & Wine* on Sichuan Peppercorns, page 218)

For the spicy oil

¾   cup peanut or corn oil

1½ tablespoons chili bean paste

1 to 2 ounces dried red chiles, preferably Sichuanese

2   teaspoons whole Sichuan pepper (see *Food & Wine* on Sichuan Peppercorns, page 218)

1. Slightly crush the ginger and scallion for the marinade with the flat side of a cleaver or a heavy object. Cut the scallion into 3 or 4 sections. Lay the fish fillets on a cutting board and, holding your knife at a shallow angle to the board, cut them into slices ¼ to ½ inch thick. Place the slices in a bowl, add the salt, wine, ginger, and scallion, and leave to marinate while you prepare the other ingredients.

2. Snip all the chiles in half with a pair of scissors and shake out as many seeds as possible.

3. Prepare the base flavorings: peel and thinly slice the ginger and garlic. Discard the coarse outer leaves of the scallions, crush them slightly with the flat side of a cleaver blade or a heavy object, and then cut them into 2- to 3-inch sections. Heat 3 tablespoons of oil in a wok over a high flame. When it is just beginning to smoke, turn the heat down a little, add the chili bean paste, and stir-fry until the oil is red and fragrant. Then throw in the ginger, garlic, scallions, dried chiles, and Sichuan pepper and continue to stir-fry until they all smell delicious and the scallions are tender. The oil should be hot enough to keep them sizzling, but take care not to burn them. When they are ready, transfer them into a deep serving bowl.

4. Bring a pot of water to a boil over a high flame. Discard the ginger and scallion from the fish marinade, add the cornstarch mixture, and stir well to coat all the fish slices. When the water is boiling, drop in all the slices. (Do not stir them before the water has returned to a boil or the starch coating will fall away.) Allow the water to return to a boil. When the fish slices are just cooked, remove them with a slotted spoon and scatter them over the base flavorings in the serving bowl.

5. Working quickly, heat ¾ cup of oil over a high flame until it is just begining to smoke. Add the chili bean paste and stir-fry until the oil is red and fragrant. Add the remaining chiles and Sichuan pepper and stir-fry until they are crisp and fragrant—the longer you fry them, the more fragrant and spicy the oil will become. Again, the oil should be hot enough to keep everything sizzling, but the spices must not burn—remove the wok from the stove for a few seconds if it seems to be overheating. Finally, pour the oil with the spices all over the fish. Serve immediately, while it is still sizzling.

# The Maccioni Family Cookbook

**EGI MACCIONI WITH PETER KAMINSKY**

INTERVIEW BELOW WITH EGI MACCIONI

**BACKGROUND** Born in Montecatini Terme, Tuscany; lives in New York City.

**HOW SHE CAME TO THE UNITED STATES** "My husband, Sirio, and I were engaged for six years, with him here and me in Italy, seeing each other only once a year for just a month. At the time I was a professional singer. He was waiting for his citizenship to come through. When it did, in 1964, he found me a singing contract, I moved to New York and we married that year." (Sirio Maccioni is co-owner, with his three sons, of New York City's Le Cirque and four other restaurants.)

**EXPERIENCE** "I have been cooking at least since I was seven years old. I have always been interested in the kitchen—I would be the 'little helper' for my grandmothers even when I could barely reach the table. Later, I would do the cooking at home. In America I cooked for my husband, and then my three sons, Mario, Marco and Mauro. And when my husband and sons opened Osteria del Circo eight years ago, they said, 'Mum, why don't you come help us?'"

**EARLIEST FOOD MEMORY** "It was very beautiful to watch my grandmother make fresh pasta, using only a rolling pin, not a pasta machine. She would roll out the dough so thin, and then cut out all kinds of shapes, little ones, big ones, tortellini—with just a sharp knife."

**HOW "THE MACCIONI FAMILY COOKBOOK" CAME TO BE** "For 40 years I've been writing down recipes. When I cook something and the dish turns out well, I will write down what I did. Almost all the recipes in the book are traditional Tuscan ones. They came from my family, from the region—they are what every woman in Tuscany cooks. All the women in Italy are very dedicated to good food."

## WHY ITALIANS LOVE PASTA
"We associate pasta with being a child: It's the first food you eat. You start with only little pastini in chicken soup, and eventually move on to all different kinds."

HOW THE COOKBOOK IS ORGANIZED "I was talking with the food writer Peter Kaminsky about how different recipes are associated with different memories and experiences, and he suggested organizing the book into chapters: my childhood in Tuscany, my husband's favorites, our time in New York and the restaurant."

FAMILY FAVORITE Pizza. "My sons insisted I include it in the book. I used to make it every Sunday before we went to church, then when we came back we would eat it. No church, no pizza."

MOST MEMORABLE MEAL "One night Frédy Girardet, the famous Swiss chef, came to our house for dinner with Danny Kaye, who was a great gourmet, and I made polenta with white truffles and mascarpone. They were so delighted! I didn't put that recipe in the book, though, because it was an improvisation of the moment."

**SIGNATURE DISH** "I'd make my ricotta and spinach ravioli at home and bring them to Le Cirque. But too many people wanted them, so I had to give the recipe to the chef. Now, we could never take them off the menu."

MISTAKES AMERICANS MAKE WHEN COOKING ITALIAN FOOD "Too many herbs; people put in ten sprigs when all they need is one. Too much garlic; it's overpowering. Too much salad dressing; you should be skimpy with the oil and dress less overall. Too much pasta sauce; sometimes there's more sauce on the plate than pasta."

HOW TO COOK LIKE A TUSCAN "Use very few ingredients. Many times, we even use just one herb, such as sage or rosemary, which are traditional."

ESSENTIAL TUSCAN INGREDIENTS Good olive oil, good red wine vinegar and good fresh-ground pepper.

FAVORITE RESTAURANTS IN TUSCANY La Mora in Lucca, Da Romano in Viareggio and Lorenzo in Forte dei Marmi. "And in Florence, a very famous restaurant, run by friends of ours, called Enoteca Pinchiorri. It is fabulous."

WHAT SHE MISSES MOST ABOUT TUSCANY Fagioli di sorana. "They are moist, soft white beans. They are expensive because they are grown only on a certain small farm, nowhere else. You cook them simply with sage, garlic, oil, salt and pepper."

FUTURE PROJECT "Perhaps one day an Italian cookbook for the little ones."

# Ricotta and Spinach Ravioli

**SERVES 4**

Nonna Augusta was a great ravioli maker. They were also a great favorite on our picnics in the hills on the day after Easter. When Le Cirque was on Sixty-fifth Street I would send twenty portions a day over to the restaurant. I had this super-secret and quite wonderful ravioli machine that I bought in Viareggio more than twenty years ago. In fact it was so great I bought two of them. Good thing, because when I loaned one to our chef, he messed up the handle. I took it right back and it has never left my house since. I tried to buy another one for the restaurant but it turned out that the man who made the originals had sold the mold to a competitor who broke the mold. My machines will now never leave my house!

Ravioli dough

2    cups all-purpose flour

3    eggs

1    teaspoon olive oil

¼    teaspoon salt

Filling

½    cup ricotta cheese (fresh, if possible)

⅓    cup grated Parmesan cheese

⅓    cup cooked spinach, squeezed of excess water and finely chopped

1    tablespoon finely chopped fresh parsley

¼    clove garlic, minced

Freshly grated nutmeg

Salt and pepper

Sauce

3    tablespoons butter, melted

16 to 20 fresh sage leaves

⅓    cup grated Parmesan cheese

Pepper

For the ravioli dough Combine all of the ingredients in a food processor and process to make a soft dough. Add a little flour if the dough is too sticky. Transfer the dough to a small bowl and refrigerate, covered, for 1 hour.

For the filling In a large bowl, beat together the ricotta, Parmesan, spinach, parsley, and garlic until thoroughly combined. Season with the nutmeg, salt, and pepper to taste (make it a little extra salty since some of the saltiness will be lost when the ravioli are boiled). Set aside.

For the topping In a medium skillet, melt the butter over medium-low heat. Gently stir in the sage leaves. Set aside. (Best if done at the last minute before serving.)

Assembling the ravioli Fill a large soup pot three-quarters full of water and bring to a boil.

Using a pasta machine, make rectangular strips as thin as possible from the ravioli dough. Cut the strips into 3- to 4-inch squares. Put a small spoonful of filling in the center of half of the squares. Be careful not to add too much filling, or the ravioli will not seal well. Cover the filled squares with the remaining dough squares. Press the edges of each ravioli firmly closed with your fingers or the tines of a fork. (If the dough does not stick, you can seal it with a little beaten egg.)

Cook the ravioli in the boiling water, stirring very gently only occasionally to make sure they do not stick to each other. Cook them to your preference, between 3 and 8 minutes.

For the sauce Gently drain the ravioli and place in a warm serving bowl. Toss very gently with the butter and sage. Sprinkle with the Parmesan and pepper to taste. Serve immediately.

# Sausage Stew with White Beans

**SERVES 4**

When Sirio wants some real Italian cooking in the middle of a day at Le Cirque he walks two blocks over to Circo, our Italian restaurant on Fifty-fifth Street that I run with my sons. Quite often he asks for sausage stew. It is one of the recipes that his grandmother made for him. Sometimes when we have friends over and Sirio wants to show off my cooking, he requests sausage and beans. And even if he is showing off, I know he is genuinely hungry for some, too.

½ pound dried cannellini (Great Northern) beans (about 1½ cups)

2 cups hot water

2 leaves fresh sage

1 clove garlic plus 2 cloves garlic, finely chopped

½ cup plus 2 tablespoons olive oil

8 Italian sausages

1 large red onion, peeled and coarsely chopped

1 bay leaf

2 tablespoons white wine

2 cups canned crushed tomatoes

Salt and pepper

2 cups Polenta (recipe follows)

In a large saucepan, combine the dried beans and hot water and bring to a boil. Boil for 2 minutes. Cover and let sit for 1 hour. Drain the beans and return to the pot.

Add the sage, whole garlic clove, and 1 tablespoon of the olive oil to the large saucepan. Cover with water and bring to a boil. Boil just until the beans are tender, 10 to 15 minutes. Drain. Discard the garlic and sage. Set the beans aside.

Puncture the sausages with a fork so that they will release their fat as they cook.

In a large pot, cook the sausages with 1 tablespoon of the olive oil over high heat until browned. Set the sausages aside. Discard the juices from the pan. Reduce the heat to medium-high. Add the onion, bay leaf, and remaining ½ cup of olive oil and cook just until the onion begins to soften. Add the chopped garlic and cook for 2 minutes. Add the wine and cook for another 2 minutes. Reduce the head to medium-low, add the tomatoes, and return the sausages to the pot.

Cover the pot and cook for about 30 minutes, checking and stirring often to prevent sticking. If the stew becomes too dry or begins to stick, add ¼ cup water. When the stew is almost ready, add the reserved beans and cook for 5 minutes. Season with salt and pepper to taste.

Serve the stew with a large spoonful of polenta.

NOTE The stew can also be made without the beans.

## Polenta

**SERVES 4 WITH PLENTY FOR LEFTOVERS**

Nonna Augusta was very fond of polenta. She would usually serve it with something stewed, especially rabbit. After she made the polenta but before it was served, she would put a towel on a big wooden board. Then she would put the polenta on top of the towel and wrap it up. The cloth would absorb the extra water in the polenta so that it was never soggy. The next day my grandmother would fry it, and I liked it even more.

1    quart water

1    teaspoon salt

1    cup yellow cornmeal

Olive oil, for leftovers

Bring the water to a boil in a large, nonstick pan. Add the salt and reduce the heat to a simmer. Add the cornmeal very gradually and stir constantly and rapidly until thoroughly incorporated. Continue simmering, stirring frequently, until the polenta comes away cleanly from the sides of the pan, 20 to 30 minutes. Remove from the heat.

Drape a large, clean kitchen towel into a large bowl. Carefully transfer the polenta to the towel in the bowl. Let sit for 5 to 10 minutes. The towel will absorb some of the water from the polenta, and it should firm up a bit. Then, using the towel, lift the polenta from the bowl, and transfer the towel and polenta to a serving tray. Serve immediately.

**NOTE** After the meal, leave any leftovers on the towel. Flip the edges of the towel on top of the remaining polenta to cover it. Put it in the refrigerator to chill and set overnight. The next day, transfer the polenta from the towel to a cutting board. Cut into ½- to ¾-inch slices. Cook the slices in approximately 1 to 2 tablespoons olive oil in a nonstick pan until it begins to turn golden. Serve immediately.

# Maccheroni al Sugo di Salsiccia

*pasta with sausage sauce*

**SERVES 4**

A true peasant dish and one that you can make very fast. Sausage is inexpensive and usually on hand. Throw in some tomatoes, garlic, and onions and you're done. In Italy we were very fond of the sausage that Sirio's uncle, Alberto, made. Once when Alberto came to visit us, my Uncle Renato took him to the races at Aqueduct. It is a beautiful track with a very pretty overhang to protect the spectators from the sun and the rain. Alberto spent a long time looking at it, even when the races were going on. Finally he turned to Renato and said, "This would be a terrific place to dry sausages."

2   tablespoons olive oil

1   large red onion, finely chopped

2   sweet Italian sausages, finely chopped

3   cloves garlic, peeled and finely chopped

2   tablespoons white wine

2   cups peeled and crushed tomatoes

Salt

Black pepper

Crushed red pepper

1   pound pasta (any chunky shape)

In a medium saucepan, heat the olive oil over medium-high heat. Add the onion and sausages and cook until the sausage meat is just cooked through, about 5 minutes. Add the garlic and cook for 2 minutes. Add the wine and cook for 2 minutes. Add the tomatoes and season with salt, black pepper, and crushed red pepper to taste. Reduce the heat to low and simmer for 30 minutes.

In a pot of boiling, salted water, cook the pasta until al dente according to the directions on the package. Drain.

Toss the pasta with the sausage sauce and serve immediately.

# Farro Pesto del Menesini

*menesini's farro with pesto*

Farro is a grain that they served a lot in Lucca, which is about twenty miles from Montecatini, but I have only started to cook with it in the past fifteen years. It tastes and looks somewhat like barley.

### Pesto

**MAKES ABOUT 2½ CUPS PESTO**

| | |
|---|---|
| 1 | cup extra-virgin olive oil |
| ½ | cup pine nuts |
| 4 | cups fresh basil leaves |
| 4 | cloves garlic |
| ¾ | cup grated Parmesan cheese |

Salt

Put all the ingredients except the salt in a blender or food processor. Mix well but do not puree—the basil leaves should be well broken up into tiny bits, and you should be able to see bits of the pine nuts. Incorporate salt to taste.

### Farro

**MAKES 2 CUPS**

| | |
|---|---|
| 1 | cup whole-grain farro (also called spelt) |
| 2 | cups water |
| ½ | cup Pesto (see recipe above) |

Soak the farro in the water for 24 hours.

Drain. Put the farro in a medium saucepan, and cover with cold water. Bring to a boil on high heat. Cover, reduce the heat, and simmer for 20 minutes. Drain, and rinse in cold water. Drain well.

Toss the farro with the pesto.

*food & wine tip*

Look for brands of farro that don't require 24 hours of soaking. Fast-cooking farro can be boiled in 20 minutes.

# The Slow Mediterranean Kitchen

## PAULA WOLFERT

### the book
*The Slow Mediterranean Kitchen: Recipes for the Passionate Cook* by Paula Wolfert (Wiley), $34.95, 350 pages, color photos.

### the gist
Mouthwatering recipes that employ slow-cooking techniques such as low-temperature roasting.

### the ideal reader
The seasoned cook who enjoys the process of cooking.

### the extras
Invaluable bits of cooking information in boxes within each chapter and in recipe introductions.

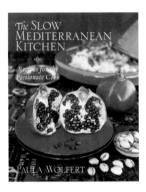

**BACKGROUND** Born in Brooklyn, New York; lives in Sonoma County, California.

**EDUCATION** Studied literature at Columbia University, in New York City.

**NUMBER OF COOKBOOKS SHE'S WRITTEN** Eight.

**NUMBER OF COOKBOOKS SHE OWNS** Around 4,000.

**FIRST FOOD MEMORIES** "During World War II, I lived on a farm in New Jersey with my grandparents, who were Serbian immigrants. We had a victory garden. Fresh food was a part of their heritage—blackberries in season, goat's milk, homemade cheese—and it became a part of mine."

**HOW SHE CAME TO WRITE ABOUT FOOD** "When I decided to get married, I approached Dione Lucas, the great New York cooking teacher, for lessons. I left college and went to work for her. That was in the day when you had to get an Mrs. degree. I discovered that I absolutely loved cooking. Then my husband and I went to Morocco and lived in Tangier for a year. I toured Yugoslavia for six months to find my relatives, then we settled in Paris, where I worked at *The Paris Review*. We went back to Morocco in 1968. Now, I thought, I'll write about Moroccan cuisine."

**MENTORS** "I met everybody—James Beard, Paula Peck, John Clancy, Gael Greene, Diana Kennedy, George Lang, Barbara Kafka. I was just this very enthusiastic person—I cared so much, I almost hyperventilated. Everybody played a role in my career. Everybody helped me for some reason; you'll have to ask them why."

**PHILOSOPHY ABOUT COOKBOOK WRITING** "When I wrote *Couscous and Other Good Food from Morocco,* in 1973, I didn't make any compromises. If you couldn't find cardoons, too bad. One day you will. And my editor allowed me to do that—I was so lucky. People go traveling abroad, taste something new and then come home and want to make it. Do they want a washed-out version? No. They want the real thing."

**CULINARY GOLDEN RULE** "With real estate, it's location, location, location. With food, it's ingredients, ingredients, ingredients."

THE APPEAL OF THE MEDITERRANEAN "I always stayed with the Mediterranean because I realized it was a bottomless pit. I even extended the area to include Soviet Georgia! I've covered greens and grains, and now I'm writing about slow cooking because it's such an inherent part of Mediterranean cuisine. By looking with a fresh eye at the same portrait, I see something new. My work is a continuum."

RAISON D'ÊTRE FOR THIS COOKBOOK "Slow cooking is simply cooking food at a lower temperature for a longer period of time. But wow, everything comes together when you do it—ingredients are transformed in a subtle way. Warm spices and herbs flavor the food. Incredible smells emanate from the pot. The process is an amazing alchemy."

BEST TIME TO SLOW COOK "You don't want to be doing this if you're coming home from work at 5:30 P.M.—then you want a fast sauté. But for weekend cooking or whenever you have more time, this method is superb."

**FAVORITE COOKWARE** Clay pots. "I'm intrigued by the relationship between the potter and the cook. The shape of a pot has meaning and purpose. You know, a bean pot has shoulders to keep in the moisture as the beans cook."

BEST USE FOR THE CROCK-POT "Certain kinds of slow cooking can be done in the Crock-Pot. For example, it's perfect for making stock. Or for cooking onions overnight to make them wonderfully caramelized."

FAVORITE CAUSE The Slow Food Movement, an international campaign launched in Turin, Italy, that aims to preserve and protect the artisanal methods of food production. "I'm fighting homogenization and globalization. Regionalism is such a strong aspect of Mediterranean life—I love the diverse traditional ways of cooking. I'm not a big fan of fusion cooking, for instance. I'm definitely a traditionalist."

UNDERAPPRECIATED INGREDIENT Molokhiya, a leafy green from Egypt. "The viscous texture is similar to that of okra—people love it or hate it. Three times I've tried to get a stew recipe using molokhiya into my book and three times it's been nixed by editors who say they can't stand it. Something about its gooey quality."

MOST SUCCESSFUL RECIPE The *canelés de Bordeaux*, cakes with a rich, custardy interior and a thin, burnt sugar shell. "I stopped everything for three months to work on that recipe. I'm not a professional baker—I consider that a triumph."

# Slow-Cooked Duck with Olives

**SERVES 4**

1 duckling (5 to 6 pounds), fresh or thawed

2 medium onions, coarsely chopped

1 large celery rib, sliced

8 garlic cloves, halved

1½ tablespoons chopped fresh thyme

¼ cup plus 2 teaspoons coarsely chopped flat-leaf parsley

2 bay leaves

2 teaspoons sea salt

1 teaspoon freshly ground pepper

1 teaspoon herbes de Provence

Green Olive Sauce (recipe follows)

Steps 1 through 3 can be done early in the day or the day before.

1. Preheat the oven to 475°F. Halve the duckling, setting aside the back, neck, and wing tips for the sauce. In a 9-by-11-inch roasting pan, make a bed of the onions, celery, garlic, thyme, ¼ cup of the parsley, and the bay leaves. With the tines of a fork, prick the duck skin every ½ inch. Rub the duck with a combination of the salt, pepper, and herbes de Provence and set it on top of the vegetables, skin side up. Roast, uncovered, for 10 minutes.

2. Reduce the oven temperature to 275°F, cover the contents of the pan with foil, and leave the duckling to cook for about 3½ hours, or until it is very tender. Turn off the heat and let the duckling cool in the flavored fat in the oven for 30 minutes.

3. Carefully transfer the duck to a work surface. Remove and discard any loose bones, chopped vegetables, and clumps of fat. Reserve 1 teaspoon of the fat for Step 5. (Reserve the remaining fat for another use.) Quarter the duck; gently squeeze or press each portion to maintain its shape, and wrap

## on wolfert's nightstand

**Elizabeth David** and **Richard Olney** are two of my favorite cookbook authors. And **Diana Kennedy**. I read my friends' books, too: **Faith Willinger, Molly O'Neill, Alice Waters, Aglaia Kremezi.** I don't read chefs' books very much, except for **Thomas Keller's** *The French Laundry Cookbook,* which I think is brilliant. I also love **Judy Rodgers's** *The Zuni Café Cookbook.* That's a great book—my favorite in the last couple of years.

*food & wine* **tip**

———————————

This is an excellent
recipe for entertaining,
since the duck is
actually better when it's
made in advance.
All it needs is some
quick reheating.

individually in foil or plastic wrap to prevent drying out. Set aside in a cool place or in the refrigerator.

**4.** About 30 minutes before serving, unwrap the duck quarters and generously season the flesh side with salt, pepper, and more herbes de Provence.

**5.** About 10 minutes before serving, preheat the broiler and set the rack about 10 inches from the heat source. Dab the duck skin with a little duck fat and run under the broiler to reheat the duck and crisp the skin.

**6.** Pour the sauce with the olives into a shallow, warm serving dish, place the duck on top, sprinkle with the remaining parsley, and serve at once.

NOTE Be sure your oven is calibrated. If the duck is baked at a higher temperature it will overcook and will taste reheated.

## Green Olive Sauce

**MAKES ABOUT 2½ CUPS**

Neck, back, and wing tips of the duck

1   medium onion, sliced

1   tablespoon tomato paste

½   cup dry white wine

Pinch of sugar

1   cup poultry stock

1½  cups (7 to 8 ounces
    drained weight) green olives,
    rinsed and pitted

¼   teaspoon herbes de Provence

Salt and freshly ground pepper

1. Slowly brown the duck neck, back, and wing tips in their own fat in a covered nonstick skillet. Add the onion and continue cooking until the onions are glazed and browned, about 10 minutes. Pour off any excess fat.

2. Add the tomato paste to the skillet and cook until lightly charred. Quickly deglaze the pan with the white wine. Add the sugar, stock, and 3 cups water. Bring to a boil, reduce the heat, and simmer for 1 hour; then strain, degrease, and boil until reduced to 1 cup. Reserve, covered, in the refrigerator.

3. About 10 minutes before serving, reheat the sauce, add the olives, and simmer for 10 minutes. Correct the seasoning with salt and pepper, and herbes de Provence to taste.

# Spicy Mussels with Herbs and Feta Cheese

**SERVES 4 TO 6**

This dish certainly isn't slow in the traditional sense if you prepare it the way they do in Thrace—quickly in a skillet with hot peppers, garlic, and butter. It is this last ingredient that "only a wacky Thracian" would add. And it is possible to take a slow approach with excellent results.

In this adapted recipe, a variation on the famous Macedonian mussels *saganaki*, the mussels are partially prepared in the morning not merely to remove the sand, shells, and beards but also to infuse the mussels with a Thracian herb and spice mixture. When it's time to serve, simply reheat the mussels and mount their juices with butter.

Try to serve with glasses of ouzo and thin slices of toasted baguette sticking out of the broth, useful for soaking up the spicy juices.

| | |
|---|---|
| 3 | pounds small mussels |

Sea salt

| | |
|---|---|
| 4 | tablespoons unsalted butter |
| 1 | cinnamon stick, 2 inches long |
| ⅔ | cup dry white wine |
| 1 | teaspoon freshly ground black pepper |

Juice of ½ lemon

| | |
|---|---|
| ¼ | cup slivered fresh basil |
| ¼ | cup chopped flat-leaf parsley |
| 1 | long dried red chile pepper, about 3 inches long |
| 2 | teaspoons tomato paste |
| 2 | teaspoons chopped garlic |
| 3 | ounces cow's milk feta |

Salt

Garlic toasts

1. Scrub the mussels, pull off the beards, and rinse in several changes of water. Place the mussels in a bowl of lightly salted cool water and let stand for at least 1 hour so they purge themselves of sand. (Farmed mussels do not need soaking; if soaked, they lose all their flavor.) Drain the mussels.

2. Heat a large nonreactive shallow pan until hot, add 1 tablespoon of the butter, and allow to sizzle. Add the cinnamon stick, mussels, and wine all at once, cover, and cook over high heat until the mussels open, about 2 minutes. If the shells are just beginning to open, leave them 1 minute longer, but do not overcook. Transfer the mussels to a bowl in order to catch their juices. Strain the cooking liquid through a fine sieve and reserve. Discard the cinnamon stick. Shell the mussels and season them with the black pepper and the lemon juice.

3. Wipe out the pan, add another tablespoon of the butter, and set over medium heat. Add half the basil, half the parsley, and the chile pepper and cook for 1 minute, stirring. Add the tomato paste, reserved mussel cooking liquid, and garlic; quickly bring to a boil. Cook over medium heat for 2 minutes, or until the liquid has reduced to about 1 cup. Remove from the heat, add the mussels, and set aside to cool. If making in advance, cool, cover, and refrigerate.

4. About 30 minutes before serving, bring the mussels to room temperature if prepared in advance. If the feta is very salty, soak it in cold water to remove excess salt. Drain the feta and cut into small slices. Dice the remaining 2 tablespoons butter. Scatter the feta and butter over the mussels. Slowly cook until almost boiling. Swirl to allow the butter and cheese to thicken the sauce. Correct the seasoning of the sauce with salt, pepper, and lemon. Garnish with the remaining basil and parsley and serve at once with the garlic toasts.

# Glazed Carrots with Green Olives

**SERVES 4**

1   pound large organic carrots

2   tablespoons butter or olive oil

3   ounces picholine olives (about 24)

1   large garlic clove, sliced

1   tablespoon chopped flat-leaf parsley

2   sprigs of thyme

Salt and freshly ground pepper

3   tablespoons heavy cream

**1.** Peel the carrots, cut in half crosswise, quarter the thicker ends lengthwise, and halve the thinner ends. Place in an electric slow-cooker or a heavy skillet wide enough to hold the carrots in one layer.

**2.** Add half the butter, cover the slow-cooker, set the heat to high, and cook, stirring once, for 2 to 3 hours, or until very tender. If substituting a skillet on top of the stove, set on a heat diffuser over very low heat. Add a few tablespoons water, cover with a round of parchment paper and a tight-fitting lid, and cook until very tender, about 1 hour.

**3.** Drain the carrots on paper towels and let rest. Meanwhile, pit the olives by gently tapping each one with a wooden mallet, halve, remove the pit, rinse, and drain.

**4.** About 10 minutes before serving, melt the remaining butter in a medium skillet over moderate heat. Add the garlic and parsley and cook, stirring, for 1 minute. Add the carrots, thyme, olives, and salt and pepper. Cook, stirring, until glazed. Pour in the cream, cover, and reduce the heat to low. Cook for 5 minutes and serve.

# The Tante Marie's Cooking School Cookbook

MARY RISLEY

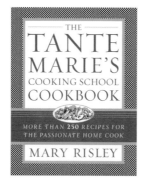

**BACKGROUND** Born in Waterbury, Connecticut; lives in San Francisco.

**EDUCATION** "I was raised to get married, but instead I went to secretarial school in Boston and worked in an office for eight years. Though I imagine I'm not alone in having spent a lot of that time trying to figure out how *not* to work in an office. I taught myself how to cook by reading Julia Child's *Mastering the Art of French Cooking,* and I saved enough money to take a short course at Le Cordon Bleu in London. I also took classes at La Varenne in France and with Lorenza de' Medici in Italy."

**EXPERIENCE** "I started teaching cooking classes at home in San Francisco in 1973, and after six years I launched Tante Marie, which I've owned for over 15 years."

**HOW SHE CAME TO LOVE FOOD** "My dad was a great eater and always took us to the finest restaurants. My mom was a great provider: I grew up eating smoked salmon and steamed artichokes in the 1950s, when no one was eating stuff like that. When I was nine I started pasting recipes from magazines such as *Family Circle* in scrapbooks. I also pasted in pictures of chickens and tea cups from *The New Yorker*."

**MENTORS** Jacques Pépin and Madeleine Kamman. "From Jacques I learned a lot about the classics and embellishing. He loves to decorate and will carve a mushroom for 45 minutes. From Madeleine I learned all about sauces, such as how to correct them when you've done something wrong."

**WHY SHE WROTE THE BOOK** "A lot of cookbooks are simply recipe collections that teach you how to follow specific recipes. I wanted to write a book that would teach people how to cook *without* recipes—because no recipe will tell you how much juice is going to come out of a pork roast, or how much salt to use for a ratatouille, or how to deglaze a pan with white wine. The goal is to get people to cook with confidence and ease. I wanted my book to be a real teaching tool."

**COOK'S TIP** "Don't beat your egg whites for a soufflé before your oven is ready."

**BIGGEST FEAR SHE OVERCAME TO WRITE THE COOKBOOK** "For so long I was scared to write it at all because I never went to college. I just went to secretarial school, and was even a bad typist, to boot."

**HOW SHE DEVELOPED HER RECIPES** "Half were developed with the teachers at Tante Marie and the others came from my travels and eating experiences. I've been to restaurants all over, and whenever I liked a dish, I'd write down what I thought went into it and then credit the chef."

**RECIPES THAT MADE THE CUT** "Those that I thought readers could learn the most from. I tried to include everything a good cook should know. If you cook your way through the book, you will learn every technique that a good cook knows."

**IDEAL COAUTHOR** Placido Domingo. "I love opera and have always wanted to write about food and opera. Also, we were born in the same year, 1941."

**RECIPES THAT DIDN'T MAKE THE CUT** "I only put in recipes I'd make at home, so I skipped pâtés and croissants, though we teach them at the school."

**DEFINITION OF A GOOD CHEF** "A good chef is someone who takes a good dish and proceeds to make it infinitely better."

**MOST COMMON COOKING MISTAKES** "Beginning cooks stir too much—I think out of nervousness—and over too low a heat. My advice is to just let the food cook. Don't push it around. Stirring meat that you're trying to brown will only steam the food, which turns it gray. You won't have a nice crust and you won't get good caramelized meat juices. Beginners should also stop opening the oven to check on a roast because each time you do that the oven temperature can drop by 50 degrees. They should also stop being so strict about measuring. It doesn't matter if you put in an extra two or three teaspoons of butter, or are a little off with the amount of wine or salt you're supposed to add."

**COOKBOOK TRENDS** "I've seen a lot of dessert books out there, as well as some really nice books from people in the wine country. Puzzlingly, there are expensive cookbooks that don't have any recipes, like Pierre Gagnaire's book. It has lots of beautiful pictures of pitted plums and juicy blueberries with sugar crystals, and there's a saying under each picture. It's more philosophy than cookbook."

# White Bean Crostini with Wilted Greens

SERVES 8

Every once in a while it is a good idea to eat something really good for you, and this is it; a healthful hors d'oeuvre that is delicious too: Little toasts with a light coating of olive oil, spread with white bean puree and covered with cooked winter greens, go perfectly with a glass of chilled white wine.

½  onion, chopped

4  tablespoons extra-virgin olive oil

Coarse salt

2  garlic cloves, minced

1  cup cooked white beans, such as cannellini or Great Northern

¼  cup chicken or vegetable stock

1  tablespoon tomato paste

Cayenne pepper

½  teaspoon finely chopped fresh rosemary

Freshly ground black pepper

1  baguette

½  pound Red Russian kale or other mild winter green, washed but not dried, stemmed, and cut in 1-inch lengths

To make the bean puree, cook the onion with 2 tablespoons olive oil and ½ teaspoon salt in a medium-size saucepan over medium-high heat, stirring constantly, until the onion is soft, about 5 minutes. Add half the garlic and cook for a minute longer. Add the cooked beans, chicken stock, tomato paste, a few grains of cayenne, and rosemary and cook over medium-low heat until most of the liquid has evaporated. Remove from the heat and mash with a potato masher in the pot. Add salt and pepper to taste.

To toast the bread, slice it as thin as possible and lay in one layer on a baking sheet. Broil until golden on both sides, watching carefully so that the pieces don't burn. Remove from the oven but leave the toasts on the pan.

To cook the greens, put 2 tablespoons olive oil and the remaining garlic with a sprinkling of salt in a medium-size sauté pan and cook over medium-high heat. When the garlic is soft, add the greens, cover, and cook for a minute. Remove the cover and turn the greens over on themselves with wooden spoons until they are wilted. Turn off the heat.

To assemble, spread a teaspoonful of the bean puree on each toast, top with a little of the wilted greens, and serve. (The toasts, bean puree, and wilted greens can all be made ahead. They should be reheated slightly before serving.)

NOTES When cooking dried beans or legumes, always sort through them carefully and discard any small rocks you find. To do this, put the beans on a baking sheet and go over them systematically. To cook dried beans, soak the beans overnight in plenty of cold water. The next day, cook the beans, covered in fresh water with half an onion and a dried red chile pepper, until the beans are tender. This may take anywhere from 30 minutes to 1½ hours, depending on the age of the beans. Drain and proceed with the recipe.

Alternatively, the quick-soak method for cooking dried beans is to put the beans in a heavy pot, cover generously with water, bring to a boil, turn off the heat, cover, and let sit for an hour. Drain the beans, return them to the pan, and proceed as above, cooking them with half an onion, a dried red chile pepper, and plenty of fresh water until they are tender. This may take anywhere from 30 minutes to 1½ hours, depending on the age of the beans. Drain and proceed with the recipe.

If using canned beans, place the beans in a sieve and rinse well to remove the canned taste.

## on risley's nightstand

My two current favorite books are **Georgeanne Brennan's** *Potager: Fresh Garden Cooking in the French Style* and **Jacques Pépin's** *A French Chef Cooks at Home.*

# Penne with Roasted Eggplant, Tomatoes, and Smoked Mozzarella

**SERVES 6 AS A FIRST COURSE OR 4 AS A MAIN COURSE**

This is a simple, easy to prepare dish that's best served before grilled chicken or meat or as a vegetarian main course with good cheese and a green salad. Think eggplant or mushrooms when preparing a vegetarian meal, because both have the texture of meat and adapt well to a variety of dishes.

5    tablespoons olive oil

4    Asian or 1 large eggplant, trimmed but unpeeled, and cut into ½-inch cubes

Coarse salt

Freshly ground black pepper

1    large red onion, chopped

2    garlic cloves, minced

⅛    teaspoon red pepper flakes

6    red, ripe tomatoes, peeled, seeded, and chopped, or one 28-ounce can Italian plum tomatoes, coarsely chopped

1    tablespoon tomato paste

1    pound dried penne or other short tubular pasta

4    ounces smoked mozzarella, cut in ¼-inch cubes

1    cup freshly grated Parmesan

3    tablespoons minced fresh Italian parsley

To cook the eggplant, heat 3 tablespoons of the olive oil in a medium-size sauté pan until very hot. Toss in the eggplant and season generously with salt and pepper. Cook, while stirring over very high heat, until the eggplant looks lightly colored and slightly crispy, about 10 minutes.

To make the sauce, put the onion with another 2 tablespoons of the olive oil and ½ teaspoon salt in a medium-size sauté or frying pan over medium-high heat. Cook, stirring from time to time, until the onion is soft, about 5 minutes. Stir in the garlic and red pepper flakes and cook another minute. Add the tomatoes and tomato paste and continue cooking for 5 minutes to meld the flavors. Stir in the eggplant. Add salt and pepper to taste. (The eggplant sauce can be made ahead and kept in the refrigerator for up to a week.)

To cook the pasta, fill a pasta pot or other large pot with water and bring to a boil over high heat. Add a tablespoon of salt and stir in the pasta. Cook, stirring from time to time, until the pasta is al dente; in other words, until the pasta is cooked through but is still firm when tasted, about 8 minutes.

While the pasta is cooking, gently reheat the sauce, stirring. Drain most of the cooking liquid from the pasta and return the pasta to the pot with the heat turned off. Quickly toss in the pasta with the sauce, smoked mozzarella, half the Parmesan, and the parsley. Add salt and pepper to taste. Serve immediately on warmed plates sprinkled with the remaining Parmesan.

NOTE To cut the eggplant, trim both ends, cut the eggplant lengthwise into ½-inch-wide slices, stack the slices on a board or counter, and cut into ½-inch-wide strips. Turn these and cut in the opposite direction. This is called dicing.

*food & wine tip*

Save some of the cooking water when you drain the pasta. You might want to add some to the sauce to thin it slightly when you toss it with the pasta.

# Roasted Whole Fish with Brown Butter Vinaigrette

**SERVES 2**

Traci Des Jardins, the brilliant chef of Jardinière in San Francisco, taught the students of Tante Marie's how to make this brown butter vinaigrette. The trick is to make it at the last moment. Try this sauce on poached eggs or sautéed chicken breasts as well as fish. This fish would go well with roasted new potatoes.

Two 1-pound whole fish, such as trout

6    tablespoons olive oil

Coarse salt

Freshly ground black pepper

4    tablespoons (½ stick) butter

2    tablespoons good-quality balsamic vinegar

3    tablespoons capers, rinsed

4    scallions, equal parts white and green, thinly sliced at an angle

2    tablespoons minced fresh Italian parsley

To roast the fish, remove any fins from the fish with scissors and rub the fish generously with 4 tablespoons of the olive oil. Season the fish well with salt and pepper. Place the fish in a small roasting pan and roast on the bottom rack of a 450-degree oven until it's firm to the touch or flakes easily when prodded with a fork, 10 to 15 minutes.

To make the vinaigrette, put the butter in a small saucepan over moderately high heat. The butter will melt and then begin to brown. When it is a deep chestnut color, remove the pan from the heat and let stand for a minute. Stir in the vinegar, capers, and scallions with the remaining 2 tablespoons of olive oil. Immediately pour the sauce over the fish, sprinkle with minced parsley, and serve.

NOTES When cooking whole fish, make sure there is absolutely no blood down the inside of the backbone because it turns very bitter when cooked. The blood must be washed out with running water prior to cooking.

To eat a whole trout, cut down the center of one side of the fish from the gills to the tail. With the knife or fork, pull the fish away above the cut from the bones. Do the same with the flesh below the cut. The exposed frame of the fish can then be lifted, again with the knife and the fork, from the tail to the head and put on a plate to be discarded. This is how waiters used to serve whole fish at tableside in fancy restaurants in the old days.

*food & wine tip*

Use a nonstick roasting pan for the fish because it has a tendency to stick. Failing that, just fillet your fish right in the pan instead of serving it whole.

# Roast Chicken with Spring Vegetables and Butter Sauce

**SERVES 4**

*food & wine tip*

If you're pressed for time, don't use carrots that require trimming. Instead, opt for the small carrots sold in plastic bags or real baby carrots from a specialty market.

Thank goodness butter is making a comeback! Don't be alarmed by the amount of butter in this dish. As with beurre blanc for fish, you are not going to eat it all. It makes food taste so good, especially the sauce for this chicken.

One 4-pound chicken

Coarse salt

Freshly ground black pepper

1 pound small carrots, peeled and cut into 1½-by-½-inch pieces, trimmed to look like baby carrots

1 pound small white turnips, cut into 1½-by-½-inch wedges

1 pound small green beans, trimmed

½ cup dry white wine

¾ pound (3 sticks) butter, between refrigerator and room temperature, cut into 16 pieces

To cook the chicken, sprinkle it generously inside and out with salt and pepper, place it in a roasting pan in a 475-degree oven, and let it roast until it is well browned, about 1 hour. You can baste the chicken once or twice toward the end of the cooking time by removing the pan from the oven, closing the door to the oven, filling a bulb baster with the juices from the bottom of the pan, and squirting the juices on parts of the chicken that need to brown before returning it quickly to the oven.

To cook the vegetables, bring a large pot of water to a boil. Drop the carrots into the water with ½ teaspoon salt and boil until they are tender when pierced with a fork. Remove them with a slotted spoon to a strainer and run them under cold water until chilled. Do the same with the turnips and then the green beans.

When the chicken is nicely browned, the juices in the thick part of the thigh run clear when pierced with a knife, and the skin has started to shrink from the legs, remove the chicken from the pan and let it rest for 10 minutes. Let the chicken juices cool as well.

To make the sauce, pour off any fat that rises to the top of the chicken juices. Place the roasting pan over high heat and pour in the wine, scraping the brown bits on the bottom of the pan. This is called deglazing. Boil vigorously for 2 to 3 minutes. Strain the juices into a small saucepan and heat over moderately high heat. When the chicken juices are reduced to 3 tablespoons, remove the saucepan from the heat and whisk in two pieces of the butter. When the mixture appears creamy, return it to a low heat and start whisking in one piece of butter at a time. As one disappears, add the next. It is best not to watch the mixture while you're whisking or you will slow down. If the mixture bubbles around the edges of the pan, remove the pan from the heat and let the heat of the pan cook the sauce. When all the butter has been incorporated, remove the saucepan from the heat and add salt and pepper to taste. Cover with a pot lid.

When ready to serve, reheat the vegetables briefly by putting them in a wide frying pan with a tablespoon of butter and shaking them over a high flame for a couple of minutes. Cut the chicken into 4 or 8 pieces and place them on a warmed serving platter surrounded by the vegetables. Spoon some of the sauce over each piece of chicken and serve the remaining sauce separately in a warmed sauceboat.

NOTE This is really a beurre blanc type of sauce made with chicken juices. It will keep warm for up to an hour. Some cooks store it in a Thermos for up to 4 hours.

# Tom's Big Dinners

**TOM DOUGLAS WITH ED LEVINE, SHELLEY LANCE AND JACKIE CROSS** INTERVIEW BELOW WITH TOM DOUGLAS

## the book

*Tom's Big Dinners: Big-Time Home Cooking for Family and Friends* by Tom Douglas with Ed Levine, Shelley Lance and Jackie Cross (Morrow), $32.50, 278 pages, color photos.

## the gist

More than a dozen festive and delicious menus, from a Puget Sound crab feast to a Chinese extravaganza.

## the ideal reader

The cook who loves to entertain large groups of friends and family.

## the extras

Detailed wine pairings and cocktail recipes to match each menu.

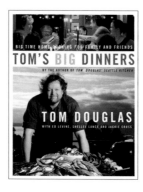

**BACKGROUND** Born in Cleveland; grew up in Newark, Delaware; lives in Seattle.

**EDUCATION** "I was never formally trained as a chef. I had two helluva good grandma cooks; plus my mother, who raised eight children, was a great cook. When I was young I would make my parents breakfast in bed on Saturday mornings. Later I realized that they really wanted to be making love—my dad was a traveling salesman who was on the road Monday to Friday. In high school I took home economics courses and worked as a cook at the Hotel du Pont in Wilmington."

**EXPERIENCE** "I was driving around the country when I was 19 and happened to run out of cash in Seattle, so I settled here. I got a job working in a kitchen, but I also built houses, sold wine and cut steel on the railroads. Eventually, I lost one job and couldn't get another, so I borrowed 50 grand and in 1989 my wife and I opened Dahlia Lounge. Etta's Seafood, Palace Kitchen and the Dahlia Bakery followed. Now we also have a catering company."

**WHY HE WROTE THE BOOK** "We heard that people were getting together and having what they called 'Tom Douglas Big Dinners,' inviting five couples who would make a dish from my first book, *Tom Douglas' Seattle Kitchen*. So *Tom's Big Dinners* came next, focusing on simple menus for a home setting, with do-ahead ideas and tips, rather than recipes from the restaurant."

**MENU INSPIRATIONS** "The Chinatown menu is based on recipes we always made at home, like shrimp rolls and ribs. We created Grandpa Louie's Dream Greek Vacation for my wife's grandfather Louie. His wife was not too enamored of his Greek heritage, so Louie never had the chance to revisit his homeland before he died. Louie's menu includes dishes that he would have eaten on a trip back to Greece."

**TOP TIMESAVER** "Be sure to read a recipe all the way through before you cook. The time it saves you in the long run is invaluable."

**COCKTAIL INSPIRATIONS** "Most of the themed cocktails, like the Santorini-tinis, were invented for the book. But the Bianco is something we make at home every summer, putting herbs like rosemary, lemon balm and lemon zest in white wine and letting the drink sit for three hours."

**HOW TO USE THE COOKBOOK** "Don't get bogged down in a menu. If you're having a cocktail party, select appetizers from different chapters."

**FAVORITE BIG DINNER** "There's something majestic about a 30-pound Chinook salmon roasted and served whole—people get excited when you present it with the head and tail on. It has beautifully browned skin and extraordinary bright red flesh when you cut into it."

**HOW TO PLAN A BIG MEAL** "Think like a chef: Prepare everything you can in advance like a short-order cook does. Then you can just reheat food rather than do all the cooking at the last minute."

**HOW NOT TO GET STUCK IN THE KITCHEN WHEN GUESTS COME** "Have them help with the cooking. If you're having 10 people over for dinner, everyone will say, 'What can I bring?' and if you say, 'I can manage' or 'Just some wine,' then you're stuck preparing 10, 20, 30 plates of food."

**ESSENTIAL INGREDIENTS** Ginger, lemons, soy sauce. "Fish from a good fishmonger is absolutely essential, too."

**MOST UNDERAPPRECIATED INGREDIENT** Pork butt. "It's underutilized and it's cheap: The other day I saw it in an expensive store for 99 cents a pound."

**ESSENTIAL EQUIPMENT** A bamboo steamer. "They're only about 10 dollars and they make beautiful servers as well. At home we use one for everything, not just Chinese dishes. Sometimes we'll buy fresh tamales and steam them in it."

**BEST WAY TO SERVE A BIG GROUP** "I won't put out just one bowl of mashed potatoes. I'll have two smaller bowls at either end of the table. It's much simpler, and because people aren't waiting for food to be passed, they're eating hotter food."

**FAVORITE PLACE TO EAT OUT WITH A BIG GROUP** Seattle's Sea Garden, a Chinese seafood place. "I love the round tables with lazy Susans in the middle."

**COOKBOOK TREND**

"Every chef is writing a book. It's a chef-y thing, having the insatiable ego to imagine people can't live without us."

# Mac and Cheese Salad with Buttermilk Dressing

**6 SERVINGS**

My take on mac and cheese is a chilled pasta salad with creamy buttermilk dressing and ricotta salata. In the spring, toss in some blanched and sliced asparagus or blanched fresh peas. The buttermilk dressing would also be tasty on a salad of poached shrimp, cucumbers, and Bibb lettuce or mixed into a bowl of steamed and chilled baby red potatoes.

For the buttermilk dressing

½ cup mayonnaise, homemade (recipe follows), or good-quality store-bought

½ cup sour cream

½ cup buttermilk

1 tablespoon chopped fresh dill

¼ cup thinly sliced fresh chives

2 teaspoons minced garlic

2 teaspoons minced shallot

2 teaspoons freshly squeezed lemon juice

Kosher salt and freshly ground black pepper

For the salad

1 pound shaped pasta such as fusilli, farfalle, or cavatappi

¼ cup thinly sliced scallion

3 ounces ricotta salata, grated (about ¾ cup)

5 cups loosely packed mâche or baby spinach leaves

**douglas on ricotta salata**

Ricotta salata is a slightly tangy Italian sheep's milk cheese. Grate it on the finest holes of a box grater. If you can't find ricotta salata, substitute pecorino, another Italian sheep's milk cheese.

A STEP AHEAD Cook the pasta a few hours ahead, run cold water over it, and drain. Spread the pasta in a single layer over a lightly oiled baking sheet. Cover the pasta with plastic wrap and refrigerate. Make the dressing early in the day, but toss the pasta salad with the dressing only when you are ready to serve.

To make the buttermilk dressing, whisk together the mayonnaise, sour cream, and buttermilk in a bowl. Add the dill, chives, garlic, shallot, and lemon juice and whisk again. Season to taste with salt and pepper.

Mâche, sometimes
called corn salad or
lamb's lettuce, has small
dark green leaves
with a mild nutty flavor.
Tender young pea
sprouts would also be
nice here. Baby spinach
or small arugula leaves
will do the trick, too.

Bring a large pot of salted water to a boil, add the pasta, and cook until al dente. Drain the pasta and immediately run under cold water until it is completely cool. Drain well.

Put the pasta in a large bowl and, using a rubber spatula, fold in enough dressing to coat it generously. Fold in the scallion, cheese, and mâche. Mound the salad on a large platter and serve.

## Mayonnaise

MAKES ¾ CUP

2   large egg yolks

1   teaspoon freshly squeezed
    lemon juice

1   teaspoon Dijon mustard

⅔   cup vegetable oil, pure olive oil,
    or a mixture

Kosher salt and freshly ground
    black pepper

A STEP AHEAD Store mayonnaise in the refrigerator, covered, and use it the same day it is made.

Put the yolks, lemon juice, and mustard in the bowl of a food processor. Gradually pour in the oil with the machine running and process until emulsified. Season to taste with salt and pepper.

NOTE It's important to be aware of the potential dangers of salmonella and other harmful bacteria and take precautions. Use very fresh grade A or grade AA eggs (check the expiration date on the carton before buying) and always keep your eggs refrigerated. Don't keep eggs at room temperature for more than an hour, and always wash your hands, work surface, and equipment thoroughly before and after using raw eggs. Use products that have been made with raw eggs within one day.

# Crispy Shrimp Rolls with Sweet Chile Sauce

**MAKES ABOUT 18 SMALL SPRING ROLLS, SERVING 6 TO 8**

Make and freeze these shrimp-stuffed fried spring rolls well ahead, but don't fry them until your guests arrive.

Keep the spring roll wrappers covered with a damp kitchen towel as you work to prevent them from drying out. If your wrappers are bigger than 6 inches square, you can cut them down to size, using a ruler and a sharp knife to cut through the entire (unwrapped) stack at once.

| | |
|---|---|
| 1 | pound raw shrimp, peeled and deveined |
| 2 | tablespoons finely chopped fresh cilantro |
| 2 | tablespoons finely chopped scallion, both white and green parts |
| 1 | tablespoon Chinese chile garlic sauce |
| 1 | tablespoon toasted sesame seeds |
| 2 | teaspoons peeled and grated fresh ginger |
| 1 | teaspoon minced garlic |
| ¾ | teaspoon kosher salt |
| 1 | large egg |

18 to 20 spring roll wrappers, 6 inches square

Cornstarch for dusting

Peanut or vegetable oil for frying

Sweet Chile Sauce (recipe follows)

**A STEP AHEAD** Form the spring rolls up to 4 hours ahead. Line them up, without touching each other, on a wax paper–lined baking sheet dusted lightly with cornstarch, cover them with plastic wrap, and keep them refrigerated. Or form them up to a few weeks ahead and freeze them. Line them up on baking sheets as described and place them, uncovered, in the freezer. When they are frozen solid, remove them from the baking sheet, seal in a plastic bag, and store in the freezer. Fry the spring rolls when you are ready to

## on douglas's nightstand

*Chez Panisse Menu Cookbook* by **Alice Waters,** *China Moon Cookbook* by **Barbara Tropp,** *The Zuni Café Cookbook* by **Judy Rodgers,** *La Technique* by **Jacques Pépin,** *The Cake Bible* by **Rose Levy Beranbaum, Edna Lewis** and **Scott Peacock's** *The Gift of Southern Cooking,* **Julee Rosso** and **Sheila Lukins's** *The Silver Palate Cookbook, Joy of Cooking* and *Blue Trout and Black Truffles* by **Joseph Wechsberg,** a 1950s *New Yorker* writer.

serve them. If they are frozen, fry them directly from the freezer, without thawing them. Frozen spring rolls will take about 5 minutes to fry.

Place the shrimp in the bowl of a food processor and process by pulsing a few times until very coarsely pureed. There should still be some chunks of shrimp. If the shrimp is wet, it is important to squeeze out as much liquid as possible before pureeing. In a bowl, combine the shrimp, cilantro, scallion, chile garlic sauce, sesame seeds, ginger, garlic, and salt. Mix thoroughly.

To make an egg wash, beat the egg with 1 teaspoon water. Set aside.

Place a spring roll wrapper diagonally on your work surface. Place about 1 tablespoon of filling, formed into a 3½-inch log, slightly below the center of the wrapper, leaving a 1-inch border without filling on either side of the log. Use a pastry brush to paint the two upper sides of the wrapper with egg wash. Pull the bottom point of the wrapper up over the filling, roll once, then fold in the sides, continue rolling, and seal. Repeat this procedure with the remaining wrappers and filling. Place the finished spring rolls, without touching each other, on a baking sheet lined with wax paper dusted lightly with cornstarch. Cover the spring rolls with plastic wrap as you are working so they don't dry out.

Preheat the oven to 200°F. Fill a straight-sided pot with at least 1½ inches of oil and heat to 350°F, checking with a frying thermometer. Fry the spring rolls in small batches until golden, about 3 minutes, rolling them over occasionally with a skimmer or slotted spoon so they brown evenly. Remove them from the oil and drain on paper towels. Keep the spring rolls warm in the oven until all are fried.

Pile the spring rolls on a platter and serve hot with small ramekins of Sweet Chile Sauce.

## Sweet Chile Sauce

**MAKES 1 CUP**

A red jalapeño is the ripe version of a green jalapeño pepper. We like the red color here, but if you can find only a green jalapeño, use it instead. Wash your hands immediately after working with hot chile peppers or wear rubber or disposable gloves. Be especially careful not to touch your eyes after handling hot chiles.

Sambal oelek is an Indonesian condiment of ground fresh chiles.

½  cup sugar

¼  cup freshly squeezed lime juice

3  tablespoons peeled, seeded, and finely diced cucumber

1  tablespoon plus 1 teaspoon seeded and minced red jalapeño pepper

1½ teaspoons sambal oelek

Kosher salt

**A STEP AHEAD** Make the sauce up to 1 day ahead and keep it covered and refrigerated, but don't add the cucumber until right before you plan to serve it.

Combine the sugar and ½ cup water in a small saucepan over high heat. Bring to a boil and cook, stirring, until the sugar is dissolved. Remove from the heat, pour into a small bowl, and cool. Stir in the lime juice, cucumber, jalapeño, and sambal oelek and season to taste with salt.

# Spring Chickens with Green Marinade

MAKES 6 TO 8 SERVINGS

2    chickens (about 3½ pounds each), cut into 8 pieces each
     (2 breasts, 2 legs, 2 thighs, and 2 wings), or 16 pieces total

For the green marinade

1    cup chopped scallion, white and green parts

½    cup chopped fresh flat-leaf parsley

½    cup sliced fresh chives

¼    cup chopped fresh tarragon

3    tablespoons chopped fresh rosemary

3    tablespoons chopped fresh marjoram

2    tablespoons chopped fresh thyme

2    tablespoons chopped garlic

1    tablespoon freshly grated lemon zest

2    teaspoons kosher salt

1    teaspoon freshly ground black pepper

¾    cup extra virgin olive oil


About ¼ cup olive oil, as needed, for browning the chicken

1    lemon, cut in half


A STEP AHEAD Make the marinade and marinate the chicken a day ahead.

Trim excess fat from the chicken pieces. Rinse them under cold running water, pat dry with paper towels, and place them in a nonreactive pan.

Combine the scallion, herbs, garlic, lemon zest, salt, and pepper in the bowl of a food processor and process until smooth, gradually adding the oil last to emulsify. The marinade will be very thick, like a pesto. Pour the marinade over the chicken pieces and coat the pieces on both sides. Cover with plastic wrap and refrigerate overnight.

**food & wine tip**

Before browning the chicken, be sure to wipe off any excess marinade with a paper towel so it doesn't burn. Then season the chicken pieces well with salt and pepper and cook.

To cook the chicken, preheat the oven to 450°F. Heat 2 large sauté pans over medium-high heat with about 2 tablespoons of oil in each pan. If you don't have 2 large sauté pans, brown the chicken in batches. Remove the chicken from the marinade, reserving any excess marinade. Put the chicken pieces in the pans skin side down and sauté until the skin is nicely browned. Turn and brown the other side, adjusting the heat between medium and medium-high as necessary so you don't burn the chicken. When the chicken pieces are browned on both sides, 8 to 10 minutes total for each piece, transfer them to a roasting pan. Squeeze the lemon halves over the chicken and throw the lemon halves into the pan. Scrape any extra marinade into the roasting pan. Put the roasting pan in the oven and roast until the chicken is cooked, the juices run clear, and the thigh meat reads 175°F on an instant-read thermometer, 20 to 25 minutes. Remove the chicken from the oven.

Remove the chicken from the roasting pan and arrange on a platter. You can cut the chicken breasts in half first so your guests can choose both white and dark meat. Whisk the pan juices to break up any clumps of the marinade and drizzle a little over the chicken. Pour the rest of the pan juices into a gravy boat, discarding the lemon halves, and pass with the chicken.

# The Vineyard Kitchen

## MARIA HELM SINSKEY

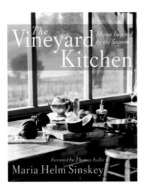

**BACKGROUND** Born in Albany, New York; lives in Napa Valley, California.

**EDUCATION** Attended California Culinary Academy.

**EXPERIENCE** "Before I went to cooking school, I worked in catering as a sideline to an advertising career, but it wasn't really considered a business. I was doing it illegally out of my own kitchen, which I'm sure wasn't up to code." Sinskey went on to land a job at San Francisco's PlumpJack Café, where she became a FOOD & WINE Best New Chef 1996.

**HOW SHE CAME TO LOVE FOOD** "I grew up in a large family that was obsessed with food. It rubbed off. We spent all of our holidays at my grandparents' houses, which were two blocks from each other. My paternal grandmother was from Alsace; her table was always piled high with strange meats and sea creatures. Beef tongue and sauerkraut were a highlight. My maternal grandmother was the daughter of Italian immigrants. I couldn't get enough of her meatballs, lasagna and pastini in chicken broth with Parmesan. I also loved my great-grandmother's manicotti and braciola."

**HOW SHE CAME TO LIVE IN WINE COUNTRY** "In 1997, while I was the chef at PlumpJack Café, I met and married Rob Sinskey of Robert Sinskey Vineyards in Napa. I stayed on at PlumpJack while working part-time for the winery. Six months after my first daughter, Ella, was born, in 1998, I took over as culinary director at the winery so that I could be closer to home."

**WHY SHE WROTE THE BOOK** "When I was at PlumpJack Café, many people asked me to write a book because they loved my food. But I was too busy. Then I got married and had two kids, and amidst all of the chaos, the timing was suddenly right. The bulk of the book poured out in four weeks. In the process I glanced at other cookbooks to see what they looked like. I found them so confusing that I just

**WHY GLUTTONY'S GOOD**
"A passion for food, wine and nature unites vineyard chefs around the world. It's a good kind of gluttony!"

closed them and put them away. I realized that I knew what I wanted to do, and it wasn't really very complicated."

MENTOR Carol Field. "I've always loved her books. I think her writing is so good and her books are so well done. She inspired me."

ESSENTIAL EQUIPMENT "My stove, a 60-inch Viking range. I love it because it has stood by me through thick and thin. It has its quirks, but I don't know any stove that doesn't. I love it so much that I bought a second one for the winery's test kitchen. I can't cook without it."

**FAVORITE CHEESE** "Gruyère has a wonderfully nutty taste with a hint of salt. It melts and browns beautifully— it makes a killer cheese sandwich on peasant bread. And I just love it in gougères, Burgundian cheese puffs."

ESSENTIAL STAPLE INGREDIENTS "Butter and eggs. Also thyme, shallots and cheese. And don't get me started on cheese."

FAVORITE SEASONAL INGREDIENT Tomatoes. "I don't eat them all winter long, but when they come in, I just eat them constantly until the season is over. And of course, the ones I grow myself are the best."

ON PAIRING WINE AND FOOD "My favorite pairing is roasted squab with Pinot Noir; my least favorite is fish with a heavy red wine. I don't think that tomatoes are as difficult to pair with wines as some people say they are. You simply need a wine that is high in acid with bright fruit, like a Sangiovese or Dolcetto, or a nice Pinot Grigio. In general, my best advice on pairing wine and food is, don't be afraid. You can always open up another bottle if you make a mistake."

ON COOKING WITH WINE "Always simmer and reduce wine after adding it to a dish. This burns off the raw alcohol edge and concentrates the flavors. Wine adds a nice acidity to an almost-finished dish."

ON COOKING FOR KIDS "If you involve your kids in making something—by having them roll out the pasta, say, or season the meat—they will eat it. I know this for a fact. My kids like to help with anything sweet, especially cake. They can't wait to lick the beaters. They'll also try anything once, and that's all I ask. If they don't like it, they don't have to eat it. Fighting over food issues can create lifelong problems."

COOKBOOK TREND "I've noticed a trend toward simpler food and home cooking."

# Grilled Hanger Steak with Lemon and Arugula

**SERVES 8**

Hanger steak, the popular *onglet* served in French bistros, used to be an overlooked cut of beef in the United States. Also known as a butcher's steak or hanging tender, it is an odd-shaped, oblong piece of meat that hangs inside the rear end of the rib cage, thus earning the name hanger steak. There being only one steak per steer made it difficult for a small neighborhood butcher to sell in quantity, so he would often take it home for his own use, hence the nickname butcher's steak.

Hanger steak is an extremely flavorful cut that does best cooked over high heat to medium-rare; undercooked it is chewy, overcooked it becomes tough and dry. This preparation is similar to that of a *bistecca alla fiorentina*, which is a thick-cut steak of Tuscan beef similar to a porterhouse that is prepared with lemon. The cut comes from Chianina breed of cattle and is known throughout the world for its significant tenderness and flavor. The *bistecca* is cooked on the coals to rare, then finished with a squeeze of lemon as it comes off the fire. The result is a crisp crust that holds in the juices of the flaming red interior. The lemon juice sizzles as it hits the crust of the meat, providing just enough acidity to balance its richness. It is often served with greens drizzled with very good olive oil. The hanger steak fares very well with this preparation and is quite delicious.

½  pound arugula

8  hanger steaks or substitute 4 porterhouse steaks cut 2 inches thick

6  lemons

1  tablespoon extra virgin olive oil, plus more for rubbing the lemons

Salt

Freshly ground black pepper

1  cup shaved Parmesan

1. Trim the arugula, stem it, and wash well. Drain and spin dry. Reserve.

2. Hanger steaks are usually long, thick, and rectangular. If they are too thick they will take forever to cook. A good way to remedy this is to butterfly the steaks, which will greatly improve their proportions and their cooking time. To do this, make a cut down the center of the steak lengthwise stopping ¼ inch before cutting through the back side. Spread the steak along this cut like a pair of butterfly wings, hence the name. You will now have a thinner squarish steak versus a long thick chunky one.

3. Preheat the oven to 500°F.

4. Cut four lemons in half, remove the pits, and rub them well with olive oil. Roast them in the preheated oven until they are caramelized, about 10 to 15 minutes. Cover them with foil to reserve their warmth until ready to serve.

5. Season both sides of the steaks well with salt and pepper. Heat a grill pan, indoor grill, or large sauté pan over high heat. Add a tablespoon of olive oil to the pan and then the steaks. Grill or pan fry them over high heat for 5 to 7 minutes on each side, depending on thickness, for medium-rare. If the pan smokes, reduce the heat to medium. The porterhouse steaks will take about 10 minutes per side. Squeeze the juice of two lemons over all just before removing from the pan. Let the steaks rest on a rack for 5 minutes before slicing.

6. Slice the steaks on the bias across the short width of the steak, or across both wings if the steaks are butterflied. If you are using a porterhouse, remove the meat from the bone and slice the steaks in the same manner. Place the sliced meat on a large platter.

7. In a large bowl, toss the arugula with a little extra virgin olive oil to moisten, season with salt and pepper to taste. Top the sliced meat with the arugula. Sprinkle the shaved Parmesan cheese over the arugula and drizzle generously with olive oil. Garnish with the roasted lemon halves, one for each person, to squeeze over all after the steak is served.

## on sinskey's nightstand

**Carol Field's** *The Italian Baker* is one of my all-time favorite cookbooks. Another one I really love is *I Am Almost Always Hungry* by **Lora Zarubin.** She really captures the essence of ingredients, and the recipes aren't difficult. It's also a good read.

# Herbed Cheese Beignets

**SERVES 8; MAKES 36 SMALL BEIGNETS**

*food* & *wine* tip

Though expeller pressed vegetable oil (oil that is extracted at a cool temperature to preserve its flavor) may be ideal, any regular, flavorless vegetable oil, like canola, works well, too.

Beignets are wonderful served warm from the fryer tucked inside a linen napkin lining a big wooden platter or willow basket. Have your guests gather around the kitchen table with a glass of wine and nibble away as they await the entrée. For a more formal presentation, make the beignets smaller and serve them with lightly dressed greens. Served either way they make a hearty winter appetizer.

| | |
|---|---|
| 1 | cup whole milk |
| 8 | tablespoons (1 stick) unsalted butter |
| ¼ | teaspoon cayenne pepper |
| 2¼ | teaspoons salt |
| 1 | cup all-purpose flour |
| 4 | large eggs |
| 2 | teaspoons chopped fresh thyme or 1 teaspoon dried |
| ½ | teaspoon chopped fresh rosemary or ¼ teaspoon dried |
| ½ | cup grated Parmesan cheese |
| 1 | heaping cup grated Emmenthaler or Swiss Gruyère cheese |
| 2 | quarts expeller pressed vegetable oil for frying |

1. Bring the milk, butter, cayenne, and salt to a boil in a heavy-bottomed saucepan. When the butter has completely melted, remove the pan from the heat and stir in the flour. Place the pan back on the heat and beat with a wooden spoon until the mixture is smooth and pulls away from the sides of the pan.

2. Place the batter in the bowl of a standing mixer fitted with a paddle attachment or beat the eggs in by hand. Add the eggs, one by one, beating well after each addition, about 15 seconds. Add the chopped herbs and then the cheeses. Reserve at room temperature for up to 4 hours until ready to fry.

3. Preheat the oven to 250°F.

4. Pour the oil into a 4-quart saucepan. The oil should rise no higher than halfway up the side of the pan. If it is any higher you risk having the oil boil over the sides of the pan. Heat the oil to 375°F. To test, drop a small piece of batter into the oil. It should dance merrily.

5. Drop the batter, one rounded tablespoon at a time, into the oil. Be careful not to let the temperature of the oil drop too low. Each addition of dough should elicit the same amount of sizzle as the first. Adjust the heat under the pan accordingly. A small ice cream scoop can be used to scoop the batter into the hot oil. Be careful not to drop the dough into the hot oil too abruptly or you risk being spattered.

6. Fry the beignets until they are golden and puffed on one side, then turn them over with a slotted spoon and repeat on the other side. Remove them from the oil with a slotted spoon and drain on clean lint-free cloth or paper towels. Keep the beignets warm in a 250°F oven until all of the batter is cooked. Serve the beignets warm.

# Salt and Herb–Crusted Prime Rib with Horseradish Cream

SERVES 8 TO 10

## sinskey on meat

Ask your butcher to trim off any excess fat and leave ¼ inch of it all around. If you desire, he can remove the roast from the bone and then tie the bone back on for easier slicing. You can also carve the meat off the bone just before serving in order to make it easier to slice.

**Horseradish cream**

¼ pound fresh horseradish root

2 tablespoons white wine vinegar

Salt

Freshly ground black pepper

1½ cups Crème Fraîche (recipe follows)

3 tablespoons chopped Italian parsley

**Prime rib**

¼ cup chopped fresh rosemary or 2 tablespoons dried

¼ cup chopped fresh thyme or 2 tablespoons dried

¼ cup extra virgin olive oil

3 tablespoons cracked black pepper

8 garlic cloves

One 4- to 5-rib prime rib roast, 8 to 10 pounds

1 cup coarse sea salt

1. Prepare the Horseradish Cream: Peel the horseradish root with a vegetable peeler and trim off the ends. Grate or chop in a food processor until very fine. Add the vinegar and season with salt and pepper.

2. Whisk the Crème Fraîche in a bowl until it thickens slightly. Fold in the horseradish and chopped parsley; season with salt and pepper to taste. Prepare 1 day in advance to allow the flavors to develop. Store tightly sealed in the refrigerator.

3. For the roast: In a small bowl, combine the herbs, ½ cup of olive oil, and the cracked pepper.

4. Peel, trim, and cut the garlic cloves in half. Make a small slit in the meat with a small sharp knife. Stick a piece of garlic in the cut before it disappears. Continue to make small slits all over the prime rib and fill them with garlic slices as you go, until the garlic is finished.

5. Rub the herb mixture all over the roast and let it marinate, well wrapped, in the refrigerator, overnight.

6. Remove the roast from the refrigerator 1 hour before roasting.

7. Preheat the oven to 450°F.

8. Moisten the salt with 2 tablespoons of cold water and press it into the fat side and ends of the roast. Place the roast in a large roasting pan and then in the preheated oven. Roast for 25 minutes.

9. Turn the oven down to 350°F and roast for 1½ to 2 hours. The internal temperature should read 120°F for medium/medium-rare when you remove it from the oven. The meat will continue to cook as it rests.

10. If you like your rib roast rare, remove it from the oven when the thermometer hits 118°F. Let the meat rest for 20 minutes before slicing to allow the juices to redistribute evenly.

11. Scrape the excess salt off of the roast. Using the bones as a guide, slide your knife down the ribs, keeping the blade flat against the ribs. When you reach the bottom of the ribs, run your knife under the boneless eye of meat. The cut should be parallel to the cutting board and closely follow the bone. You may have to raise and lower your cut slightly to accommodate ridges in the bones. Place the meat on a cutting board.

### sinskey on horseradish

You need to be careful when you are pureeing fresh horseradish. Do not place your face over the vent or top of the food processor when you are running it or when you remove the top. The fumes from the horseradish are very sharp and can cause quite a shock to your system.

12. Slice the boneless roast into medium-thick slices. Cut the bones apart and serve them on the side for those who relish chewing on them. Serve with the Horseradish Cream on the side. Accompany with potato gratin, or mashed or baked potatoes.

## Crème Fraîche

**MAKES 2 CUPS**

Substitute this delicious homemade Crème Fraîche for the more expensive commercial variety.

2  cups heavy cream

4  tablespoons cultured buttermilk

1. Combine the cream and buttermilk in a very clean glass container.

2. Cover with cheesecloth secured by a rubber band or a piece of plastic wrap that has been perforated with a toothpick twenty times or more.

3. Let the mixture sit at room temperature overnight or for up to two days. If you prefer a mild Crème Fraîche with just a bit of tang, stop the culture by refrigerating the Crème Fraîche after one night. If you prefer more tang, let the cream sit for one more night. Transfer to an airtight container and refrigerate.

# Slow-Roasted Pork with Fennel, Tomatoes, and Olives with Flat Bread

**SERVES 8**

This dish can be thrown together in a pot and then forgotten about for a few hours. You can use that time to make the Flat Bread or use store-bought flat bread. Wrap the fragrant tender chunks of pork in the Flat Bread and top with the olives and vegetables. The juices will dribble down hands and chins as they are eaten, so provide plenty of napkins. Good flat breads can be purchased at most Indian and Middle Eastern grocery stores.

| | |
|---|---|
| 1 | tablespoon fennel seeds |
| 2 | medium yellow onions |
| 2 | large fennel bulbs |
| 5 | pounds pork shoulder, cut into 2-inch cubes |

Salt

Freshly ground black pepper

5 to 8 tablespoons extra virgin olive oil, plus more for drizzling

| | |
|---|---|
| 6 | large garlic cloves, peeled and trimmed |
| 1 | cup white wine |
| 1½ | cups canned whole peeled tomatoes, seeded and chopped |
| 2 | cups pitted mixed olives (Picholine, Niçoise, Kalamata) |
| 2 | bay leaves, fresh or dried |
| 2 | tablespoons chopped Italian parsley |
| 12 | Flat Breads (recipe follows) or store-bought flat bread |

1. Preheat the oven to 400°F.

2. Spread the fennel seeds in a small ovenproof pan and toast in the preheated oven until their perfume is released, about 6 minutes. Cool and reserve.

3. Reduce the oven temperature to 325°F.

## food & wine tip

The roasted pork and vegetable mixture may be slightly oily. To correct this, let the dish rest for 5 minutes when it comes out of the oven, then skim off any excess fat with a spoon.

4. Peel the onions and remove the root core. Slice the onions into thin ¼-inch wedges. Reserve.

5. Wash and trim the fennel bulbs. Cut them in half and remove the core in a triangular wedge. Slice into thin ¼-inch wedges. Reserve.

6. Season the meat well with salt and pepper. Heat a large braising pan over medium-high heat and add 3 tablespoons of olive oil to cover the bottom. Add one layer of pork to the pan. It should sizzle instantly when it hits the pan. Add more olive oil if necessary. You might have to sear the meat in two or three batches depending on the size of your pan. Sear the meat until it is golden and crisp on all sides. This will take about 15 minutes for each batch of pork. Reduce the heat in the pan if it begins to smoke or burn. Remove the pork from the pan and let it rest on a plate. Drain the fat from the pan.

7. Add 2 tablespoons of olive oil to the pan. Add the onions, garlic, and fennel and sauté until they are wilted, about 15 minutes. Add the white wine and reduce by half, 5 minutes. Add the tomatoes, olives, bay leaves, and fennel seed and stir. Add the meat back to the pan and place in the oven, uncovered.

8. Roast until the juices are thick and the meat is tender, 2 to 3 hours. Turn the meat over after 1 hour. Add water, 1 cup at a time, if the juices evaporate before the meat is tender. Salt and pepper to taste.

9. Prepare the Flat Bread according to the recipe while the pork is roasting.

10. To serve, remove the bay leaves and spoon the pork and vegetables into flat bowls with some of the olives and juice. Garnish with the chopped parsley and a drizzle of extra virgin olive oil. Serve the Flat Breads on the side.

## Flat Bread

**MAKES TWELVE 10-INCH FLAT BREADS**

4 cups all-purpose flour

1 tablespoon salt

1 teaspoon yeast

1¼ cups warm water

¼ cup extra virgin olive oil

1 tablespoon chopped fresh thyme leaves

1. Combine the flour and salt in a mixing bowl. Make a well in the center. Whisk together the yeast and water in small bowl to dissolve. Pour it into the well in the flour and let it sit for 10 minutes.

2. Add the olive oil and thyme leaves to the well. Mix everything together and knead until you have a soft pliable dough, about 5 minutes. Add more water if necessary.

3. Let the dough rise, covered with a damp towel or plastic wrap, until doubled, about 2 hours, depending on how warm your kitchen is. If you have a cool kitchen it might take even longer.

4. After the dough has doubled, punch down and divide into twelve equal pieces. Roll each piece out as thinly as possible and place the rounds on parchment-lined sheet pans. Let the Flat Breads rise covered with a towel for 20 minutes.

5. Heat a 12-inch cast-iron or heavy-bottomed sauté pan over medium-high heat. Place a Flat Bread in the pan and let it brown and puff on one side, turn it over, and let the other side brown and puff. The Flat Breads may also be cooked directly on a hot grill.

6. Remove the Flat Bread from the pan and wrap in a towel to keep warm. Repeat with the remaining dough. Adjust the heat as necessary to prevent the pan from smoking and the Flat Breads from burning. Serve warm.

### sinskey on flat bread

You must have patience when you make these Flat Breads. The small amount of yeast in the dough causes them to rise ever so slowly. This slow rising develops the taste and texture of the bread, so your efforts will be duly rewarded. Allow at least 2 hours for the Flat Breads to rise.

# Pan-Roasted Ling Cod with Sweet Red Peppers, Capers, and Lemon

**SERVES 8**

Fishermen used to throw ling cod back into the water. It was not considered a commercially viable fish. When other species became scarce, ling cod came into fashion. It is an excellent eating fish despite its unglamorous name. It's tender and succulent with large flakes. It is a flavor chameleon, readily taking to all the flavors with which it is prepared. The sweet peppers, salty capers, and zesty lemon make your taste buds dance. The fish can be served with simple steamed rice, couscous, or the accompaniment of your choice. (Unfortunately, at this writing, ling cod is now scarce. Substitute line-caught Atlantic cod, Pacific cod, or Alaskan halibut.)

Sweet red peppers and capers

| | |
|---|---|
| 4 | medium red bell peppers or 8 small gypsy peppers |
| ½ | medium lemon |
| Salt | |
| Freshly ground black pepper | |
| ½ | cup extra virgin olive oil |
| 2 | medium garlic cloves, peeled, trimmed, and sliced |
| 3 | tablespoons capers |
| 2 | tablespoons chopped Italian parsley |

Eight 6-ounce ling cod, halibut, or Atlantic or Pacific cod
Sea salt
Freshly ground black pepper

| | |
|---|---|
| 2 | tablespoons extra virgin olive oil |
| 2 | lemons, cut in half, pips removed |

1. To prepare the peppers: Roast the peppers over an open flame until the skin is charred or roast in the oven (see Note on next page). Place them in a paper bag, close the bag, and cool. Remove the skin by rubbing it off with a clean kitchen towel. Cut the peppers in half and remove the core and seeds. Dice into ½-inch squares, place in a small bowl, and squeeze the ½ lemon over. Season the peppers with salt and freshly ground black pepper. Reserve.

2. In a medium sauté pan heat ½ cup of olive oil over medium heat. Add the sliced garlic and cook until it is toasted and golden. Remove the pan from the heat and let the oil cool for 10 minutes.

3. Add the capers and peppers to the oil. Heat the peppers gently over medium heat until the capers sizzle, about 2 minutes. Turn off the heat and add the chopped parsley. Season to taste with salt and pepper. Cover to keep warm.

4. Preheat the oven to 400°F.

5. Season the fish on both sides with salt and pepper.

6. Heat a large sauté pan over medium-high heat. Add 2 tablespoons of olive oil to the pan. Add the fish to the pan and sear until golden on one side, about 5 minutes. Turn the fish over and roast in the preheated oven for 5 to 10 minutes, depending on the thickness of the fish, until the fish flakes when gently pressed in the middle. Remove the pan from the oven and squeeze the lemons over the fish.

7. Spoon the sweet red peppers over the fish and serve from the pan.

NOTE  The peppers may also be roasted in the oven. Cut them in half and remove all the seeds. Place the cut side down on a sheet pan and drizzle with olive oil. Roast in a 500°F oven until the skin puffs and blackens. Place in a paper bag and proceed according to the recipe.

## sinskey's variations

Serve the sweet red peppers and capers with grilled skewers of big fat prawns or chicken. Use as a topping for pizza or toasted slices of bread. Spoon them over grilled calamari or seared sea scallops for an appetizer or light entrée.

# Credits

**The American Boulangerie: French Pastries and Breads for the Home Kitchen**
Text © 2003 by Pascal Rigo. Photography © 2003 by Paul Moore. Used by permission of Bay Books, an imprint of BAY/SOMA Publishing.

**BBQ USA: 425 Fiery Recipes from All Across America**
Excerpted from *BBQ USA*. Copyright © 2003 by Steven Raichlen. Used by permission of Workman Publishing Co., Inc., New York. All rights reserved. Cover photographs by Greg Schneider, Fernando Diez, Rory McNamara, Stan Schier, Jim Barcus/Kansas City Star, Scott Eastman Photography, Tom Stewart/CORBIS.

**Bernard Clayton's New Complete Book of Breads**
Reprinted with the permission of Simon & Schuster Adult Publishing Group from *Bernard Clayton's New Complete Book of Breads: The 30th Anniversary Edition* by Bernard Clayton. Copyright © 1973, 1987, 1995, 2003 by Bernard Clayton, Jr. Cover photographs by Maria Robledo.

**BitterSweet: Recipes and Tales from a Life in Chocolate**
Excerpted from *BitterSweet*. Copyright © 2003 by Alice Medrich.

Photographs copyright © 2003 by Deborah Jones. Used by permission of Artisan, a division of Workman Publishing Co., Inc., New York. All rights reserved.

**The Bread Bible**
From *The Bread Bible* by Rose Levy Beranbaum. Copyright © 2003 by Rose Levy Beranbaum. Used by permission of W. W. Norton & Company, Inc. Cover photograph by Gentl & Hyers.

**The Cakebread Cellars Napa Valley Cookbook: Wine and Recipes to Celebrate Every Season's Harvest**
Reprinted with permission from *The Cakebread Cellars Napa Valley Cookbook* by Dolores and Jack Cakebread with resident chef Brian Streeter. Copyright © 2003 by Dolores Cakebread and Jack Cakebread, Ten Speed Press, Berkeley, CA. Available at Ten Speed Press at 800-841-2665 or www.tenspeed.com. Photographs copyright © 2003 by Maren Caruso.

**César: Recipes from a Tapas Bar**
Reprinted with permission from *César* by Olivier Said and James Mellgren with Maggie Pond. Copyright © 2003 by Olivier Said and James Mellgren, Ten Speed Press, Berkeley, CA. Available at Ten Speed Press at

800-841-2665 or www.tenspeed.com. Photographs by Olivier Said.

**Come for Dinner: Memorable Meals to Share with Friends**
From *Come for Dinner* by Leslie Revsin. Copyright © 2003 by Leslie Revsin. All rights reserved. Reproduced here by permission of Wiley Publishing, Inc. Cover photograph by Christopher Hirsheimer.

**East of Paris: The New Cuisines of Austria and the Danube**
From *East of Paris* by David Bouley, Mario Lohninger and Melissa Clark. Copyright © 2003 by David Bouley. Reprinted by permission of HarperCollins Publishers Inc. Ecco Press. Photographs by Thomas Schauer.

**Everyday Greens: Home Cooking from Greens, the Celebrated Vegetarian Restaurant**
Copyright © 2003 by Annie Somerville. Used by permission of Scribner, used under license by Simon & Schuster, Inc. Cover illustration by Mayumi Oda.

**Food Network Kitchens Cookbook**
Excerpted from *Food Network Kitchens Cookbook*. Published by Meredith Books © 2003. Reprinted by permission only. Photographs by Mark Ferri and Robert Jacobs.

# Index